The Samurai Castle Master

The Samurai Castle Master

Warlord Todo Takatora

Chris Glenn

FRONTLINE BOOKS

First published in Great Britain in 2022 by
Frontline Books
An imprint of
Pen & Sword Books Ltd
Yorkshire – Philadelphia

ISBN 978 1 39909 658 4

A CIP catalogue record for this book is
available from the British Library.

Typeset by Mac Style
Printed in the UK by CPI Group (UK) Ltd, Croydon, CR0 4YY.

Pen & Sword Books Limited incorporates the imprints of Atlas,
Archaeology, Aviation, Discovery, Family History, Fiction, History,
Maritime, Military, Military Classics, Politics, Select, Transport,
True Crime, Air World, Frontline Publishing, Leo Cooper, Remember
When, Seaforth Publishing, The Praetorian Press, Wharncliffe
Local History, Wharncliffe Transport, Wharncliffe True Crime
and White Owl.

For a complete list of Pen & Sword titles please contact

PEN & SWORD BOOKS LIMITED
47 Church Street, Barnsley, South Yorkshire, S70 2AS, England
E-mail: enquiries@pen-and-sword.co.uk
Website: www.pen-and-sword.co.uk

Or

PEN AND SWORD BOOKS
1950 Lawrence Rd, Havertown, PA 19083, USA
E-mail: Uspen-and-sword@casematepublishers.com
Website: www.penandswordbooks.com

Dedication

To my First Hero, John Glenn.

Contents

Acknowledgments

I am indebted to Kato Yuka for helping to source materials, checking details and following me countless times to castles, battle sites and Takatora-related locations.

To Professor Miura Masayuki, Japan's foremost expert on samurai castles and a man most generous with his limited time and unlimited knowledge. Medieval castle specialist, Professor Nakai Hitoshi of Shiga University, and Professor Fujita Tatsuo of Mie University for their answering of endless questions.

Many thanks also Mr Kasai Kenji of Iga Ueno City, the curators of Iga Ueno Castle, and the Osaka Castle Museum. Koura's Mayor Nose Kikuo, the caretaker of Takatora's grave, Miyabe Ryoyu of Kansho-in Temple, Tokyo and the priests of Nanzen-ji Temple, Kyoto. Many thanks also to the countless people in city hall offices and education department researchers and specialists in Ichinomiya, Imabari, Kami-cho, Kinokawa, Kyoto, Osaka, Shizuoka, Tamba Sasayama, Tokyo, Tottori, Toyooka, Tsu, Uwajima, Matsusaka, Yabu, Yamato Koriyama, Yamazaki, and others across Japan who took my repeated calls and answered my questions. Thanks to Omi Tourism Board's Kojima San and Naiki San, and to the Frontline team.

List of Plates

1. 1907 copy of an Edo period portrait of Todo Takatora. The original was lost to an air raid in 1945, while this copy is kept in the Kansho-in Temple in Tsu.
2. The armour worn by Todo Takatora during the Battle of Osaka, now part of the Osaka Castle collection.
3. This distinctive *Tokan Kabuto* (Chinese cap-shaped) helmet was presented to Todo Takatora by Toyotomi Hideyoshi just prior to Hideyoshi's death in 1598. The helmet was later given to a relative, who wore it in the 1615 Summer Siege of Osaka. This helmet is now on display in the Iga Ueno Castle Museum.
4. Todo Takatora's *umajirushi* battle standards as recorded in Edo-period books of samurai heraldry, and the Todo clan Sekigahara battle flag of white *mochi* on a black background.
5. Koriyama Castle ruins in Nara Prefectures' Yamato Koriyama City.
6. Wakayama Castle, designed and continually improved over a number of years by Todo Takatora.
7. The ruins of Akagi Castle's central precincts carved from a 50m-high mountain and shored up by thick walls of piled natural stone.
8. Looking across the site of Akagi Castle's front gates to the main *honmaru* enceinte at the top.
9. A *masugata* gate system, showing a smaller gate leading to the courtyard and requiring a right-hand turn to the *yagura-mon* gatehouse, surrounded by connecting corridor-like *tamon yagura*. Illustration from an original copy of the *Gunshi no Maki* (軍詞之巻) dated 1716, collection of the author.
10. Form and function – Imabari Castle's graceful and elegant lines mask its military strengths.
11. Wide moats, high, straight stone walls with *inubashiri* at the base, square outline with corner watchtowers, *tamon yagura* and thick clay

walls surrounding it, and a towering keep. Imabari is one of Takatora's masterpieces.

12. The wide moats and stone-walled ruins of Takatora's excellent Tsu Castle.

13. Tsu Castle's reconstructed tower.

14. Strong, square and sturdy Sasayama Castle ruins.

15. Wide *inubashiri* can be seen skirting the base of Sasayama's high stone walls.

16. Iga Castle's impressive stone walls stand 27m high above the moats, about the height of a modern-day ten-storey building. Until Osaka was redeveloped by Takatora in the 1620s, Iga Ueno's walls were Japan's highest.

17. Iga Ueno Castle's 1935 reconstructed *tenshu* keep.

18. At 30m, Osaka Castle lays claim to having the highest stone walls of any samurai castle. Todo Takatora was responsible for the overall design and wall construction techniques.

19. The staggered wall sections of Osaka Castle provide coverage at all angles.

20. Kyoto's largest Sanmon Gate belongs to the ancient Nanzen-ji Temple, and was donated and constructed by Todo Takatora. The upper section, not open to the public, houses a statue of Tokugawa Ieyasu, with Todo Takatora to his right. The Buddhist memorial tablets of seventy-one of Takatora's closest vassals and family members killed in battle at Osaka are also kept here.

21. Wooden effigy of Todo Takatora, housed in the upper section of the Nanzen-ji Temple's Sanmon Gate. Taken with the permission of the Nanzen-ji Temple.

22. The typical straight, clean, squared lines of a Takatora-designed castle are evident at Suncheon Castle in South Korea. The *tenshu* tower keep base can be seen upper center.

23. Ozu Castle in Ehime Prefecture, Shikoku, was owned by numerous warlords, with Todo Takatora being the major contributor to the overall outline of the current structure.

24. Flanked by the original wings, Ozu Castle's soaring tower keep was reconstructed using authentic techniques and traditional craftsmanship.

Introduction

In a time when the average Japanese man stood between 150cm to 165cm tall, Todo Takatora, at 190cm, was a giant among men. By comparison, of the three eventual unifiers of Japan, Oda Nobunaga stood 169cm, Toyotomi Hideyoshi was 154cm, and Tokugawa Ieyasu was just 157cm tall.

It wasn't just his large size that made him stand out, but his many abilities and achievements. Todo Takatora was without a doubt one of the most intelligent of men of the Warring States period. As a warrior, he took part in many of the major battles of his day, often in the front ranks, being wounded time and again, yet showing extraordinary bravery each and every time. Together with Kato Kiyomasa and Kuroda Kanbe, Todo Takatora is regarded as the premier samurai castle planner and architect. He greatly influenced castle design and construction with his many innovative ideas and plans, designing, building or at least assisting and advising on the construction of over thirty of the finest castles across Japan and even Korea. Takatora made castles with such fine defensive reputations that no one wanted to attack them. Aside from his remarkable architectural innovations, Takatora's political acumen, negotiating skills and ideas changed Japanese politics during the highly volatile late sixteenth and early seventeenth centuries, with lasting effects throughout the feudal period.

History has been unkind to Todo Takatora. He has, until now, never properly received the attention, the praise or respect afforded countless lesser men of his time. As we shall discover, his contribution to Japanese warfare, architecture, politics, history and culture is immense. Indeed, it is difficult to name another more influential historical character.

One of the reasons for this lack of respect and attention is that his reputation was sullied in the early Edo period for his having been instrumental in a number of – at the time – highly controversial policies and practices. Takatora was deemed 'unreliable' by many *daimyo* and scholars, particularly in the later Edo period and Meiji period when unflinching loyalty to a single lord was seen as a virtue, as he had changed masters a record seven times to serve ten men, and as will be fully explained, was a *tozama daimyo*, an outsider, who had worked his way into a position of trust within the inner sanctum of the Shogunate. Not once did he ever misuse his position or influence. This sincere, austere man, earnest and diligent in his dealings, worked to serve his masters, for the good of the nation.

Takatora was originally closely allied with the Toyotomi clan, former rulers of the nation, and yet he became not only one of the most trusted men in the Tokugawa Shogunate, but one of the closest personal friends of Tokugawa Ieyasu, and an equally trusted personal instructor and advisor to the second and third Shoguns, Tokugawa Hidetada and Tokugawa Iemitsu. His skills in battle equalled those in negotiation, tactical planning, leadership and, importantly, castle construction. Skills that made him invaluable to the rulers of the nation, and in turn the cause of envy amongst other ruling *daimyo* and the elite *hatamoto* samurai. His advice played a major role in shaping the policies of the Tokugawa government, and the history and culture of Japan.

A giant among men, Todo Takatora lived a life that unfolds like a drama. This is his story.

Pre-Glossary

Please note, Japanese names are given in the traditional order, family name first, then personal name. In the case of the samurai, names changed often, and so only the better-known names of each individual warrior are used.

Dates are often confusing, as Japan used an Imperial period name and a lunar calendar system. Where possible, modern Gregorian calendar dates are provided.

In an effort to educate and improve understanding and appreciation of Japanese castles, Japanese terminology has been used throughout this book. Although there is a full and detailed glossary of terms in the back section, here are some words and terms that will appear frequently throughout. To assist readers in understanding and becoming familiar with the terms, please read this Pre-glossary.

Bakufu – Lit. 'tent government', refers to the ruling administration.

Borogata Keep – An old architectural style of keep building based on temple construction techniques.

Daimyo – A warlord or feudal lord.

Dorui – An earthen wall or embankment.

Edo Period – 1601–1868, named after Ieyasu's Edo Castle, seat of the Tokugawa *Bakufu*.

Fudai daimyo – *Daimyo* historically and closely associated with the Tokugawa clan.

Honmaru – the main central, and most important, of castle baileys and walls.

Hori/bori – Water-filled or dry moat.

Inubashiri– Lit. 'dog's run', a narrow space around baileys.

Ishigaki – Piled drystone castle walls.

Kuruwa – A highly fortified castle bailey, enceinte or precinct, and usually assigned a name or number. An older name for a *maru*.

Masugata – A highly fortified double-gate system, better remembered as a 'Death Box'.

Maru – Like *kuruwa*, a fortified castle bailey, compound, enceinte or precinct. *Maru* is used as a prefix to a name. For example, *ni-no-maru*, the second bailey, *nishi-no-maru*, the Western bailey etc.

Mon – A castle gate. *Mon* is used as a suffix, such as *ote-mon*, main gate, *higashi-mon*, east gate etc.

Ronin – A masterless samurai.

Sotogata Keep – An architectural style created by Todo Takatora to build castle keeps.

Sumi yagura – A corner watchtower.

Tamon yagura – A single-storey corridor-like watchtower structure running along the tops of castle walls.

Tenshu – The castle's iconic main tower keep or donjon.

Tozama daimyo – *Daimyo* not originally associated with the Tokugawa clan.

Umadashi – Lit. 'horse opening', a fortified barbican-like defence space in front of castle gates for cavalry and infantry to muster and exit.

Yagura – A watchtower.

Yagura mon – A gatehouse.

Yashiki – A single-storey samurai residence.

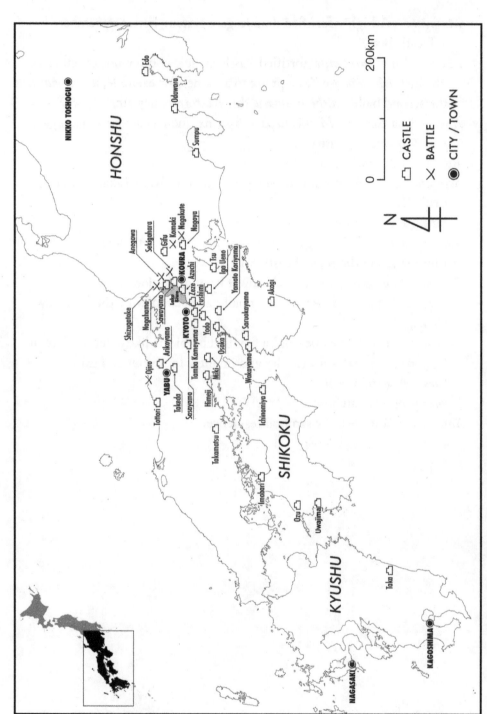

Map of Japan showing places and locations associated with Todo Takatora.

Chapter 1

The Early Years

Like many a hero, Todo Takatora was born in a time of turmoil, one of near-constant civil war and political unrest at the height of Japan's Sengoku or Warring States period on 16 February 1556,[1] in the village of Todo[2] in Omi Province.

Takatora was the second son of Todo Torataka (1516–5 December 1599). Previous biographers and many historians have made the mistake of believing that because Takatora's father lived and worked in a remote and rural setting, he must have been a *jizamurai*, among the lower ranking of country samurai – but well above *ashigaru* status – and of *dogou* or *kokujin* class, meaning that he was a minor landlord making his living through collecting taxes from his estate workers. However, the size of the Todo family property and house, and the clan's history, among other reasons to be revealed later in this book, suggest otherwise, and it would be safe to surmise that the Toda family were formerly of the aristocracy, and had been sent to what is now the township of Koura as regional guardians. What is without a doubt, is that they were warriors of merit, and Todo Takatora would once again bring distinction to the clan name.

Takatora's father, Torataka, had also been born in Omi Province, the second son of Mitsui Noritsuna, the master of Omi Namazue Castle, a fine fortress built in a strategic position above the ragged cliffs of the Aichi River. At a young age Torataka had left Omi Province and using the surname of Aichi, a name taken from the river running close by his birthplace at Namazue Castle, joined the feared Takeda clan of Kai, serving Lord Takeda Nobutora (11 February 1494–27 March 1574), father of the

---

1. On the sixth day of the first month in the second year of the Imperial Koji period, Year of the Rabbit, by the old Japanese lunar calendar. Of interest, the warlord Uesugi Kagekatsu was born on 8 January that year, samurai commander and nephew of General Shibata Katsuie Shibata Katsutoyo was also born in 1556, while the 'Viper of Mino', the warlord Saito Dosan, was killed on 28 May in battle against his own son that very year.
2. Modern-day, Jo-no-uchi, Zaiji, Koura Cho, Inukami-Gun, Shiga Prefecture.

great warlord Takeda Shingen (1 December 1521–13 May 1573). He had received the 'Tora' or 'Tiger' part of his name from Lord Nobu**tora** as a reward for his excellent services and merit in battle.[3] Torataka was admired by Lord Nobutora for his intelligence and great courage in battle, traits that, like the auspicious part of his name, were later passed down to his son. On his return to Omi, Torataka had married O-Tora, the daughter of the local elite land-owning warrior, Todo Tadataka, and was adopted into the Todo clan. O-Tora herself had been born to the head priest of the ancient Taga Taisha,[4] one of Shiga Prefectures' most important Grand Shrines, and adopted as a child into the Todo clan.

The Todo clan ancestry begins nine generations before the birth of Takatora with Todo Mikawa no Kami Kagemori, an exceptionally strong warrior and a close vassal of the fourth Ashikaga shogun, Ashikaga Yoshimochi (12 March 1386–3 February 1428) during the Muromachi period (1336–1573). Kagemori was the first to adopt the Todo name. On the orders of the Shogunate he relocated to become guardian of Todo Village, modern-day Koura-cho. The family name Todo (藤堂) translates directly to 'Wisteria Pavilion'. According to legends and to signs posted in the grounds of Takatora's hometown, Shiga Prefecture's Koura Village Hachiman-sha Shrine, the Todo family name is believed to have been taken from the *fuji* wisteria said to have planted there by Prince Toneri Shinno, the son of the 40th traditional Emperor of Japan, Emperor Temmu (c. 631–1 October 686), and still growing in the shrine grounds. The *kanji* for wisteria, *fuji* 藤 is also read as *tou* (as in the common names of Kato, Saito, Ito, etc.), and while most families with the character for *fuji* in their name use a variation of the wisteria crest, the Todo clan crest was a version of the *Tsutamon*, a crest featuring the leaf of the *tsuta* vine, or Japanese Ivy (*Parthenocissus tricuspidata*).[5]

---

3. Receiving a character from the name of one's lord was considered a very high honour indeed.
4. Taga Taisha Grand Shrine was established in 620 according to the ancient *Kojiki* chronicles. The Grand Shrine's gardens are a nationally designated Place of Scenic Beauty and contain a stone bridge constructed by Toyotomi Hideyoshi. The Grand Shrine is associated with long life, successful marriage and good fortune, and its specialty is a pounded rice cake known as an *itokiri-mochi*, the serendipitous relevance of which will become evident later in the life of Todo Takatora.
5. *Parthenocissus tricuspidata* is a flowering plant commonly known as Japanese Ivy, Japanese Creeper, Grape Ivy and Boston Ivy, although it is not a true ivy, as it belongs to the Vitaceae or grape family. Known as *tsuta* in Japanese, it is native to Japan, Korea and northern and eastern China. Incidentally, the plant's Chinese name, 爬牆虎, translates to 'Reposed Tiger', most fitting as Takatora's name, 高虎, translates directly to 'High Tiger'.

The Todo clan's *Tsutamon* crest.

Ivy was believed to be an auspicious plant because of its fast growth, vitality, and its ability to spread and climb. As such, it was considered a symbol of prosperity, and as it became widely used among numerous samurai clans, it was recognised as an authoritative family crest. There are 290 variations of the *Tsutamon* crest, and the Todo family's crest is also known as the 'Todo Ivy' with well-defined leaf veins, wider than the general ivy crest.

The Todo clan were wealthy warrior landowners controlling several villages in the Inukami-gun region. As was often the case in the turbulent times of the fifteenth and sixteenth centuries, the family fortunes and power had diminished by the time Takatora was born. As such, his father Torataka loyally served the Kyogoku clan, and later the Azai clan, warlords of the centrally-located and battle-wracked Omi Province.

The samurai often changed their names at various and auspicious times in their lives, and as an infant, Takatora was named Yokichi. His wet nurse was unable to satisfy his insatiable demands and so a number of other women in the village were called upon to supply him with milk. He was apparently breast fed until the age of three, by which time he was said to have been capable of eating three to five *mochi,* pounded sticky rice cakes, in a single sitting. *Mochi* rice cakes appear to have remained a firm favourite of the man, and as we shall soon discover, would continue to play an important role later in his life. The young Takatora was said to have been rarely ill and would never complain of any injuries sustained in childhood adventures. Takatora's elder brother Takanori was six years his senior, but by the time he was seven years old, Takatora had surpassed his brother in height. Besides this, little is known of his formative years, but he would have undergone a proper education, learning to read and write along with training as a warrior befitting his father's position.

There is, however, one early episode that shows the bravery and tenacity of the man who would make such an impact on Japanese history, warfare, politics and culture. Takatora's village was raided by bandits in 1568, and his father took it upon himself to punish the marauders. Takatora's father was accompanied in his mission by his elder son, Takanori, then around 18 years of age. Takatora had also wanted to be part of the action but aged just 12 was deemed too young to go with them. Having been told by his father countless times to go home, the boy finally relented and did just that. The stubborn youth went home as ordered, though it was only so he could collect one of his father's swords and follow after his father and brother to the bandits' encampment, positioning himself at the rear. As his father and elder brother attacked from the front, a number of the bandits quickly exited out the back, where the large boy was able to cut them down and take their heads. It is recorded in the Todo clan diaries that despite his having disobeyed his orders, Torataka was later very pleased and impressed with his younger son's brave actions and abilities, and word of Takatora's exploits soon spread around the local villages.

Loss of a Brother

By the following year, 1569, the charismatic warlord Oda Nobunaga (23 June 1534–21 June 1582) was fast emerging as a major political and military force. Nine years earlier Nobunaga had made a name for himself in defeating an invading force of an estimated 25,000 troops under the warlord Imagawa Yoshimoto with just 2,500 of his own samurai in the Battle of Okehazama. He had continued to strengthen his position within his own domain of Owari Province, and in forming an alliance with Tokugawa Ieyasu, the master of neighbouring Mikawa, Nobunaga was in control of what is now modern-day Aichi Prefecture. Shortly after, by defeating his nephew Saito Tatsuoki, Nobunaga claimed the strategically important lands of Mino Province. He now controlled the critical central Japan region, the heart of Japan. With Mino in his grasp, Nobunaga relocated his base to his former father-in-law's mountain fortress, and along with re-naming it Gifu Castle, announced his ambitious bid for sole control of the nation. He intended to unify Japan under one leader – himself – in an effort to put an end to the incessant fighting between the *daimyo* warlords.

The next step of his plan required the annexation of the Owari-adjoining Ise Province (modern-day Mie Prefecture) held mostly by the noble Kitabatake clan, who had long been the *Kokushi*, or provincial governors, of Ise. Although he had officially retired and had made his son, Tomofusa, Lord of Ise, it was the old lord, Kitabatake Tomonori, who continued to pull the political strings.

During June 1569, Nobunaga's general Takigawa Kazumasu had orchestrated to have the master of Kozukuri Castle, Lord Kitabatake's younger son Tomomasa, betray his own father and liege lord elder brother, Tomonori, by turning to assist the Oda in capturing Ise. Becoming aware of the intrigue, Tomonori promptly ordered an attack on his younger brother's Kozukuri Castle. This siege lasted over three months before the Kitabatake received word that Nobunaga, having settled other conflicts, was now turning his attentions to Ise and with over 70,000 troops was now heading towards the Kitabatake territories.

Nobunaga departed Gifu Castle on 20 August 1569, and arrived at Kozukuri Castle on the 23rd. By this time the 16,000-strong Kitabatake army had already lifted its siege, with old Lord Tomonori and his son Tomofusa taking refuge in their main stronghold of Okawachi Castle with 8,000 troops, while another 8,000 Kitabatake samurai were dispersed to man Okawachi's smaller surrounding protective satellite castles.

To capture a medieval samurai castle, a ratio of at least three attackers to every one defender was required. Even then it was not a simple matter. Samurai castles were taken via either overwhelming force, or by prolonged siege leading to attrition and the starvation and thirst of the defenders. Other ways included through treachery, or even through peaceful, diplomatic means. Trickery and treachery seem to have played the biggest roles, with the men inside these castles often being coerced through various methods such as bribery, or threats to family members outside the castle, to open the gates, or cause fires or even an insurrection from within.

Battering rams are often depicted in movies and TV as being used to smash down the castle gates by attackers. This may have been the case in European warfare, but there are no documented cases of Japanese castles ever having been brought down or gates being breached through the use of such devices. That is pure fiction. Besides, any samurai carrying a battering ram or similar siege device and approaching the heavily defended castle gates would be an obvious target for the defenders within. Samurai castles were also designed so that gates and their approaches were built at angles, preventing direct, easy access, and remained under watch at all times.

Smaller protective satellite fortresses often surrounded larger castles as a means of making an attacking force split into smaller units in order to attack the smaller castles and fortresses simultaneously, or risk having the samurai of these nearby related guardian castles come to the aid of those under siege. The splitting of the main attack force not only weakened the attackers, but could lead to communication, cohesion and logistical problems, exactly the sort of confusion those being attacked greatly desired.

In the Battle of Okawachi, fought between 29 August and 3 October, Nobunaga's forces brazenly bypassed these smaller surrounding fortresses, and despite the risk to their rear, instead laid siege directly to the Kitabatake clan's main central Okawachi Castle. This had been constructed in 1451 and was an exceptionally well developed and defended castle. Built on the northern end of a hill in Okawachi of what is now a part of Matsusaka City in Mie Prefecture, it was surrounded by natural obstacles. Okawachi was guarded by the Yatsu River to the north, and the Sakanai River to its east. The southern and western flanks were protected by deep valleys, making it a difficult castle to take. By 28 August the Oda forces had completely surrounded Okawachi on four sides, and erected log palisades in rows two and three deep around the castle. The two-month siege had begun.

Numerous violent attacks were launched in an effort to topple the Kitabatake and their castle. Takatora's elder brother, Todo Takanori, had joined the ranks of the Azai clan, and was among the troops serving as reinforcements alongside the Oda allied Kyogoku army. During one of the more daring attacks, the 19-year-old Takanori was killed.

On 3 October, the Kitabatake were ready to capitulate, and reached a settlement favourable to the Oda under the conditions that Nobunaga's second son, Nobukatsu, would become the adopted heir of Tomofusa, and therefore would become the lord of Ise and the Kitabatake domains. Okawachi Castle was to be vacated and turned over to Nobukatsu. Kitabatake Tomofusa and Tomonori would withdraw to other castles, Tomonori to the clan manor at Kiriyama Castle, while Tomofusa went to Sakanai Castle. Under the control of Nobukatsu the Kitabatake would retain some of their authority for at least four years until late in the summer of 1573, when Nobukatsu would kill them all.

With the death of Todo Takanori, Takatora was made heir to his father Torataka's estate. Becoming heir did not mean that Takatora would be treated any differently or protected from risk in any way. In fact, the following year Takatora himself would join the ranks of Azai Nagamasa's forces and soon see action in one of the most violent battles of the Warring States period.

The Azai Years

The Azai clan were the feudal lords of north-eastern Omi Province (Shiga Prefecture), based in Odani Castle. The Azai had risen to prominence in the early 1500s while serving as vassals of the Kyogoku clan, governors of Omi, eventually becoming independent by the 1540s. Located at Kohoku, not far from modern-day Nagahama City, Odani Castle was an exceptionally large and fine castle built in a horseshoe shape along the highly fortified mountain ridges around a central 800m-long, 200m-wide valley, hence its name, O-dani, the Big Valley Castle. Along with Kasugayama Castle, Nanao Castle, Kannonji Castle and Gassantoda Castle, Odani Castle is counted among Japan's Five Greatest Mountain Castles, and the impressive ruins can be enjoyed to this day.

Odani had been built by Azai Sukemasa (1491–21 January 1542) around 1521, but in losing to the regional rival Rokkaku clan, he had fled to the central Mino region (Gifu Prefecture), maintaining independence thanks to an alliance of convenience with the neighbouring Asakura clan, allowing him to return to Odani some years later. After Sukemasa, Odani Castle was inherited by Azai Hisamasa (1526–3 September 1573).

The Azai had long been at war with the Rokkaku clan, a well-established military house descended from the noble Minamoto clan and with roots in central Omi Province going back to the thirteenth century.

The Rokkaku had been appointed the constabulary of Omi, and as such had a fine castle, Kannon-ji, built on Mount Kinugasa overlooking the vital highways and plains of what is now the eastern districts of Azuchi City. This castle had been captured during the Onin Wars of 1467–77, the precursor to the Sengoku or Warring States period, and as a result the Rokkaku had lost a great deal of power and prestige. Looking to restore their position and fortunes, they had set their sights north to the lands of the Azai, and attacked!

The Rokkaku were initially successful in subjugating the Azai, with the second clan head, Lord Azai Hisamasa, proving to be both a weak and ineffectual leader, easily surrendering his lands to the Rokkaku in early 1560, a move that greatly angered his own men who later forced him to hand power to his son, Nagamasa. Azai Nagamasa (1545–26 September 1573) then became the third head of the Azai clan. Nagamasa had shown his competence in defeating a 25,000-man Rokkaku force over twice the size of his own 11,000 men in the Battle of Norada, fought in the late summer of 1560. The once powerful Rokkaku clan would never fully recover from the battle, ceding much of their territory to the Azai.

These territories were situated directly in between the first of the National Unifiers Oda Nobunaga's lands of Owari and Mino, and the capital, Kyoto. Nobunaga required the Azai's lands in order to traverse the region freely, and to control Japan. Now the master of Odani Castle, Azai Nagamasa would find himself forced to form an uneasy alliance with the mighty Oda Nobunaga. Nobunaga offered an affiliation with the Azai, being a pact of familiarity; he gave his younger sister O-Ichi to Azai Nagamasa as a wife. Nagamasa and O-Ichi's marriage in 1564 sealed the political alliance which held until 1570, when the Oda commenced their subjugation of the Asakura clan of Echizen (northern Fukui Prefecture). Since the days of Azai Nagamasa's grandfather, Sukemasa, the Azai had held a mutual alliance with the Asakura, and rather than turn against their close allies, the Asakura, Azai Nagamasa boldly decided to turn against his brother-in-law, Nobunaga.

The story goes that knowing her husbands' plans, O-Ichi sent her brother a bag of azuki beans, intriguingly tied shut by strings at both ends. It was a sign Nobunaga recognised as a warning of entrapment, and he quickly extracted himself, decamping to the safety of Kyoto. Nobunaga would soon seek revenge. His target would be his brother-in-law, Azai Nagamasa, and Odani Castle.

The Battle of Anegawa

As the Oda forces laid siege to Odani and Yokoyama Castles, the Azai and their Asakura allies reacted accordingly. Azai Nagamasa called on support first from Asakura Yoshikage, ruler of Echizen (now Fukui Prefecture), to halt the Oda's advances, leading to the Battle of Anegawa, also remembered as the Battle of Nomura by the Oda and the Azai clan scribes, and as the Battle of Mitamura by the Asakura historians.

At around 6 a.m. on the morning of 30 July 1570, Oda Nobunaga and Tokugawa Ieyasu heading a joint army of 28,000 faced an Azai-Asakura coalition army of around 18,000 men from opposite sides of the narrow, shallow River Ane. The Oda samurai took on the Azai upstream while the Tokugawa's 5,000 samurai concentrated on the Asakura downstream. Nobunaga is said to have had some 500 matchlockmen in his front lines.

Among the Oda front-line forces was a 33-year-old general who had used his sharp intellect to work his way from being a low-ranked *ashigaru* foot soldier to becoming a general under the great Nobunaga himself. Anegawa would be that general, Toyotomi Hideyoshi's first time leading troops into battle, as Nobunaga had assigned him the honour of being in the vanguard.[6] Leading the rear guard in this particular skirmish was the ever-reliable Oda stalwart Sassa Narimasa, with support provided by the armies of Ikoma Ienaga, Yamauchi Kazutoyo, and Hideyoshi's associate, Hachisuka Masakatsu.

Leading the second division, Tokugawa Ieyasu positioned the troops under the respected generals Honda Tadakatsu and Sakakibara Yasumasa on the Asakura's left flank and then had his immediate troops spread out so as to almost surround Asakura Kagetake's men.

---

6. Born Kinoshita Hiyoshi-maru on 27 March 1537 in Nakamura Village, now Nakamura Ward of Nagoya City, Toyotomi Hideyoshi was a foot soldier who rose in the ranks to become a samurai, general, statesman and ruler of Japan. His father, Yaemon, died shortly after his birth, and his mother remarried a lowly samurai who treated the boy harshly. As a child he was sent to a nearby temple to become a priest, but absconded at age 15 to join the army of Matsushita Yukitsuna as an *ashigaru* foot soldier. In 1558, Hideyoshi was given six *ryo*, a fair sum of money, to purchase a coat of chain-mail for his master. However, the young man ran away and used the money to buy himself light armour and weapons and, returning to Owari (Aichi Prefecture), entered the services of Oda Nobunaga as a sandal bearer. The story goes that one cold winter's morning he warmed his master's straw sandals in the breast of his kimono, attracting the attention of Lord Nobunaga. History books tell us his master, Nobunaga, called him 'Saru', or 'Monkey', however that is apocryphal, a later Edo period fiction, as diaries and letters show Nobunaga referred to him as the 'Bald Rat'.

The battle began as many samurai field battles since time immemorial had begun. Not with a sky-filling exchange of arrows or clouds of smoky gunfire, nor through brave spear or cavalry charges as may be expected, but with the throwing of rocks. In fact, 10 per cent of deaths in Sengoku-period samurai battles were caused by thrown rocks. Bows and arrows accounted for the majority of deaths at 41 per cent, matchlock guns claimed 19 per cent, spears made for 18 per cent, while swords resulted in a mere 4 per cent of samurai deaths in battle. There was plenty of initial ammunition lying at the feet of the warriors along the riverbanks, and no doubt, the tall, strong Todo Takatora was among those insulting the nearby opposition with a hail of fist-sized river stones before the desperate battle commenced.

Despite being fought in and around a riverbed, the hot, dusty conditions and smoke from the continual firing of matchlocks at Anegawa made it hard to see and breathe, and it added to the confusion of the close hand-to-hand combat. Very few reliable sources regarding the details or tactics at the Battle of Anegawa remain, including actual casualties, nonetheless, the official Diary of Lord Nobunaga, the *Shincho-koki* notes that some 1,100 Asakura clan samurai perished in the action. It is plausible, however, to expect that many thousands more men may have been killed in the violent action as the heads of common *ashigaru* foot soldiers were rarely included in these counts, and front-line *ashigaru* numbers far outnumbered actual samurai in the armies of this time. The *Mikawa Fudoki* (the Mikawa Provincial Chronicles) provides one of the best descriptions of the disorientation and turmoil of Anegawa, and proudly points out that the bulk of the 3,170 enemy heads taken by the joint Oda-Tokugawa forces were collected by Ieyasu's warriors.

According to notes made from the *Shinpitsu Tomegaki*[7] and the remaining *Koshitsu Nenpu Ryaku*,[8] a diary of the Todo clan, Takatora was among the total 46,000 men on the field at the Battle of Anegawa on

7. The *Shinpitsu Tomegaki* (親筆留) and many other important documents related to Todo Takatora have been lost over the years, particularly during the air raids of the Second World War, when incendiary bombs destroyed a research centre in Tsu.

8. *Koshitsu Nenpu Ryaku* (公室年譜略) is a compilation of the achievements of Todo Takatora, his son Takatsugu, and grandson Takahisa, by the feudal lord Kitamura Noritsune. The title gives the impression of a monotonous simplified chronology of the Todo clan lords, but the contents are extremely detailed and contain a wealth of information not obtained from other historical books.

30 July 1570 as a spear wielding 15-year-old. It is believed his father, Torataka, was at his side and both were fighting under the direct command of Isono Kazumasa (1523–8 October 1590), a senior retainer of Lord Azai Nagamasa. Isono Kazumasa was an exceptionally brave and able veteran warrior, and as such had been in the vanguard of most of the Azai forces' battles and would shine particularly at Anegawa. He and his unit fought with great courage during the skirmish, seeing some of the most violent action of the day.

During one daring advance, Isono's horse was shot from under him, and having crashed to the earth, Isono quickly recovered, mounted a spare, and returned to the action, leading his men even deeper into the Oda forces. As a unit, Isono's men broke through the forward formations of both of Oda Nobunaga's leading generals, Shibata Katsuie and those of Toyotomi Hideyoshi. Having done so, they then came very close to reaching Nobunaga's main command post but were stopped only by the quick actions of Mori Yoshinari (1523–19 October 1570) and Sakuma Nobumori (1528–18 February 1582) who quickly redirected their troops to intercept the Isono advance and protect Nobunaga.

Unable to continue any further, and deep within enemy-held ground, Isono's small force then had to beat a hasty retreat, extracting themselves by fighting their way back out through the Oda troops to the safety of the Azai forces' front lines. This near direct attack on the Oda encampment remains one of the highlights of the Battle of Anegawa, and is recorded in the Azai clan diaries, the *Azai Sandaiki* (浅井三代記) under the title, 'Kazumasa's eleventh stage collapse of Anegawa' (員昌の姉川十一段崩し). Takatora took his first head in battle at Anegawa, a *kubi kabuto*, being the head of a ranked Tokugawa samurai claimed while still enclosed in its helmet, and deemed a fine prize indeed, but because his master lost at Anegawa, the young Takatora was neither recognised nor rewarded for the meritorious deed.

The battle ended around 2 p.m. with the deaths of an estimated 3,000 warriors. The river was said to have flowed red from the blood of those killed on both sides. So much blood was spilled that the fields around the battle site were renamed *Chihara*, the 'Blood Fields', while another nearby site is known as *Sen-nin-kiri no Oka*, the '1,000 Killed Hill'. Victory in the Battle of Anegawa was claimed by the joint Oda-Tokugawa forces.

Attack on Usayama

Later in October that same year during an attack on Usayama Castle (Otsu City, Shiga Prefecture) Todo Takatora would again come to his master's attention. Usayama Castle had been constructed by Mori Yoshinari on the orders of Oda Nobunaga not only to watch over the main route along the banks of the wide ocean-like Lake Biwa, but to protect Nobunaga's rear from the Azai and Asakura as he commenced fighting with the militant monks of the highly fortified Hongan-ji Temple in Osaka. The castle was commanded by Mori Yoshinari and supported by Oda Nobuharu, Nobunaga's younger brother. Both Mori Yoshinari and Oda Nobuharu were killed in action on 19 October 1570 when the castle fell to the overwhelming numbers of the Asakura and Azai. On the front lines of the attack, Todo Takatora bravely took another enemy head in combat, for which Azai Nagamasa presented the youth with a sword and a signed letter of commendation.

Although Todo Takatora had well and truly cut his teeth in battle, more than proving his worth and had finally come to the attention of Lord Nagamasa, he would not remain with the Azai clan for long. In 1572, Takatora had an argument with Yamashita Kasuke, a retainer of the Azai, that escalated into a fight, in which the much larger Takatora struck him down with his sword, killing him instantly.[9] For this he was forced to flee from Odani Castle with a contingent of Azai samurai in hot pursuit. Takatora is said to have often worn a colourful patterned *haori*, a loose jacket worn over a kimono and sporting a large family crest on the back. His pursuers asked the townspeople if they'd seen anyone wearing a *haori* matching the one Takatora was known to have worn, however all answered in the negative. How such a giant of a man running at breakneck speed through the town managed to evade the notice of the townsfolk remains a mystery, but Takatora is believed to have turned the flamboyant jacket inside out to mask the pattern and the crest to aid his escape.

---

9. One story has it that the cause of the argument was Yamashita Kasuke's ridiculing of Takatora's wide nose.

The Atsuji Period

Following his escape from Odani Castle, Todo Takatora then entered the service of Atsuji Sadayuki (1528–7 July 1582). Atsuji was a vassal of the Azai, and master of Yamamotoyama Castle, just 7km south-west of Odani Castle, near Nagahama along the north-eastern side of Lake Biwa. Like many mountain castles of the day, the castle's baileys, walls, gates and protective features were carved from the earth, and then built upon. The earthen embankment surrounded ruins of the *honmaru* or main bailey, and the *ni–no–maru* second bailey, located atop 324m-high Mount Yamamoto, still remain in relatively good condition to this day.

Atsuji Sadayuki appears to have been most pleased to have the young Takatora among his warriors, treating him well and providing him with a good position. Unfortunately, this situation was also not to last long. Two of Sadayuki's leading vassals, Atsuji Natasuke and Hirobe Tokube, for some reason failed to obey their master Sadayuki's direct orders, and a quarrel broke out between them and the impetuous Takatora, who again drew his weapon and killed them both for insubordination. For this, he was instantly dismissed from service and having been expelled within a year had once again became a *ronin*, a wandering, masterless samurai.

Incidentally, upon the fall of Odani Castle and the Azai clan, Atsuji Sadayuki had quickly allied himself with the forces of Oda Nobunaga and served under Nobunaga's most trusted general, Akechi Mitsuhide. He was party to the Honno-ji Incident of 1582 in which Nobunaga was attacked and killed by Akechi Mitsuhide's troops, and the subsequent Battle of Yamazaki in which Toyotomi Hideyoshi defeated the Akechi forces. Todo Takatora would also see action at Yamazaki against the Akechi forces. The 54-year-old Atsuji Sadayuki survived the battle, and made his escape back to Yamamotoyama Castle, where he was later attacked, captured and executed along with his family by Toyotomi Hideyoshi on 7 July 1582.

The Isono Years

Having only briefly served his second master, Atsuji Sadayuki, Todo Takatora roamed the land for some time until being admitted into the service of the master of Omi Ogawa Castle, Isono Kazumasa, in 1573. Takatora had served under Kazumasa at the Battle of Anagawa, and so

Kazumasa was well aware of the young man's skill and bravery. Isono Kazumasa offered Todo Takatora a generous 80 *koku*[10] to be part of his army.

Isono Kazumasa was a highly regarded warrior of the Azai clan, initially serving Lord Azai Sukemasa directly. It had been Kazumasa who had halted the enemy Rokkaku clan's attempt to take Sawayama Castle, for which the thankful Sukemasa offered him Sumamatsu Castle as a reward. When Azai Sukemasa was later overthrown – ousted by his own men and replaced by his son – Kazumasa pledged his allegiance to Azai Nagamasa, taking part in various conflicts, the Battle of Anegawa being among the most notable.

For his fine action during the attack on Odani Castle, Isono would become master of Sawayama, a large, strong and strategically important castle located in the east of modern-day Hikone City (Shiga Prefecture) overlooking the major Nakasendo route, one of the nations' five major highways.

By 1573, Oda Nobunaga had destroyed the Azai clan's allies, the Asakura, and with 35,000 troops set his sights on taking the Isono-held Sawayama Castle. Fearing humiliation in losing to Nobunaga a second time, Azai Nagamasa is said to have abducted Isono Kazumasa's elderly mother and held her hostage, threatening to execute her if Kazumasa failed to hold Sawayama. Hoping to spare his mother's life, Kazumasa and his men held out for eight months until supplies were completely exhausted, and he was forced to capitulate to Nobunaga. On hearing of the surrender, Azai Nagamasa had Kazumasa's mother killed. Acknowledging the vanquished warrior's plight, Nobunaga made Kazumasa an offer of a position within his forces and a provision of land in the Takashima district of western Omi Province.

Grateful for the opportunity, Isono Kazumasa remained in this fief, serving the Oda until 1578, when he suddenly and inexplicably fled his territory, and is believed to have spent the last five years of his life living quietly as a farmer in Omi Province. (Incidentally, Isono's yet-to-be-born grandson would become the future son-in-law of Todo Takatora.)

---

10. A *koku* is a bushel, or 180kg, of rice, said to be the amount required to feed a single man for a year, and the financial amount by which samurai and feudal lords were valued. As a comparison, at the peak of his career and while living in Kumamoto under the Hosokawa clan from 1630, the famed swordsman Miyamoto Musashi received a 300-*koku* stipend, while a well-paid professional *ashigaru* foot soldier could expect around 15 *koku*.

Following his abrupt departure, Isono's successor at Sawayama would be Oda Nobunaga's nephew, Oda Nobuzumi (1555–24 June 1582), also known as Tsuda Nobuzumi, who, in becoming the castellan of the castle, became Todo Takatora's fourth liege lord.

The Oda Nobuzumi Period

According to the *Shinke Shinpiroku* (諸家深秘録), Todo Takatora was also paid an 80-*koku* annual stipend and offered a position as a member of Oda Nobuzumi's elite *horo* brigade, a very important role during battles, and despite his large size – and the difficulty in obtaining a suitable horse in order for him to perform his job – by all accounts, it was a position that Takatora excelled at.

The *horo* brigade were mounted *tsukai-ban* messengers, orderlies or persons of noted rank in a unit. *Horo* were large cloth balloon-like devices carried on the backs of certain mounted samurai. These *horo* were first popular in the Kamakura period (1192–1333), and were a type of silk or fine cotton cape worn tied to the top and waist of the armour and left opened at the sides allowing it to billow out like a parachute when charging. Around a century and a half later, use of these capes were revived and a frame of bamboo or whale baleen was used to hold it in an inflated shape. Although the real reason is lost to history, it is believed the *horo* served a number of functions, including to intimidate an enemy, rather like a puffer-fish bloating itself for protection, or in imitation of the Gods of Wind and Thunder, who were often depicted with air-filled capes billowing out behind them. *Horo* are also believed to have been used for catching arrows shot by the enemy, but appear mostly to have been used as a form of identification on the battlefield.[11] For example, Oda

---

11. There have been a number of experiments conducted and documentaries made showing how the *horo* may have caught an arrow, and while the re-enactments look plausible, the *horo* only really works if 1) Your back is to the enemy . . . not a good position for a samurai. 2) The cape is inflated with wind, . . . i.e. it wasn't effective while stationary, or when the wind is from behind you, which is most probably the reason for adding the frame later (in this case, the *horo* cape has to be loosely fitted around the frame, as being kept taut will allow the arrow to pierce it easily). . . . and 3) at some distance from the enemy, whereby the momentum of the arrow is mostly spent. Considering that any Sengoku-period samurai of rank carrying such a device would have been wearing armour strong enough to be able to withstand arrows, the *horo* appears to be more a means of identification than for protection

Nobunaga had units of *tsukai-ban*, messengers and orderlies, and elite *Kinju* samurai kitted out with red or black *horo*, while Nobunaga's general and successor, Toyotomi Hideyoshi, had units with yellow or red *horo* on their backs. Often samurai who had shown great valour were permitted to wear the *horo* as a sign of bravery. The *horo*-wearing member of a unit could be seen by the commander and his staff from a distance, indicating the positions, depth of enemy penetration and distribution of their forces. For that reason, they were an attractive target for the enemy, and the capture of such a warrior's head was most desirable by any enemy wanting to make a name for himself.

The *Hosokawa Yusai Oboegaki*, the diary of Hosokawa Yusai (1534–1610), also suggests that the taking of an elite *tsukai-ban* messenger's head was a most desirable prize. In it is written; 'Having taken a *horo* warrior's head, wrap it carefully in the silk of their *horo*. In the case of an ordinary warrior, roll it up in their *sashimono* battle flag.' This shows both the degree to which a *tsukai-ban* was held in esteem, and also the inherent danger of being a *horo* bearer.

Takatora may well have excelled in this position, but it appears that Oda Nobuzumi failed to recognise his talents and reward him accordingly, and so a disgruntled Takatora soon took his leave and once again became a *ronin*.

The master of Sawayama Castle, Oda Nobuzumi, would end up being executed by his cousin, Oda Nobutaka, in 1582, immediately after the Honno-ji Incident in which Akechi Mitsuhide's forces attacked the great unifier Oda Nobunaga while he was resting in the lightly guarded Honno-ji Temple in Kyoto, leading to his death. Despite no evidence at the time, nor ever since, Nobuzumi was accused of a possible collaboration with his father-in-law, Nobunaga's once trusted general, and deprived of his head.

At this stage in his life, the 19-year-old Takatora was still going by the youthful name of Yokichi, but on finding employment with his next master in 1576, a number of major changes were about to occur. First, the change in liege lords would lead to his change in name from Yokichi to Yoemon. The change in lords, the change in name, and the change in position would also see a major change in Takatora's attitude, and can be seen as a considerable turning point in this remarkable man's life.

Chapter 2

The Hashiba Hidenaga Years

The then 20-year-old Takatora came into the service of General Hashiba Hidenaga in 1576. Hidenaga was born in Owari's Nakamura Village (modern-day Nakamura Ward of Nagoya City) and, as the younger half-brother of the Oda clan general Toyotomi (Hashiba) Hideyoshi, held an important position in his brother's military.

Almost forgotten by the Japanese history books, Hashiba Hidenaga (8 April 1540–15 February 1591), also known at various stages in his life as Kinoshita Koichiro, Hashiba Nagahide, and Toyotomi Hidenaga, was one of the most powerful and influential warlords of the late 1500s and can be regarded along with Kuroda Kanbei as both the brains and the brawn behind much of his half-brother Toyotomi Hideyoshi's successes, often formulating fine tactical plans and fearlessly leading the vanguard in Hideyoshi's battles.

Quite the opposite of his often brash, outspoken, ostentatious elder brother, Hidenaga was a quiet and thoughtful man. He was well liked within the samurai community, and his friendships with many of the leading lords led him to being made the prefect of Hideyoshi's *daimyo*. Trusted by all, he often took the position of intermediary between the *daimyo* and Hideyoshi when problems arose, further endearing him to the other warlords.

Hidenaga offered the young *ronin* 300 *koku*, quite a handsome stipend for someone so young. Hidenaga was not a man to take a gamble. In those days of incessant warfare, no one could be fully trusted. As such, Hidenaga would have done his 'due diligence' and thoroughly researched Takatora's background before making such an offer. He would have discovered the Todo clan's impressive family history, its connection to the former shogunate of Kyoto and clan service records, and have asked around Takatora's homelands in the Omi region and the areas of his past masters for information on his character and intents. No doubt he was impressed enough to take him on, and Takatora was singled out as having great potential.

At the time, Hidenaga was in command of a huge army, and had between 100 and 150 immediate vassals. Although highly ranked men of undoubted great military talent, very few of these men were able, or even permitted, to report directly to him. There was a chain of command, yet Takatora was soon made one of the few retainers who could freely enter Hidenaga's presence and speak directly to him. From early on in the service of Hidenaga, Takatora found someone he could fully respect. Hidenaga's military skills, his attention to detail, his calm and rational attitude, and his way with people influenced the intelligent young man for the better.

Nagahama Castle

One of Takatora's earliest experiences under Hidenaga was to work on Nagahama Castle. For his fine services to Oda Nobunaga, Toyotomi Hideyoshi had been awarded the captured Azai clan's Odani Castle as his domain, but Hideyoshi considered the mountain castle to be inconvenient, and its position difficult for controlling the province. He decided to relocate, and with Nobunaga's permission commenced construction of a fine castle right on the banks of Lake Biwa near the village of Imahara. On the orders of Hideyoshi, Hidenaga's forces were involved in the construction of this castle between 1575 and 1576, and Takatora took part. Under his new master, Takatora would see a great deal of action against various castles and in each and every campaign, he would distinguish himself. Each attack exposed him to new dangers, but at the same time increased his knowledge and understanding of fortification design and defence. These skills would come to serve him well in the years ahead.

The castle and village at Imahara were renamed Nagahama by Hideyoshi, the 'Naga' part coming from his master, Nobu**naga** and 'hama' meaning beach or coast. Nagahama was to play an important role in the 1583 Battle of Shizugatake, after which the warrior Yamauchi Kazutoyo was made castellan. Naito Nobunari replaced him after the 1600 Battle of Sekigahara. Nagahama Castle was demolished in 1615, and various parts were recycled in the construction of the now National Treasure-designated Hikone Castle.

The Chugoku Campaign

Oda Nobunaga had been rapidly expanding his hold on the central western areas of Japan known as the Chugoku region but was finding the powerful Mori clan to be more difficult to deal with than expected. For this campaign, Nobunaga had ordered Toyotomi Hideyoshi to secure Harima Province (now Hyogo Prefecture). With Hidenaga by his side, Hideyoshi was able to capture much of the region with relative ease and had advanced his forces to the former Kuroda stronghold of Himeji Castle and relocated his base there. During this time, Hideyoshi supervised the redevelopment of the castle.

During the campaign of 1577, Takatora accompanied Hidenaga to Harima Province where, as part of Hideyoshi's army, they attacked Tamba. The Tamba region consisted of four basins, the Hakami and Sasayama basins in what is now Hyogo Prefecture, and the Kameoka and Fukuchiyama basins in Kyoto. Because the Tamba region was close to Kyoto, the capital, and as it was the gateway to the western districts' San'in Region, Tamba was considered an important objective.

Another Harima Province castle that came under Toyotomi control around that time was the mountaintop Takeda Castle. Takeda was originally built in 1441 overlooking the township of Asago and the Tajima region. In 1577, the Toyotomi captured Takeda and it came into the possession of Hashiba Hidenaga who, although not the castle's commander, is known to have made some repairs and changes to the layout. Although there is no surviving documentation, it could be speculated that given the shape and layout of Takeda Castle, Takatora's position under Hidenaga and his skills in castle design, and the use of the Omi-based Anoshu stonemasons, that Takatora was most probably involved in the castle's redevelopment. Kuwayama Shigeharu was made commander of the castle upon completion of the reworking but he was transferred to Wakayama Castle in 1584 and replaced by Akamatsu Hirohide. Takeda Castle was burned down in suspected arson by Akamatsu Hirohide and abandoned following the Battle of Sekigahara. Akamatsu would be forced to commit *seppuku* for his actions. The stone ruins of Takeda Castle are often promoted as 'Japan's Machu Pichu' and have become a popular tourist spot. Incidentally, Takeda Castle is also known as Torafusu Castle – the Sleeping Tiger Castle.

The Siege of Miki Castle

As part of Hideyoshi's forces and under the orders of Oda Nobunaga, from the spring of 1578 until January 1580 Todo Takatora was engaged in the protracted siege of Miki Castle against the Mori allied Bessho clan.

The key to conquering Harima Province was the capture of Miki Castle. The township of Miki had been formed in a basin area surrounded by the Rokko Mountains immediately west of modern-day Kobe City and bordering the Harima Plains where the wide Minogawa River and the bustling Miki Highway came together. Besides being of military importance, the handy location and well-established land and river-borne trade and transport routes had attracted many craftsmen, making it a prosperous manufacturing region. Centrally located and watching over these strategically important routes and the town below was Miki Castle.

The castle site was well chosen and well defended being surrounded by natural barriers including rivers, ragged cliffs, steep mountains and deep valleys, leaving only the south-eastern sections of the castle exposed, but well-guarded nonetheless. The castle featured three main baileys covering around 500m² and was spread over the river terraces. Outer earthworks including moats and earthen walls provided extra protection.

Miki Castle was established by Bessho Noriharu (?–1513) in 1492 as the clan's main base. The Bessho clan were a branch family of the highly ranked and highly regarded Akamatsu clan, retainers to the Muromachi Shogunate and governors of the Settsu, Harima, Bitchu and Mimasaka regions (modern-day Okayama Prefecture). The Akamatsu clan's fortunes had faded as a result of a failed coup d'etat staged against the Muromachi Shogunate by the clan but had recovered their prestige following the Onin Wars of 1467–77.

The Akamatsu clan had returned to govern Harima after the Onin Wars, but the rival Yamana clan, warlords of the San'in region who had formerly held Harima, attempted to retake it. The Akamatsu and Yamana clans fought a fierce war in which the Akamatsu were supported by Bessho Noriharu, and finally Harima was recovered. As a reward for their contribution, the Akamatsu appointed Bessho Noriharu as a deputy governor of the eastern half of Harima Country. In a show of strength and as a political stronghold, the Bessho had constructed Miki Castle.

Around 1550, the powerful Miyoshi clan, which dominated the Kinki region around Kyoto and Osaka, sought to increase their land holdings and acquire Harima Province and so they attacked the Bessho. The clan head at the time, Bessho Yasuharu, fought well against the Miyoshi but being outnumbered was forced to submit to them. The Miyoshi clan soon lost a great deal of power due to internal conflicts following the death of their leader Miyoshi Nagayoshi in 1564, allowing the Bessho clan to regain independence and prominence in eastern Harima Province. During this time Miki Castle was greatly expanded and enhanced.

By 1568, Oda Nobunaga had increased his influence as far as Kyoto and had full control of Japan's central districts. Initially the Bessho clan offered their support for Nobunaga's military actions, and so maintained their status under him. Almost ten years later, in 1577, as Nobunaga continued his expansion into the Chugoku region, he appointed Toyotomi Hideyoshi as the regional commander. Hideyoshi's huge entourage lead by his trusted commanders including his brother, Takatora's master, Hidenaga, entered Harima Province and quickly secured it. At first Bessho Nagaharu (1558–2 February 1580), the grandson of Nariharu and the then leader of the clan, supported Hideyoshi and his appointment. However, the Bessho suddenly turned against the Oda forces under Hideyoshi and with around 7,500 samurai, locked themselves inside Miki Castle in March 1578.

There are a number of theories regarding the sudden turning. One of the speculations involves Nagaharu's uncle, Bessho Yoshichika, who is said to have felt insulted at having to place himself under Hideyoshi, a man whom he considered an upstart farmer making a name for himself. Yoshichika is said to have talked his nephew and his men into refusing to submit to Hideyoshi, arguing that by being placed under him the Bessho lost their status as an independent power. Hideyoshi's forces at the time were of moderate strength and so the powerful Mori clan, masters of the Chugoku region, concerned at the probability of a future Oda invasion of their lands, supported the Bessho revolt to prevent a full takeover by the Oda clan. Further, at around the same time, the family of Nagaharu's wife, the Hatano clan, warlords of Tamba county (currently the central Hyogo and north-western part of Kyoto Prefectures) also turned against Nobunaga.

During this siege, Takatora was positioned amongst the front lines of Hidenaga's troops on Mount Hiraiyama overlooking Miki Castle from the east. They were directly alongside and to the left of Hideyoshi's main command post, and based right in front of the troops of Hideyoshi's famed tactician, Takenaka Hanbei.

Hideyoshi's armies first attacked the smaller outlying castles surrounding and protecting Miki Castle. Hidenaga's troops, Takatora among them, were tasked with attacking the fortress on Mount Tanjo, in turn cutting off the main supply routes to the castle. Hidenaga's troops then attacked nearby Kouzuki and Awakawa Castles but were repelled. Their siege kept the occupants of both castles from being of concern to the Toyotomi, and from being of assistance to Miki Castle.

With the satellite castles taken, Miki was then surrounded by at least 20,000 Toyotomi troops. The Bessho had long expected this siege, and had prepared well, having ensured their storehouses were very well stocked, after which the Mori navy had made some daring secret resupply missions keeping the siege going, and on numerous occasions the Bessho attempted to break the siege, sallying forth to attack the various encampments and units surrounding the area. Hideyoshi then ordered defensive earthworks and log palisades to be built around Miki Castle, preventing anyone inside from getting out, and to prevent any supplies from getting in.

To compound matters, while the siege was reaching its climax in October 1578, Araki Murashige (1535–86), one of the generals supposedly supporting Hideyoshi, rose up against Nobunaga from his castle at Itami, near Osaka, causing great concern for the troops around Miki Castle as their rear was now vulnerable. According to a much-loved tale, after being accused of treason by Akechi Mitsuhide, Araki was called before Lord Oda Nobunaga. As was the custom, before entering Nobunaga's audience chambers he stopped at the threshold and bowed low. The story goes that Araki had sensed great danger on entering, and before bowing, had cleverly placed his iron-ribbed *tessen*, folding war fan, in front of him as was the custom, but in the tracks of the sliding *fusuma* door. Nobunaga's plan was to have a guard slam the sliding doors on Araki as he bowed, killing him. Araki's fan preventing the doors from closing, and so his life was spared. Araki would later become an apprentice to the great tea master Sen no Rikyu, and eventually come to serve Hideyoshi as a tea specialist.

With the unwavering support of his loyal generals and captains, including the ever-active Todo Takatora, Hideyoshi's forces maintained the long siege of Miki Castle. It was during this extended siege that the brilliant tactician Takenaka Shigeharu, better known as Hanbei, died of illness. Soon after, Hideyoshi's legions found themselves in a desperate situation as the enemy Mori advanced and executed a pincer attack with the Mori becoming a threat to one flank and the Bessho clan to the other. Hideyoshi ordered the attack on Kouzuki Castle to be abandoned and priority was given to the attack on Miki Castle.

Various skirmishes broke out over the next 20 months as repeated attacks were made directly on the castle, supply missions were intercepted, and sorties made by those within attempting to break out through the besiegers were contained. Hideyoshi's men were able to gradually strengthen their positions and defeat the Mori and Bessho. Bessho Nagaharu's younger brother, Harusada, lost his life in one such skirmish. During one of these battles Takatora again distinguished himself, taking a number of heads, including that of the mounted samurai Kago Rokuroemon. Having dispatched the highly ranked Kago, Takatora kept the man's horse, adding it to his spoils as Miki Castle weakened. The horse was a large, powerful beast Takatora renamed 'Kako-kuro', Kako after its' late owner, and Kuro from its jet-black coloring. Native Japanese horses of the time were small, shaggy-haired, stocky animals, looking more like a modern-day pony than a horse. Despite their small size, they were fast, nimble creatures, and surprisingly strong. While Takatora's feet would hang low, almost touching the ground when riding an average native Kisouma horse, this steed's back was 140cm above the ground, a good 20cm taller than average, and was strong enough to carry the 190cm tall, 110kg man and his hefty armour, believed to have weighed around 20kg.

After suffering a severe defeat in the maritime Battle of Kizugawa River in November 1578, the Mori clan lost their sea route supply line to the castle, yet the defenders held on. Almost a year later, in October 1579, the Ukita clan of Bizen (Okayama Prefecture) turned their support to Hideyoshi. Now there was to be no possibility of either aid nor assistance from the Mori clan.

In the bleak January of 1580, with supplies having long been depleted, and his men suffering from hunger and the cold, Bessho Nagaharu decided to capitulate, stating by letter to Hideyoshi that he would offer his own life in the manner of the samurai, on the condition that his troops within Miki Castle were spared. Having gained Hideyoshi's signed agreement, the brave warrior took the lives of his family first by his own hand, and then cut himself open on 2 February 1580. His death poem read: 'In offering my life to save others, I hold no remorse'. Bessho Nagaharu was aged just 27. Upon his demise, his uncle, Bessho Yoshichika was then set upon by his own men and killed for his role in having been the cause of the prolonged siege.

After its capture, Miki Castle was maintained as a regional administrative base until being demolished along with thousands of other castles in 1616 as part of the Tokugawa Shogunate's new policy of allowing only one castle per province. Now the former castle's central enclosure at the edge of the upper terrace remains as a park, and although it has been developed, the terrain of the surrounding areas still maintains traces of the former castle site.

This battle later came to be regarded as one of Hideyoshi's three most famous sieges, the others being the Siege of Tottori Castle (Tottori Prefecture) and the Siege of Bitchu Takamatsu Castle (Okayama Prefecture). Naturally, Todo Takatora played a role in all three.

Takatora's Battle of Ojiro

Throughout the Siege of Miki Castle Takatora had continued to be of excellent service to his lord and gained great fame for himself though his valiant actions. While the siege dragged on, a little-known insurrection known as the Battle of Ojiro welled up, and it was Todo Takatora who successfully quelled this revolt.

There is little in the way of reliable historical documentation regarding this battle itself, and the remaining few records – actual local archives and the Todo family's chronology – appear to be unclear in a number of details, and in many cases, the dates also fail to concur. However, according to research conducted by the Kami Township's Board of Education, between October 1577 and early 1580, while the siege of Miki continued, Takatora's master Hashiba Hidenaga ordered the then 21-year-old warrior to crush an uprising at Ojiro, in the Shitsumi district of what is now Kami-cho in north-eastern Hyogo Prefecture.

Hidenaga had been concentrating his efforts on subjugating the Tamba area when news came of a disorder led by one Ojiro Daizen, also known as Gando, a local *jizamurai*, a low-ranked land-owning lord of a small rural domain, and at least ninety-two of his samurai at Ojiro. The Mori allied rebels had overtaken and ensconced themselves within the area's Jouyama Castle. This was in protest at Hideyoshi's attempts to subjugate the area. These samurai were simply trying to protect their own lands and support their regional overlords, the Mori clan.

Hidenaga ordered Takatora to lead a small unit of around 120 *kibatai* cavalry and matchlock-armed *mushatai* foot samurai against the belligerents harboring in Jouyama Castle above the Ojiro Valley. Being a small band, as they approached the castle, Takatora's men set fire to the various temples along the valley. This was a psychological trick the warlord Oda Nobunaga had often used in the past when attacking castles. By showing no fear of the gods nor mercy for the temples, they would strike terror into the hearts of the enemy, as anybody brazen enough to do such a horrendous act, it was thought, must be a devilish force to be reckoned with.

The initial attack appeared to have gone very well for Takatora and his troops, but the rebels proved to be very strong and capable fighters, and Takatora's samurai were soon hit by a fierce counter-attack in the form of rocks and large logs being dropped on them from the castle above, before finding themselves caught in a pincer movement.

As arrows rained down from above, fifty cavalry reinforcements under Enya Saemonnojo from nearby Tochidani Castle in Futakata-gun (modern-day Tochidani, Shinonsen Town) arrived to support the troops of Ojiro Daizen inside Jouyama Castle. Finding themselves trapped between enemy forces left and right, many of Takatora's men were killed and just as many suffered serious injuries in the sudden and close combat. In giving the signal to retreat, the badly wounded Takatora too was forced to flee for his life. Retreating some 15km via Hiroi-zaka (now Shio Hiroi, Ojiro-ku, Kami-cho) and crossing Mount Tendaki at Ichiji Pass (currently Hagiyama, Muraoka-ku, Kami-cho) and finally to Oyatani (the modern-day township of Oya in Yabu City, Hyogo Prefecture), Takatora and but a handful of surviving men sought refuge with the regional chief, Tochio Yuzen, master of Kaho Castle, and his son, Tochio Genzaemon Yoshitsugu.

Numerous assaults took place during the nearly two-year-long campaign, with Takatora and his samurai facing the enemy almost daily. During the early stages, in their efforts to capture Jouyama Castle Takatora's forces were being continually hampered in their approach along the mountain ridge by a small but very strong and strategically located fort called Yokoyuki that doubled as a satellite guard post for the main castle. In an attempt to eliminate this outpost, Takatora and another samurai named Iai Magosaku made a night-time sortie up the side of the hill and undercover of darkness entered the fort. A fierce scuffle erupted between the surprised handful of men manning the station overnight and the two lightly armed samurai. Takatora was wounded in the attack, but he and Iai were able to claim victory.

Another conflict of note was the Battle of Kuragakino, in which Takatora was yet again badly injured during a charge. His horse was struck by an arrow and brought crashing down, throwing the giant Takatora to the ground in the process, just metres away from the Ojiro samurai. With Takatora sprawled dazed in the dirt, a group of insurgents behind the palisades quickly rushed forward and attacked him, cutting and stabbing with swords and spears at the wounded Takatora as he tried to regain his footing and fight them off. It was Tochio Yuzen's son, Tochio Genzaemon Yoshitsugu, who quickly came forth to Takatora's rescue, sending the Ojiro samurai scurrying back behind their barricades, before dragging Takatora off to safety. Afterwards it was noted that Takatora's sleeveless *jinbaori* coat worn over his lacquered steel armour had been slashed in five places.

While sheltering and recuperating with the Tochio clan at their fortified residence at the foot of Kaho Castle, Ojiro Daizen and his men discovered Takatora's whereabouts. Gathering around thirty of their best fighters, they surrounded the manor and made a daring attack. Takatora, his few remaining men, now likewise numbering around thirty, and those of the Tochio clan were trapped. A siege-like situation developed, and this small but violent confrontation went on for a couple of days before Takatora and his samurai managed to break out, and in a final show of fierce fighting around the southern banks of the Oya River, subdued and captured the attackers. To make an example of them, Takatora had the surviving rural samurai displayed spread-eagled on double-beamed wooden crosses along one of the major roadways not far from the Tochio house, and publicly executed. The site of the battle and where the insurgents met their deaths is now known as Gando-Zuka, after their leader Dairen's other name, Gando. A 4m-high cedar timber memorial to Takatora also stands over the site welcoming visitors to the sleepy hamlet.

A stone monument to Todo Takatora has been erected near the entrance to the nearby Ayu Historical Park.

Takatora is said to have stayed in the area a little longer after the uprising had been crushed in order to maintain the peace. His hosts, the Tochio family, had taken a liking to Takatora over the time he spent with them, and so Tochio Yuzen introduced him to Lady Kyuhou, the daughter of the samurai Isshiki Yoshinao, another of the local landowning gentry of nearby Nakanomura. Shortly afterwards, Takatora's parents and clan were called from Omi, and upon their arrival the wedding ceremony of Takatora and Lady Kyuhou, or O-Ku as she was also known, was carried out in the home of Tochio Yuzen. O-ku was said to have been a gentle woman, and Takatora and his bride soon became very close. From all accounts, theirs was a happy marriage, although O-Ku was unable to have children.

Around that time, Takatora was invited to build his own *yakata* residence, beside that of Lord Yuzen's mansion at the base of Kaho Castle. Kaho and the much smaller Tawa Castle, where Takatora eventually resided with his new wife and his parents who came to live with them, were located on either side of the Oya River in Yabu City's Oya district. This would remain his official residence until 1587 when he was awarded the Kokawa region in Kii Province, becoming master of Saruokayama Castle.

According to volume 2 of the *Koushitsu Nempu Ryaku* 高山公實録, Toyotomi Hideyoshi himself is said to have stopped in the area en-route to the attack on Tottori Castle, enjoying a luncheon at the Tochio clan mansion before visiting Takatora's private residence. For having ended the insurrection and having captured and executed the ringleaders, the much-pleased Hideyoshi awarded an extra 3,000 *koku* to Takatora's 300 *koku* income. Takatora's success in Oya is believed to have been another major turning point in his career, leading to his rise in position, future successes and good fortune.

Arikoyama Castle

Married life was not to slow Takatora down. Oda Nobunaga would soon send Hideyoshi and his forces against the warlords of what is now Hyogo Prefecture, and among them the Yamana, the masters of Arikoyama.

Arikoyama Castle was a mountaintop castle in Toyooka, in the centre of Tajima Province along the route that connected Fukuchiyama in Tamba Province (north-western Kyoto) and Tango, being the northern parts of Kyoto. Arikoyama Castle was constructed in 1574 by Yamana Toyosuke as the Yamana clan base, some 320m above sea level atop Mount Shiroyama on the southern edge of the Izushi basin overlooking the Izushi River.

The Yamana were once a strong and proud clan, masters of eleven of the sixty-six provinces, mostly in the Japan Sea-facing coastal San'in regions of south-western Honshu, and laying claim to having familial ties to the Ashikaga Shogun. The Yamana had been politically and financially weakened by the Onin Wars of 1467–77, and through internal bickering had lost much of their authority and lands by the sixteenth century. Yamana Suketoyo (1511–80) had settled the clan at Kurosumiyama Castle, a site about 2km north of Arikoyama, and through subjugating a number of smaller local warlords, succeeded in restoring the clan to prominence once again. This brought them to the attention of Oda Nobunaga, who ordered his general, Toyotomi Hideyoshi, to either have them bow down to him or destroy them completely. Hideyoshi launched a successful attack, quickly capturing Kurosumiyama Castle. Realising his dangerous position, Yamana Suketoyo had then sought an audience with Nobunaga, and in submitting himself to Nobunaga's authority, was permitted to retain his lands.

Suketoyo decided that as his castle had been captured all too easily, he would build a bigger, better castle on a higher mountain. This he named Arikoyama. The Yamana served Nobunaga loyally for some years, but in 1575, during Nobunaga's bid to gain control of the Chugoku region from the powerful Mori clan, the Yamana's retainers, the Otagaki of Takeda Castle, turned to support the Mori. The Yamana were then regarded as a potential enemy, and so once again, Nobunaga sent Hideyoshi into battle against them, defeating them soundly and removed them from any future position of power. Hideyoshi was then awarded Arikoyama as part of his own domains.

Hideyoshi handed control of the battle-damaged Arikoyama Castle to his younger brother, Hidenaga. Hidenaga in turn entrusted the redevelopment of the mountain and castle complex to his talented retainer, Todo Takatora. Takatora quickly seized the opportunity to design his very first castle and turned the medieval-style mountaintop fortress into a more formidable modern castle.

Under the direction of Takatora, the sides of the mountain were shaved to increase the angles and encased in stone walling built on various levels. The main *honmaru*, central bailey, became a rectangular shape, 42m long and 20m wide, and this too was surrounded by impressive walls of natural, undressed stone. Again, this was in a time when most castles had no stone walls, yet this castle had three levels of walling each 4.5m high. The technology to have built such high walls had not been fully realised at this stage, and so these can be seen as highly innovative. Up close, and like many of the early period castle walls, they seem haphazardly put together with large gaps between the various sized stones filled with smaller stones. On the contrary, this was a remarkably sturdy construction that has stood the test of time well. The larger *senjo-jiki* enceinte to the south and east of the *honmaru* was 120m long and 80m wide and is believed to have been used for residential and administrative structures. Five terraces flanked by walls of well-placed *ishigaki* spread out along the ridge below the central bailey. The walls between the main and second enceintes are particularly impressive, being around 4m high. Each section is interconnected by pathways guarded by stone walls and stone steps, all of which remain in a line of archery or gunfire at all times.

A huge 28m-wide, 12m-deep V-shaped *horikiri*, a type of dry moat, was dug across the mountain ridgeline separating the forward hilltop area and the rear *senjo-jiki* areas to further prevent the enemy from gaining easy access. Wide, deep moats would become a standard feature in Takatora-designed castles. The width of the average mountain castle's dry moat in those days was about 5 to 15m. Twenty-eight metres was an extravagance, but it was visually and physically impressive, and it was the distance at which particularly archery, and importantly, the newest weapon in the samurai arsenal, the matchlock, began to lose effect against armoured men. The entire castle was redeveloped and rebuilt by Takatora in as little as three months. Sengoku-period castles were constructed very quickly, as the enemy could attack before the fortress was completed and put into operation.

Considering a balance of both security and convenience, the average mountain castle was built at a height below 200m. Arikoyama at over 250m is quite high. The path leading to the upper fortifications is so steep it requires a guide rope in places and takes over 30 minutes to climb. Outweighing the disadvantages of its height and sheer slopes are the views of the mountains around the Izushi basin from the top. Greatly impressed by his work, the speed at which it was undertaken and the improved defences and updated design of Arikoyama Castle, Hidenaga gave Takatora a raise from 300 to 4,600 *koku*. For the next 30 years or so, the greatly improved Arikoyama Castle watched assertively over the area. The castle structures were demolished and abandoned in 1604, and the area's new lords, the Koike clan, built a smaller fortress known as Izushi Castle at the base of the mountain. The Arikoyama site is mostly in ruins now, although many of the original stone walls remain in relatively good condition and can be accessed easily. In 2017, Arikoyama Castle ruins were also listed as one of the Extended Top 100 Castles of Japan, and designated a National Historic Site.

The Taking of Tottori

The impressive castle of Tottori was a key Mori defence against Oda clan encroachment of the central western provinces of Japan, and Toyotomi Hideyoshi's army was sent to take it. Just before Hideyoshi departed Himeji for Tottori in late 1580, he held the *Shutsujin-shiki*, the pre-war ceremony, in which Takatora took part.

The *Shutsujin-shiki* was a slow and deliberate affair held with great decorum prior to a campaign or battle to reinforce pledges of loyalty. Samurai armies were often made up of greater lords – in this case Hideyoshi – with clan members, vassals, lesser lords, and retainers joining their ranks in support. The ceremony was held to bring one and all together, primarily to confirm allegiances by submitting themselves and their men to the disposal of Lord Hideyoshi, and also develop unity and cohesion before going into battle.

One by one the generals dressed in full armour and with helmets fitted would approach and go down on their right knee[1] before their lord, who was seated on a folding camp stool known as a *shogi* and surrounded by *jinmaku*, cotton curtains featuring large prints of the lord's crest. The lord

---

1. Going down on the right knee and raising the left knee pushed the *tachi* sword to the samurai's left away from the lord and made it more difficult for the sudden drawing of the sword should a vassal decide to assassinate his master.

at this stage would be wearing his armour, but not his helmet, which would be held by an attendant to his right side. Instead, he would be wearing a tall black gauze cap known as an *eboshi*.

Bowing and opening a folded epistle with a flourish, the general would read out loud from it, stating their name, title, and the numbers of troops, for example, how many matchlockmen, mounted cavalry, spearmen, and infantry samurai they had supplied. This information would then be presented in writing to their leader. The lord would then acknowledge their loyalty, sign their documents in acceptance, and hand it back. Taking the signed letter with reverence, the general would bow again, fold the letter and holding it in both hands raised forehead high, stand, and bowing, would retreat while facing the lord to a distance, before turning and returning to his position. The next general would then approach and do the same. With these formalities completed, five pieces of *awabi*, a type of abalone shellfish, seven *kuri* chestnuts, and five pieces of dried *kombu* seaweed were presented to the lord along with three saké cups of varying size. In each case, the items served on a low tray were brought forward solemly, slowly and with a great deal of pomp and circumstance by armoured warriors, all highly trusted vassals.

First the lord would choose a piece of *awabi*. Taking it in his left hand he would bite off the widest part of it, then turning it around, bite into the narrower part to make a shape resembling Mount Fuji. This represented the Japanese figure eight, (/\) and suggested *sue hiro gari* or 'spreading influence and great fortune in battle'. The smaller of the saké cups would be brought before the lord and filled with saké, poured slowly, and in three tilts of the serving vessel by a close attendant of the lord, then drunk in three sips.

Next a single, peeled chestnut or *kachi guri* (*kachi* meaning both 'peeled' and 'to win') would then be consumed, followed by the second largest cup of saké in a similar fashion to the first. After that a strip of the *kombu* seaweed would be taken, and torn into three pieces, of which the lord would eat the middle piece, and then drink the third and largest cup of saké in three gulps. The *kombu* stood for *yoro-kombu*, meaning peace and happiness after the battle.

While the lord remained seated, his helmet bearer would approach, and his helmet would be fitted and tied. When the helmet bearer had completed this, the lord would then stand, offer words of inspiration or providence, and having drawn and raised his sword, would instruct his men to draw their weapons. Thrusting his drawn sword into the air, he led the *kachidoki* cheer. Shouting 'Ei! Ei!' his men would answer raising their swords with a rousing 'Ooh!'. Again, the lord would call 'Ei! Ei!' while lifting his sword, to which all in attendance chorused 'Ooh!'. The third chant would have all in unison shouting 'Ei! Ei! Ooh!' as they punched their blades skywards.

The lord's bow would be handed to him, a ceremonial arrow notched and fired for luck. Next, the lord's horse was brought forward. If the horse neighed while being fetched, this was considered auspicious, though if the horse neighed while the lord was mounting it from the right in the manner of the samurai, it was seen as an unlucky sign.[2] If the lord then fell from his horse it was considered unlucky if he fell to the left, yet curiously fortuitous if he fell to the right.

Having completed the ceremony, Hideyoshi then led 30,000 samurai from Himeji to 250m-high Mount Taishaku to the east of Tottori, and quickly made a castle base there. The main *honmaru* of this fortress measured 65m east to west, and 40m north to south. The base of the castle was surrounded by dry moats and *dorui* earthen walls. Hideyoshi's castle site is now known as Honjin Taiko Ganaru.

Hidenaga's command post at Tottori was a long, narrow fortress, with its main enceinte running about 70m east west along the top of a hill about 300m north-west of Hideyoshi's base. This fortress was constructed by Takatora with the assistance of other vassals. Despite its small size, the experience of constructing this well-designed fortress greatly tested and increased Takatora's knowledge and understanding of castle defence and construction.

Tottori Castle was under the command of the Mori-loyal Kikkawa Tsuneie (1547–21 November 1581). In typical style, Hideyoshi attempted first to negotiate with Kikkawa, but to no avail, and so he turned to force. A 12km-long, 8m-deep trench was dug around the castle's perimeter,

---

2. While modern-day equestrians mount their horses from the left side, the samurai always mounted a horse from the right side. One of the reasons being that the sword, in this case the *tachi*, was worn slung on the left, and while wearing armour, the shorter *wakazashi* companion sword was tied firmly into the *obi* sash to the left. Mounting from the left risks catching or hitting the *tsukagashira* sword handle end caps on the saddle. Mounting from the right keeps one's hips and shoulders pointing in the same direction as the *tsukagashira* on one's *wakazashi* or *daisho* (paired *katana* and *wakazashi*).

with rows of rudimentary palisades hastily erected around that and simple wooden *yagura* watchtowers positioned every 500m. Those local villagers finding themselves trapped within the palisades were forced to take shelter inside the castle compounds. With supply routes to the castle cut off, and extra mouths to feed, stores were quickly depleted. To exacerbate the situation, Hideyoshi then openly purchased all the available rice in the region at well above market value to ensure that no supplies would be available for smuggling in.

Anyone caught entering or escaping the castle during the 200-day siege was promptly shot or cut down by spear or sword blade. As provisions ran out, the garrison and townsfolk within Tottori Castle were said to have begun eating grass, and when that was depleted, they ate the horses in the stables, and at the sieges' six-month mark were rumoured to have been considering cannibalism when the commander, Kikkawa Tsuneie, agreed to surrender himself and commit *seppuku* on the agreement the remaining samurai and townsfolk be spared. Aged 34, Kikkawa dressed himself in a pea-green kimono and a black silk jacket, recited two poems to his gathered men, then slipping off his upper garments, took a razor-sharp dagger to slice himself once vertically across his lower stomach, and then again in a perpendicular vertical cut to form a plus-shaped wound. He then turned to his second – a trusted retainer – reminding the swordsman about to take his head that, 'Hideyoshi will be inspecting this head. Make sure you cut it off cleanly', and stretching his neck forward, was promptly decapitated, along with three other loyal retainers who followed him in death. The castle's surviving occupants were soon freed, but unfortunately, many of the famished survivors then succumbed to gorging, a most painful death from overeating the food provided to them by Hideyoshi's forces.

Azuchi

Japan is an earthquake-prone country – in fact 20 per cent of the world's earthquakes occur in Japan – and as such, stone was never used for domestic buildings, but was used extensively for castle walls. *Ishigaki*, literally 'stone hedges', are the drystone walls of Japanese castles, constructed without the use of mortar, allowing for a degree of movement in earthquakes. These walls often look haphazardly made yet are exceptionally strong. What we see from the outside is only the end of the rock itself. The bulk of the stone lies inside the wall. Samurai castle walls are built sloping inwards and with the stones set into the wall at an angle. This is not just to be able to support a heavier structure on top, but because of earthquakes. If the stones were laid flat, like Western bricklaying techniques, the stones would dislodge in times of seismic activity, and fall. Being laid on an inward angle means that in an earthquake, the force of gravity causes the stones to fall inwards, further strengthening and firming-up the walls.

Todo Takatora was still going by the name of Todo Yoemon around the time that Oda Nobunaga announced the construction of his magnificent Azuchi Castle in 1576. Nobunaga's new castle and planned power base was to be built on a mountain alongside Lake Biwa. Strategically it was an ideal position. Located in the geographical centre of Japan, it overlooked the route to Kyoto via the vital Nakasendo highway, as well as the water traffic on Lake Biwa. Toyotomi Hideyoshi had been ordered to construct certain segments of the castle, and in turn had set numerous tasks for his brother Hashiba Hidenaga to complete. Under Hidenaga, Takatora was further able to hone his considerable skills while participating in the construction work.

Even today, many people, including the Japanese, tend to believe that a castle without *ishigaki* stone walling and a *tenshu* tower keep is not a proper castle. They fail to realise that a castle is not a keep nor structures, but the fortified area within a moat. Early Japanese castles were made primarily from earth. A moat was dug, and the soil taken from it was used to build an earthen embankment inside the moat. Along the top of this high earthen wall were log or plank palisades, later stronger, more protective wattle-and-daub mud walls, and sturdy watchtowers were built. Later, these outer earthen walls came to be clad in stone. Stone walls provide a strong, impressive image, certainly demonstrating the authority and prestige of the master of the castle. Anyone who could afford to have such huge stones sourced, then brought to the castle site and manoeuvred into position by hand (i.e. without the use of cranes, bulldozers or trucks) must be someone of extreme wealth and power. Same too with the tower keep. For the majority, this was simply a highly visual symbol of authority.

Castle construction technology was extensively developed and consolidated with the building of Azuchi Castle. One of the greatest innovations adopted by Oda Nobunaga on this particular project was the widespread use of piled dry-stone walls. Nobunaga only lived at six castles;

his birthplace of Shobata, then Nagoya, Kiyosu, Komakiyama (all in Aichi Prefecture), Gifu and finally Azuchi. Only two, Komakiyama and Azuchi, he constructed himself. Komakiyama was innovative in that the top of the small 65m-high mountain had been levelled, and the sections below that carved into a multi-levelled shape not unlike a Mayan or Mesoamerican step pyramid with the sides of the upper three levels cut back to increase the angle of the walls, which were then encased in huge boulders and stones known as *ishigaki*. This imposing modification started the trend for samurai castles to be encased in walls of stone, particularly once the nation's warlords had seen the effect of Azuchi. Azuchi was encased completely in stone, and despite no structures still standing, even now remains a most impressive castle site. For a man of Takatora's skills and tastes, Azuchi would have appealed to his creative and military senses, and no doubt affected his future castle designs.

The second major innovation was the towering keep, the likes of which Japan had never seen before. It was a grand six storeys high, including the basement within the piled stone base below. Until then, most castle structures never went above three storeys, and even then were certainly nowhere near as fine as the castle Nobunaga envisaged. It was to impress and intimidate his enemies with its scale and grandeur. Further, his trusted generals including Shibata Katsuie, Toyotomi Hideyoshi, Tokugawa Ieyasu, Maeda Toshiie and all would now be close at hand, having been allocated land either side of the wide main approach to the keep on which to build their residences.

Nobunaga ordered the keep to have the awe-inspiring dignity of the tall cathedrals of Europe that he had heard about from the visiting foreign missionaries. It was an opulent structure, inside and out. Inside it was fully lacquered and featured gold leaf covering on the walls along with other rich furnishings and art. Nobunaga himself would live within the upper floors of this magnificent structure. He gave his carpenters three years to complete the assignment.

Once the enormous task of cutting the mountain and carving out the baileys and gateways, and the setting of the stone walls was completed, Okabe Mataemon and his team erected the soaring timber-framed tower and surrounding defensive buildings. Okabe Mataemon was the master carpenter of Atsuta Jingu Shrine, second only to the Great Shrine of Ise, and located in the southern suburbs of Nagoya City. His family had constructed a number of shrines and temples around the Nagoya region, and he was responsible for the maintenance and upkeep of Atsuta Shrine and its surrounding buildings. His ancestors had been master builders to the Ashikaga Shogunate during the time of the eighth Shogun, Yoshimasa, and Mataemon himself possessed remarkable talents for architectural design, specialising in the older, grander style of architecture seen in the larger, more complex temples of the capital.

Mataemon had served Nobunaga from the time of the Battle of Okehazama. In 1573, Nobunaga had ordered the construction of a warship with which to control the waters of Lake Biwa. This was 59m long, 13m wide and carried a castle-like structure on her top deck. The ship was completed by Okabe and his men in two months, well ahead of schedule. The result pleased Nobunaga immensely. As such, Okabe was made master builder of Nobunaga's grand fortress, and placed over the local Koura carpenters who also played a major role in the construction of Azuchi.

Azuchi Castle's keep is believed to have been the biggest multi-storeyed wooden structure in the world at the time. It was shaped like that of a huge temple building set atop *ishigaki* stone walls, with a fascinating tower structure on top. While the lower floors were mostly covered in white plaster with black wooden cladding, the central tower was the focal point. The upper most roof was covered in glittering golden tiles above a white-walled exterior. The floor below that was octagonal – supposedly representing heaven – topped with blue glazed tiles and surrounded by red walls and balustrades. Under that was the blue tiled, white-walled three-storey main part of the castle. It was the most splendid building Japan, possibly the world, had ever seen. The entire project took just under three and a half years.

Azuchi Castle soon became the talk of the nation. During the summer months, Nobunaga would hang paper lanterns from the eves of the tower keep, illuminating it at night and creating an entertaining spectacle for the people of the new town. From Azuchi, Nobunaga would continue his push to conquer the nation. His dream of controlling the nation was within reach, or so he believed.

The Siege of Takamatsu, the Honno-ji, and the *O-Gaeshi*

After the Siege of Tottori ended, Hideyoshi led his army around 130km south to Bitchu Province (modern-day Okayama Prefecture), for the famed siege of Takamatsu Castle. Before attacking the main castle, the surrounding supporting castles had to be eliminated. Todo Takatora was in the lead on the attack on one of those satellites, Kanmuriyama Castle, also known as Sukumozuka Castle, located about 4km away from Takamatsu. Kanmuriyama Castle was situated on a low hill about 40m high and surrounded by flat rice paddys. It was held by Hayashi Saburozaemon. Some 20,000 Oda-allied samurai descended on the area on 17 April and immediately assailed the small fortress with fervour, expecting it to fall easily. Instead, they were surprised at the repulse they received from the defenders within, so much so that the attackers were forced to retreat temporarily before doubling their efforts. Kanmuriyama was not to be brought down as easily as expected.

The continued storming of the castle resulted in a great loss of life on both sides. As per usual, Takatora was in the front lines from the start. Amid the brutal action at the base of the hill, Takatora came face to face with the enemy general, Taketomo Konosuke. In the savage hand-to-hand spear combat that ensued, Takemoto Konosuke was defeated and Takatora – now sporting new wounds – took his head as a trophy. Eight days after the attack began, fire broke out in one of the inner central compounds of Kanmuriyama and quickly spread across the confined complex, destroying the castle and forcing its 51-year-old commander Hayashi Saburozaemon and the remaining 139 defenders to commit *seppuku* amongst the roaring flames. Toyotomi Hideyoshi later singled out Takatora for his achievements in battle and presented him personally with a scarlet felt *jinbaori* war coat. The castle had been attacked with such ferocity that the defenders of another nearby satellite castle, Etta, having seen the damage inflicted on life and property, capitulated. Its master pleaded for mercy in surrender and promptly withdrew.

With Kanmuriyama and Etta Castles taken, Todo Takatora returned to his master's side. Lord Hidenaga had been assisting his brother at the Siege of Takamatsu Castle against the Mori clan from April 1582. As suggested by the tactician Kuroda Kanbei, Hideyoshi had ordered a series of levees be constructed, and then by diverting the nearby Etta and Kumozu rivers, had begun flooding the low-lying castle area. Heavy seasonal rains had simply accelerated the flooding. Fortified floating barges had been organised to allow the attacking forces to maintain a continual barrage of gunfire towards the castle as the waters rose. The rapidly rising waters struck fear into the defenders, and the constant firing of matchlocks and small cannon at the castle wore on the defenders' nerves. As the siege continued, Mori Terumoto began to amass an army said to have been nearly six times larger than Hideyoshi's forces, and so to counter this, Hideyoshi had written to Nobunaga urgently requesting reinforcements.

At the time, Nobunaga was staying in the Honno-ji, a regularly-used influential temple in central Kyoto. Nobunaga's leading generals were spread out along the borders of his expanding empire. Shibata Katsuie, for example, was in Echigo (Niigata Prefecture) facing the Uesugi. General Niwa Nagahide was involved in the invasion of Shikoku, and Takigawa Kazumasu's troops were stuck in modern-day Gunma and Nagano Prefectures in their campaign against the Hojo clan, while Toyotomi Hideyoshi was preoccupied with the attack on the Mori-held Takamatsu Castle. Nobunaga was at the centre of this empire and, believing himself safe in this Kyoto temple, was surrounded by as few as seventy guards and around as many scribes, assistants and maidservants. On receiving Hideyoshi's request for reinforcements, Nobunaga had ordered his most trusted general, Akechi Mitsuhide, to lead his men to Takamatsu in support of the Toyotomi. On the night of 20 June 1582, Akechi Mitsuhide assembled some 13,000 troops and led them out of his castle at Tamba Kameyama, but instead of leading them towards Takamatsu, he turned in the direction of Kyoto, telling his men that 'The enemy is within the Honno-ji'! They attacked Nobunaga as he slept in the temple's main hall in the early hours of 21 June.

Mitsuhide is often portrayed as leading the attack on Nobunaga at the Honno-ji personally, but in fact had positioned himself about 20km south of Kyoto when his troops surrounded the temple. As the armoured samurai poured through the temple's main gates a great cry went up from attackers and defenders alike. Woken by the cacophony, Nobunaga roused his staff, sending the women and non-military personnel from the temple and out of harm's way. Stepping outside onto the hall's wide veranda, he watched as the armoured warriors, most carrying the light blue battle flags featuring the bellflower crest of the Akechi on their backs, filled the grounds. In the ensuing few minutes of melee, Nobunaga was badly wounded by matchlock fire and arrows while fending off the attackers with bow and arrow, and then, when the bowstring snapped, a spear. Realising the situation was hopeless, the great general then retreated back into the main pavilion, and setting it alight, committed *seppuku* amongst the flames. Although there are many theories and even more stories regarding the treachery, the true reason for Akechi Mitsuhide's turning remains one of history's greatest mysteries.

Although Mitsuhide did not personally kill Nobunaga, he claimed responsibility and then claimed the title of Shogun based on his ancestry. The betrayal shocked the nation. Mitsuhide had expected little opposition to his coup, as he believed the other Oda generals to be too far away and otherwise engaged in their objectives to be of help or hindrance.

Twenty-four hours later, however, some Toyotomi samurai intercepted a letter from Akechi Mitsuhide addressed to the Mori clan explaining that Nobunaga had been destroyed and offering a plan of cooperation in defeating the Toyotomi invaders. Shortly after, Hideyoshi received direct confirmation of Nobunaga's shocking death. Hideyoshi quickly and peacefully resolved the situation with the Mori, and set out to avenge the death of his lord. Keeping Nobunaga's death a secret, he calmly suggested to the Mori that peace could be easily achieved and the men of Takamatsu spared on the condition that their master, Shimizu Muneharu, commit *seppuku*. Completely unaware of Nobunaga's demise, Muneharu complied on 23 June. Setting out from the castle in a small boat, he was rowed to a position where both sides could witness the brave lord cut himself open, and his second decapitate him. His head was then presented to Hideyoshi, and the siege was lifted.

Hideyoshi then quickly set in motion one of the greatest feats of logistics Sengoku-period Japan, or even samurai history, had ever seen, the *O-gaeshi* as it is known in Japanese, or the 'Great Return'. Within ten days he had organised his entire force, Takatora among them, to break camp, march the 205km from Takamatsu to Kyoto covering over 30–40km per day. Hideyoshi had sent messengers ahead, ordering any available horses be readied, lodging and bedding be prepared where possible, and large amounts of rice to be cooked and prepared for his samurai and *ashigaru* forces to eat on the march. By 2 July this huge army had arrived and regrouped at Yamazaki just outside the capital. Here, exhausted but eager to seek justice, they met with Akechi Mitsuhide's army, and a furious battle broke out.

The Battle of Yamazaki

Mitsuhide had been unsuccessful in his bid to raise additional troops from the local peasantry or from former allies such as the Hosokawa clan who refused to participate in disgust at Mitsuhide's actions. Mitsuhide had counted on the support of the Hosokawa, particularly as his daughter Gracia was the wife of Hosokawa Tadaoki. With limited support, Akechi Mitsuhide chose to face the Toyotomi at Yamazaki, an area south of Kyoto, and had already taken control of two key positions, nearby Shoryuji Castle, a strategic stronghold used since 1339 in the defence of the capital, Kyoto, and Yodo Castle in nearby Fushimi, where Takatora would later return to work on Matsudaira Sadatsune's castle in 1623. Yamazaki was positioned between the Yodo River protecting the south along Mitsuhide's left flank, and the 270m-high Mount Tennozan protecting his right. The area between the river and the mountain was marshland, and this, he believed, would give him an advantage over his larger opposition as the swamps made the pass even narrower causing a bottleneck in which Mitsuhide's troops could check the Toyotomi advances.

Any confidence Mitsuhide felt was soon dashed as the Toyotomi forces arrived much faster and in greater numbers than the Akechi had expected. Despite being near exhaustion, the Toyotomi regiments were ever ready to fight. Upon realising the scale of Hideyoshi's forces now bearing down on him, Mitsuhide had wisely decided not to be caught inside a castle and sent his troops forward. Mitsuhide himself led the bulk of his forces to Yamazaki, not far from where the namesake Japanese whisky is distilled and set his battalion along the banks of the narrow Enmyoji River (currently known as the Koizumi River).

On the eve of the battle Nakagawa Kiyohide and his 2,500 men and Takayama Ukon's 2,000 troops had occupied the village of Yamazaki and held the front lines along the old Saigoku Kaido highway. Hideyoshi had secured himself to the rear in the Hozumi-ji Temple. Between him and the enemy were his 20,000 men, including those seconded from his allies, Niwa Nagahide and Takayama Ukon, and another 10,000 samurai under Oda Nobunaga's third son Nobutaka. These divisions had taken their positions immediately below Mount Tennozan on the flat lands facing the Akechi troops on the opposite banks of the Enmyo-ji River.

Foolishly, especially for someone as skilled in the military arts as Akechi Mitsuhide, he had failed to secure Mount Tennozan.[3] Instead, this vital position was quickly taken by Todo Takatora's master, Hashiba Hidenaga, and alongside him, the troops of the expert tactician Kuroda Kanbei. Looking down on the Akechi formations, they could see that Akechi Mitsuhide was positioned to the rear of his forces, just south of Shoryuji Castle. Akechi's allies, Saito Toshimitsu, Ajitsu Sadayuki, Ise Sadaoki, Mizuo Shigetomo and Ogawa Suketada formed a barrier along the narrow front between the rivers and the mountain.

Under cover of darkness on the night of 1 July, Hideyoshi's generals Nakamura Kazuuji and Horio Yoshiharu are said to have ordered their ninja[4] into the Akechi encampments, where they caused fear and confusion, spreading gossip, setting tents on fire, releasing the tethered horses and the like, anything to psychologically upset the enemy.

The battle began in earnest the next morning, 2 July, as the Toyotomi troops gathered opposite the Akechi units across the Enmyoji River. A small contingent of Akechi samurai under the command of Matsuda Masachika and Nabika Kamon first attempted to cross the river below Mount Tennozan in the hopes of wresting control of the strategically important position from Hashiba Hidenaga and the Kuroda troops above, but were repelled by matchlock fire, then chased off by Toyotomi generals Kato Mitsuyasu and Ikeda Tsuneoki before they could reach the foot of the mountain.

Less than an hour later that same combination of Ikeda Tsuneoki, his son Motosuke, and Kato Mitsuyasu's troops themselves crossed the Enmyoji River covertly to check the movements of the Akechi-allied Tsuda Nobuharu along the Yodo River. Tsuda's troops suddenly found themselves coming under attack from three sides, and their ranks were

---

3. Takatora's descendants would see battle around Tennozan again some 286 years later at the end of the Edo period when the Todo clan of Tsu Domain fought in the Battle of Toba-Fushimi in 1868. It would be the actions of the Todo clan under Todo Takayuki that would turn the tide of the battle against the Tokugawa Shogunate in favour of the new imperial army.

4. Far from being the black clad, superhero-like warriors portrayed on TV and the movies, ninja, better known by the contemporary term of *shinobi*, were simply infiltrators, spies and agitators.

thrown into panic as they were decimated. Following the positive action of Ikeda's troops, Niwa Nagahide and Oda Nobutaka's troops made their move, launching a flank attack on the central body of Mitsuhide's men. Meanwhile, Hidenaga's men, Takatora among them, and those of the Kuroda had come down from their position on Mount Tennozan to join the melee and support Nakagawa Kiyohide and Takayama Ukon's troops who had been struggling against those of Saito Toshimitsu and Ise Sadaoki. Gradually the Toyotomi forces began to gain the upper hand, and the rout began. Saito soon broke away and left the battle line. Matsuda Masachika, now facing Kuroda Kanbei's well-trained troops, and Ise Sadaoki, were killed in action. Akechi's army began to retreat. With Ikeda Nobuteru reinforcing Hideyoshi's right flank, Hideyoshi's main forces were able to march directly against the Akechi.

After sending a messenger to Mitsuhide saying, 'Pull back while I die', the bravest of his retainers, Mimaki Kaneaki, and 200 of his remaining samurai put up a bold front against the rapidly advancing Toyotomi in attempt to buy some time for his master and retreating comrades. They stood their ground as Hashiba Hidenaga's men led by Takatora rapidly approached, and at the last minute, the few matchlockmen amongst them let loose the contents of their barrels. Numerous Hashiba samurai fell dead before them, but the yelling, screaming hordes of enemy samurai continued bearing down upon them. There was no time to reload the guns. The archers nervously released their arrows, yet their efforts were nowhere near enough to stop the oncoming wave of warriors. As the flood of Toyotomi closed in on Mimaki and his men, spears and swords became the final weapons of choice, but the Toyotomi samurais' momentum was such that they completely bulldozed them, slashing and cutting them down and trampling over their bloodied corpses in their desire to reach their prize, the head of Akechi Mitsuhide.

Shoryuji Castle was a strategic stronghold, a *hirajiro*, flatland castle, rectangular in shape covering 120m east to west and 80m north to south. Twelve-metre-wide water moats, with 10m-high, 5m-wide *dorui* earthen embankments, topped with sturdy walls and watchtowers made it a stable and secure castle. While Hidenaga directed from the rear, Takatora took his position at the front shouting orders and encouragement, leading the weary troops now severely depleted from the violent encounters of the day, in an intermittent advance on Shoryuji Castle. Takatora had survived the matchlock fire and the arrows and was now preparing his men to attack. Unknown to Takatora and his men was that Akechi Mitsuhide had secretly escaped from the north gate of Shoryuji Castle and was well on his way to Sakamoto Castle by the time the thousands of Toyotomi-allied samurai converged on the fortress. The trapped Akechi men fought back with matchlocks and a continuous hail of arrows, but to no avail. The 16,000 defenders were soon overrun, many at this time choosing to desert. The garrison collapsed within two hours and the Toyotomi claimed victory. The Akechi troops had been defeated by the 30,000 samurai under the supreme command of Hideyoshi and Oda Nobutaka. Despite the nearly two-to-one ratio, 3,000 Akechi samurai were killed, while the exhausted Toyotomi suffered 3,300 losses, proving that both armies had put up an extraordinarily strong fight.

Having been put to flight, the defeated Akechi Mitsuhide was attempting to reach the safety of his Sakamoto Castle on the banks of Lake Biwa in Omi. He only made it as far as Ogurusu village in southern Kyoto's Fushimi-ku area where, the story goes, he was attacked by peasants armed with nothing more than bamboo staves and killed. A most inglorious end for an elite samurai. He was 54 years old, and had been self-proclaimed Shogun for all of 13 days. Mitsuhide's head was delivered to the Toyotomi army the next day, and was put on public display before the Honno-ji in Kyoto and then at Awataguchi.

Hideyoshi's Ascension to Power

The *Kiyosu Kaigi* was Japan's first major political gathering, held on 16 and 17 July 1582, just three weeks after the death of Oda Nobunaga at the Honno-ji incident, and two weeks after the Battle of Yamazaki in which Toyotomi Hideyoshi defeated the troops of Nobunaga's attacker, Akechi Mitsuhide. The remaining vassals of the Oda were hurriedly called together at Kiyosu Castle to determine Nobunaga's successor and the future of the clan. Nobunaga's eldest son and designated heir, Nobutada, had been killed by the Akechi forces attack on Kyoto's Nijo Castle immediately after the attack on the Honno-ji. For most, there was no reason to doubt that Nobunaga's succession would be contested between his sons, Nobukatsu and Nobutaka. Both were 24 years old, born just 20 days apart to different mothers. Nobutaka was actually born first, but as his mother was of lower social rank than Nobukatsu's mother, Nobukatsu was given the honour of being named as Nobunaga's second son, and Nobutaka the third son. But who to support? Nobukatsu had been adopted as heir to the Kitabatake clan of Ise and has been described as an incompetent leader, and appears to have been unpopular among the retainers. Nobutaka, on the other hand, was more battle-hardened, wiser, and more decisive than his brother.

Once all the retainers had gathered, with the exception of Takigawa Kazumasu, who was late, Maeda Toshiie and Sassa Narimasa who were engaged with the enemy in the field, and Tokugawa Ieyasu, the two-day meeting commenced. Those in attendance included Oda Nobukatsu, Shibata Katsuie, Toyotomi Hideyoshi, Niwa Nagahide, Ikeda Tsuneoki, Maeda Gen'i and Hori Hidemasa.

In the early stages, it is believed that Shibata Katsuie, as chief retainer of the Oda clan, suggested that Nobutaka, being of the right age and disposition and because of his experience in the field, would be best suited to the position. Shibata Katsuie and Nobutaka had already established a long-standing relationship. Katsuie had officiated at Nobutaka's *Genpuku* (coming of age ceremony) almost 10 years earlier, and had since acted as an advisor and mentor to him. Having Nobutaka at the head of the Oda clan would also ensure Katsuie's position as chief retainer. This proposition further soured relations between Nobutaka and Nobukatsu who, as officially-designated second son, had expected to be automatically nominated as heir. Incidentally, while Nobukatsu was present at the conference, Nobutaka, despite having taken an active part in defeating the Akechi forces at the Battle of Yamazaki, was left out.

According to the *Tamon'in Nikki*, a diary compiled by monks covering a 140-year long period from 1478 to 1618, following Shibata Katsuie's nominating Nobutaka, Toyotomi Hideyoshi, it appears, then nominated Nobunaga's grandson, and the first son of the late Nobutada, the two-year-old Samboshi (later to be named Hidenobu) as rightful heir. This must have been a surprise to most in attendance, and especially to Nobukatsu, having now been passed over a second time. Reminding all before him of the Oda clan laws, and of the infant's position at birth, Hideyoshi, with the child in his arms, argued that Samboshi was the rightful heir. Hideyoshi's motion was supported by Niwa Nagahide. Four days later, the top four retainers would meet again, and with a three-member majority, Samboshi was chosen as leader of the Oda clan.

This caused yet another slight rift between the clan retainers. There were still many who supported Shibata Katsuie in his efforts to have Nobukatsu installed as leader, and there were those who believed Hideyoshi was correct in seeking to have Nobunaga's grandson as clan leader. How many saw the true path Hideyoshi was taking in nominating himself and appointing the infant boy's two uncles, Nobukatsu and Nobutaka, as guardians of Samboshi? The boy's uncles, Nobunaga's sons, could not see eye to eye, and that would leave Hideyoshi in the role of de facto leader, 'advising' the young lord, ruling in his stead, just as generations of the puppet Ashikaga Shogunate had been controlled by the Miyoshi and Hosokawa puppet masters.

After a day of deliberations, the decision to accept Sanboshi was made. The following day's agenda consisted of how the former Akechi lands were to be divided amongst the retainers and other Oda property was to be redistributed. A memorial service for Nobunaga was observed, and then Lord Sanboshi's succession ceremony was held. All eyes were on young Lord Sanboshi. And of course, his new mentor, Toyotomi Hideyoshi.

The *Kiyosu Kaigi* resulted in a major power shift between the retainers, lessening the influence of Shibata Katsuie and giving greater control to Hideyoshi. It also saw the start of the Oda clan's decline. It would not be long before the Oda retainers would split into two factions and go to war with one another.

Meanwhile Nobutaka had gained Mino Province, his late elder brother's lands. It fell far short of his initial expectations, and he watched as Hideyoshi further usurped his family's lands and power. In an effort to win them back and oust Hideyoshi from his ill-gotten position, he encouraged the equally disgruntled old warriors Shibata Katsuie and Takigawa Kazumasu to make a move against Hideyoshi. In response to this intrigue, Nobutaka soon found himself trapped inside his new castle at Gifu, surrounded by his brother, Nobukatsu's troops. Tensions escalated, spilling over into a battle between the armies of Katsuie and Hideyoshi. This was the Battle of Shizugatake.

The Battle of Shizugatake

Another major battle in which Todo Takatora would play an important role and once again distinguish himself, seeing front-line action and receive numerous wounds, was the Battle of Shizugatake.

As tensions between Hideyoshi and Katsuie increased, it was obvious to all that there was to be no backing down by either side. During the late winter of 1582, Shibata Katsuie and his troops had returned to their lands at Echizen (Fukui Prefecture) and while they were snowbound in the Shibata clan's Kitanosho Castle, Hideyoshi made the first strike, attacking Katsuie's son, Katsutoyo, in Nagahama Castle. The castle had been built by Hideyoshi and as he was well aware of its strengths and weaknesses, it fell within days. Nagahama was returned to Hideyoshi's hands. From there, Hideyoshi turned his attentions on Gifu Castle, where Oda Nobunaga's son Nobutaka had foolishly provoked his ire. The Toyotomi responded with such force that Nobutaka surrendered immediately.

The following January of 1583, the Shibata-allied Takigawa Kazumasu attempted an attack on Hideyoshi, but the 50,000 loyal Toyotomi troops soon deafted the Takigawa's forces. Hideyoshi then considered the very real threat of the snowbound Katsuie and Maeda Toshiie becoming mobile as spring approached and planned accordingly.

As Japan emerged from the winter cold, Hideyoshi ordered four small forts to be built on the bottleneck area of mountains between the northern most point of Lake Biwa and the southern shores of the smaller Lake Yogo – later said to have been stained red by the blood of the samurai killed in action – in an effort to prevent Shibata Katsuie's 30,000 troops from advancing along either the eastern or western sides of Lake Biwa.

The northernmost of these forts was Iwasaki-yama, which overlooked the vital Hokkoku-kaido highway. Iwasaki-yama was left in the control of Takayama Ukon. To the south of that was Oiwa held by Nakagawa Kiyohide. Below that, on Mount Shizugatake, another large fortress was constructed and held by Takatora's master, Hidenaga. On the other side of the Hokkoku-kaido running below these three castles, was Mount Tagami, upon which Hideyoshi set his command post. When Shibata Katsuie was finally able to leave Echizen he established himself 10km north of this position on Mount Uchinakao. Each side then waited and watched one another.

Another sudden insurrection instigated by Gifu-based Oda Nobutaka forced Hideyoshi to return to Gifu Castle and again he laid siege to Nobutaka. It turned out to be fortuitous for Hideyoshi, as not long after he had left the northern Biwa region, Shibata Katsuie ordered his nephew Sakuma Morimasa to take these fortresses.

Nakagawa Kiyohide (1542–6 June 1583) was in command of the fortress on Mount Oiwa. Kiyohide is among history's most curious of samurai characters. Originally an independent *daimyo* from the province of Settsu, around the northern Osaka, southern Hyogo Prefectures, Kiyohide quickly submitted to Oda Nobunaga out of fear when Nobunaga marched on Kyoto and threatened the Osaka region. Some years later, in 1578, when Araki Murashige suddenly rebelled against Nobunaga, Kiyohide in collusion with him also turned. Nobunaga promptly raised a large army against them both. Nakagawa Kiyohide soon surrendered and turned yet again, attacking Araki Murashige in the hopes of appeasing Nobunaga and escaping his wrath. After defeating Murashige, Kiyohide took part in various battles under the Oda generals Niwa Nagashige and Ikeda Tsuneoki and saw action at the Battle of Yamazaki under Hideyoshi.

Fort Oiwa was considered the securest of the strongholds constructed by the Toyotomi troops to repel the Shibata forces. Kiyohide was therefore shocked when the Sakuma army attacked Oiwa early on, and fought with great valour. Despite this, Oiwa was overwhelmed, and Nakagawa Kiyohide and his force of only a few hundred men were all killed. Hideyoshi was said to have cried upon hearing of the loss of Kiyohide and his men, and of the brave fight they had put up. Kiyohide's grave lies at the peak of Mount Oiwa. On the anniversary of his death, memorial services are held for him and his men even now.

Having captured Fort Oiwa, Sakuma Morimasa's troops then turned their attention to Fort Iwasaki-yama, bringing it down and forcing Takayama Ukon (1552 or 1553–5 February 1615) to flee for his life. Sakuma's troops then surrounded Hashiba Hidenaga's corps, including Todo Takatora, in Fort Shizugatake. Overconfident in his own abilities, Sakuma had made the fatal mistake of disobeying his uncle's orders.

'Never underestimate the Toyotomi. When you capture Fort Oiwa, move your troops into it, and hold it firm!' were Katsuie's instructions. Instead, Sakuma had left Fort Oiwa, intending to set siege line camps around Shizugatake in an attempt to take it. He knew that Hideyoshi was still at Ogaki Castle, having just attacked Oda Nobutaka at Gifu Castle again, and so Sakuma estimated it would take around three days for Hideyoshi to move his 20,000 troops back to Shizugatake, by which time Sakuma was sure he would be able to take the mountaintop fortress, leaving Hideyoshi without a secure base and therefore vulnerable. Meanwhile Hidenaga's men within the well-fortified Shizugatake feared they would not be able to hold off Sakuma's troops for long and made emergency plans for their evacuation. As they were considering their future, Hideyoshi's general Niwa Nagahide had taken a ship across Lake Biwa and arrived with 2,000 reinforcements. Niwa's arrival prevented Sakuma from taking the fortress easily.

Later that evening, Sakuma Morimasa was shocked to see thousands of flaming torches burning around the base of the mountain. The Toyotomi forces had marched 52km from Ogaki Castle and within around five hours they had moved into a position where they were threatening the Sakuma. Todo Takatora was amongst those leading troops and had assumed a position whereby they could seriously threaten Sakuma. And that is exactly what he commanded his troops to do!

Takatora sent his men in with matchlocks blazing and arrows filling the sky. The Todo samurai climbed the 421m-high mountain and, firing volley after volley, attacked with such vehemence that Sakuma Morimasa's men were forced to make an immediate retreat. The attack was so overwhelming, the Sakuma samurai are said to have abandoned their weapons on the spot and cast off their armour in order to make a hasty escape north to safety. Shortly after, Takatora led troops attacked the Shibata stronghold, forcing Shibata Katsuie to abandon his base camp on Mount Uchinakao and make a break for his castle of Kitanosho, about 50km away in Echizen, (modern-day Fukui City).

Todo Takatora had been badly injured in the close fighting, but this did not prevent him and his samurai from leading the pursuit of the fleeing Sakuma troops, who were closely followed by those of Hideyoshi's army and his generals. Katsuie realised his situation was now hopeless, but could not bring himself to surrender to the likes of the usurper Toyotomi Hideyoshi. Instead, three days after arriving at Kitanosho Castle, and surrounded by Toyotomi troops, he ordered his wife O-Ichi – his late master Nobunaga's sister – to leave the castle and escape to safety.

Although she did send her three daughters, fathered by her first husband, Todo Takatora's former master Azai Nagamasa, to safety, O-Ichi refused to leave Katsuie's side. Katsuie and his wife then retired to the main keep of Kitanosho, built by Katsuie in 1575, and at nine storeys high Japan's largest at the time, and setting it alight, took their lives in the way of the samurai as it burned around them. Sakuma Morimasa was later captured alive but instead of being allowed to commit *seppuku*, he was punished by being beheaded, executed like a common criminal.

Oda Nobutaka also surrendered. Forced from Gifu Castle, he was sent into exile in the Omido-Ji Temple, also known as the Noma Daibo in Noma, on the Chita Peninsula of Aichi Prefecture, where the warrior Minamoto no Yoshitomo, father of the first Kamakura Shogun Minamoto no Yoritomo, had been assassinated in the bath in early 1160. Under pressure from both Hideyoshi and his own brother Nobukatsu, Nobutaka committed *seppuku* on either 19 or 21 June 1583. His grave is beside that of Yoshitomo. With the demise of Shibata Katsuie and Oda Nobutaka, Toyotomi Hideyoshi now ruled the Oda territories, uncontested.

Takatora had fought well in the front lines of Hidenaga's forces in the Battle of Shizugatake, after which Hidenaga was awarded Harima and Tamba Provinces, becoming master of Himeji Castle. This castle, although on the same site as the current National Treasure and World Heritage listed one, was far from the magnificent fortress we see today. That complex would be completely rebuilt by Ikeda Terumasa, son-in-law of Tokugawa Ieyasu in 1601 following the Battle of Sekigahara. For having put the troops of Sakuma Morimasa to flight, Takatora would be richly rewarded by Hideyoshi for his significant achievement, and he received further lands and his stipend was raised to 4,600 *koku*.

The *daimyo* Niwa Nagahide gained Echizen and Kaga Provinces, worth over 1,230,000 *koku*, to become one of the most powerful of Hideyoshi's retainers. However, Nagahide died suddenly of an illness in 1585 without having achieved much else. There are theories suggesting that Nagahide did not died of an illness, but on seeing Hideyoshi eclipsing the Oda clan, committed *seppuku* from the shame of having allowed Hideyoshi to usurp power so easily.

The Battle of Komaki Nagakute

The dark clouds of war had again begun to form as Toyotomi Hideyoshi's power rose to new heights. Oda Nobunaga's son Nobukatsu had watched Hideyoshi seize his late father's power, and following the Battle of Shizugatake, Hideyoshi had invited Oda Nobukatsu and a number of the former Oda clan generals to Osaka to inspect his recently completed castle there. This splendid fortress, on a par with, if not even surpassing, Nobunaga's most elegant Azuchi Castle, was Hideyoshi's show of newly acquired authority, and to Nobukatsu, this was the final straw. He refused the invitation, knowing that attending would simply place him below Hideyoshi. Hideyoshi attempted to reach out to Nobukatsu via three of Nobukatsu's chief retainers, Tsugawa Yoshifuyu, the temporary castellan of Matsugashima Castle in Ise, Azai Nagatoki and Okada Shigetaka. Hideyoshi's contacting of these men angered Nobukatsu even further, and so these generals were accused of collaborating with Hideyoshi, and all three were executed on 16 April 1584. Hideyoshi took this snub and then the executions as justification for bringing Nobukatsu down and further cementing his power. Realising that as Hideyoshi had greater numbers he had the upper hand, Nobukatsu turned to Tokugawa Ieyasu for assistance. Accepting the risk, Ieyasu dispatched reinforcements and thus a war between Hideyoshi and Ieyasu began in March that year, lasting until November.

The main Komaki Nagakute battlefields were north of Mount Komaki, where Nobunaga had built his first castle to the north of Nagoya City, and in Nagakute to the east of sprawling modern-day Nagoya. While Hideyoshi's men had positioned themselves across the wide area between Mount Komaki and Inuyama Castle, Ieyasu and Nobukatsu's troops dug in at the remains of Oda Nobunaga's Komakiyama Castle. Both sides faced off against one another, with minor skirmishes breaking out as each jostled for position.

The two armies, Toyotomi's 40,000 against the combined 18,500 Tokugawa/Oda troops, sat watching each other for a number of weeks with very little action until a number of the Toyotomi units, realising that Ieyasu's stronghold, Okazaki Castle further behind the Tokugawa lines in Mikawa, was weakly guarded while he and his men were at Komaki, decided to go around behind the Oda-Tokugawa forces and attack Okazaki.

Lead by Ikeda Tsuneoki and his 6,000 men, a large contingent consisting of Toyotomi Hidetsugu and 8,000 samurai, supported by another 6,000 under the command of Mori Nagayoshi and Hori Hidemasa, set out for Mikawa. The plan was to make quick hit-and-run attacks on the smaller castles and fortresses along the way so as not to impede their advance to Okazaki, but Ikeda was detained when attacking Iwasaki Castle. It seems a marksman from within the castle was able to shoot at Ikeda, knocking him off his horse. Angered by the insult, he ordered a full-scale attack on the small fortress, wasting both valuable men and time in the process. Over 300 of the garrison were killed. The delay provided enough time for the Tokugawa troops to catch up and defeat the Ikeda-led forces, preventing Okazaki from being captured.

Although Ieyasu had tasted success in battle, Hideyoshi had pulled out and returned to Osaka Castle, with both men claiming victory. The two would later reconcile early the following year.

The Battle of Matsugashima Castle

In a skirmish prior to the Battle of Komaki Nagakute, Todo Takatora took the head of a *karo*-class officer, a top-ranking advisor and clan elder under the Takigawa, during an attack on the Oda–Tokugawa held Matsugashima Castle in what is now Mie Prefecture.

Matsugashima guarded the old road to the sacred Grand Ise Shrine, and facing Ise Bay, was considered a strategically strong and important sea and land position. Oda Nobukatsu's generals Takigawa Katsutoshi and Heki Daizen were acting as castellans of Matsugashima with 3,000 samurai, and a large contingent of around 100 ninja of Iga under the command of the famed Hattori Hanzo.

Toyotomi Hideyoshi had handed command of operations to Hidenaga, and serving him were the generals Tsutsui Junkei, Gamo Ujisato and his vassals Saka Genzaemon, Todo Takatora and Tamaru Tomonau. Covering the ocean were the maritime forces under Kuki Yoshitaka, forming a 20,000-strong army.

The Tsutsui forces commenced the attack but were quickly repelled by the troops of the defenders Heki Daizen and Ida Katsuzo and forced to retreat. Seeing the performance of the defenders, Oda Nobukatsu ordered the castle town be set alight. The conflagration spread so quickly that parts of the castle soon caught fire, but were extinguished by Tokugawa vassal Nakatsu Shimasuke at the risk of his own life. Both sides, defenders and attackers alike, applauded his courage.

The siege lasted for 40 days of violent fighting during which the Toyotomi allies also attacked and captured nearby Mine Castle on 24 April, followed by Ise Kameyama Castle. Meanwhile at Matsugashima Castle, the three days from the 26th to the 28th saw some of the heaviest fighting during which Takatora's unit attacked and breached the gates. Takatora was the first samurai into the enemy fortress, and while the remainder of the 3,000 defenders fought desperately to oust the attackers, Takatora battled on, taking the head of one of the leading warriors within the castle. For having breached the gates and having taken a head, he was rewarded by Hidenaga with a fine *katana* forged by the famed smiths of Bizen.

During the hard-fought battle, Lord Hidenaga was approached by a 17-year-old girl remembered as Keihou, the daughter of the local warrior Hoshiai Jinzaemon. Her husband had been killed in the fighting defending Matsugashima, and, shocked at the bloodshed, she appealed to Hidenaga to end the fighting. Hidenaga agreed to her request, and suggested she act as the go-between. She readily accepted, and on the 29th day, the castle surrendered peacefully. Many hundreds of samurai from both sides had been killed, and while the defenders would be confined to the local area, the bulk of the attackers were redeployed to the Komaki area at the top end of Ise Bay.

Matsugashima Castle was later abandoned when Gamo Ujisato relocated himself to Matsusaka Castle, using many of the surviving structures and stones from the walls in the building of his new fortress. The townsfolk of Matsugashima were ordered to relocate to the new township of Matsusaka, and Matsugashima returned to being a peaceful fishing village. Today, much of the castle's former grounds have been overtaken by private housing. A small park where the *honmaru* was, and a rise known as Tenshuyama where the castle's small keep once stood, have been preserved.

Following the Battle of Komaki Nagakute, the provinces of Yamato (Nara), Izumi (the south-western Osaka region) and Kii (Wakayama) then became the domains of Hashiba Hidenaga. Upon accepting the lands, Hidenaga relocated his base to Yamato Koriyama Castle in Nara.

Hidenaga then constructed a grand palace-like *yakata*, worthy of his now one million *koku* status, within the castle walls as his official residence. Hidenaga undertook further redevelopment of the castle, bringing it to the standards of a fortress ready and able to defend Osaka.

Yamato Koriyama Castle

The impressive ruins of Nara Prefecture's Koriyama Castle sit atop a small hill surrounded by two rivers forming natural moats. The positioning of the castle and its strong layout served it well through the final years of the violent Sengoku period and through the peaceful days of the 260-year Edo period.

Oda Nobunaga had entrusted the Yamato region to Tsutsui Junkei (1549–84) for having destroyed his enemy Matsunaga Hisahide and uniting Yamato Province (now Nara Prefecture). Tsutsui Junkei relocated from his smaller namesake Tsutsui Castle to Koriyama where he constructed a bigger, better and finer castle. Two years after its completion in 1580, Akechi Mitsuhide had attacked Oda Nobunaga in the Honno-ji Incident and turned to Tsutsui for military assistance at Horagatoge Pass. Tsutsui, who had served under the Akechi since allying himself with the Oda, is said to have taken his time contemplating his erstwhile friend's request and carefully watched the tide of events before deciding his course of action. This delayed action led to the formation of the Japanese saying '*Horagatoge wo kimekomu*' or, 'To wait and see what happens at Horagatoge', used in a negative or sarcastic context when someone is being opportunistic. In fact, Tsutsui had decided to remain neutral, and had withdrawn to the Yamato district.

A tower keep had been added in 1583 increasing the visual splendour of the fortress, but Tsutsui Junkei died the following year and his adopted son Sadatsugu became its master. Almost a year after having gained Koriyama Castle, Sadatsugu was transferred upon the orders of the Toyotomi clan to Iga Ueno Castle in Mie Prefecture.

Under Hidenaga, the castle and the town were greatly developed, and Takatora is known to have had a leading hand in the design and layout of the new town. His skill was exceptional. Part of the town planning saw the widening of the town's main roads, and businesses relocated from the city of Nara to the castle town of Koriyama. Each business sector was allocated a particular area in which to live and ply their trade. There were fourteen such towns: Honmachi (Main Town), Uoshio-cho (Fish Town), Sakai-cho (Prosperous Town), Yanagimachi (Willow Town), Imaimachi (Current Well Town), Watamachi (Cotton Town), Inomachi (Reed Town), Naramachi (Nara Town), Zakokumachi (Millet Town), Chamachi (Tea Town), Zaimokumachi (Lumber Town), Konyamachi (Dyer Town), Tofumachi (Bean Curd Town) and Kajiya-cho (Blacksmith Town). All of these historical town names still exist in modern-day Koriyama.

Todo Takatora would have been involved in the redesigning of the layout and strengthening the defences of this castle, as he had been tasked with supervising the bulk of the *ishigaki* stone walls. Visible Takatora influences can be seen, including the squaring off of baileys, the wide moats, high, straight edged stone walls and use of *tamon yagura* around the main central *honmaru* bailey.

During the reconstruction efforts, Koriyama's layout was reconfigured, developing it in a strong *rinkakushiki* layout, meaning that the important *honmaru*, covering an area of around 100m, was centrally located and protected on all four sides by the surrounding baileys and precincts. This was one of the strongest castle configurations, and one that was favoured by Takatora. The surrounding stone walls also had the Takatora characteristics of being high and steeply-angled, but straight instead of the gracefully curved stonework prominent in other castle construction. One of the castle's compounds was even dubbed the *Yoemon-maru*. This was named after Todo Yoemon Takatora, believed to have been so named in honour of his having been one of the major influences and designers in the reconditioning of the castle.

As Koriyama was hurriedly reconfigured and enlarged, various structures, such as the grand main gate of the Negoro-ji Temple, a large Buddhist temple complex, were appropriated and transferred to the castle. (The commandeering of this particular gate would prove to have negative consequences in the near future.) In old Japan, nothing ever went to waste. Everything was recycled in one way or another. Takatora, and indeed many other *daimyo*, would often use old timbers, structures and parts from other abandoned castles or temples when building their fortresses. Stones to be used in the hastily-built castle walls of Koriyama were becoming increasingly hard to come by, and so gravestones, location marker stones, parts of stone lanterns, even carved Buddhist Jizo statues

– the patron saints of children and travellers – were incorporated in the stonework. Many modern-day visitors often leave coins as offerings to these Buddhist stones within crevasses in the walls. Having been built in the 1580s, these stone walls contain an interesting mixture of traditional stoneworking methods. Upon its completion Koriyama was a strong and impressive castle.

After the death of Hidenaga in 1591, Hideyoshi appointed Mashita Nagamori (1545–1615), one of the five magistrates of the Toyotomi administration, as the commander of Koriyama Castle. Yamato Koriyama Castle is now a public park in Yamato Koriyama City, Nara Prefecture. It has undergone extensive restoration in recent years to preserve the remaining moats and stone walls. The Otemon gate, the Ote Mukai Yagura and Tamon Yagura, the Ote East Yagura, the Gokuraku Bridge and Hakutaku Gate have also been well reconstructed and are opened at certain times during the year. Koriyama Castle was made one of the Extended Top 100 Japanese Castles in 2017.

By around 1585, the growing power of the militaristic monks, the *Ikko Ikki* and the Shingon sect's warrior priests of the Negoro-ji Temple in Kii Province's Wakayama, was becoming a concern for the Toyotomi. The Negoro-ji had been established around 1087, and at its peak during the Muromachi period (approximately 1336–1573), some 2,700 temples graced the spacious complex. They had been throwing their weight around in the political arena for some time now, and in particular their support of Tokugawa Ieyasu against Hideyoshi in the Battle of Komaki Nagakute the previous year had earned them his great displeasure. That the Toyotomi clan had recently taken their gates and various structures for use in Hidenaga's castle gave them cause for greater offence.

Having watched Nobunaga before him struggle with the protracted sieges against the militant monks of the Hongan-ji Temple, and not wanting to have the same experiences himself, Hideyoshi launched a pre-emptive attack of Negoro-ji Temple. Having first attacked other local warrior-monk temples, Hideyoshi's forces approached the Negoro-ji Temple from two directions. Many of the monks quickly fled to nearby Ota Castle and Hideyoshi ordered the temples razed. Any remaining Buddhist monks fleeing the flames were cut down. Hideyoshi then turned his attentions to Ota Castle, and built dams on three sides of the castle to divert the rivers and allow heavy rains to flood the castle. Those trapped on the hill by the rising waters soon succumbed to hunger, and the samurai, monks and peasants inside finally surrendered. In a last-ditch effort, some fifty warrior monks made a final suicidal charge against Hideyoshi's forces. All were destroyed. Ota Castle was later to be rebuilt as Wakayama Castle.

Wakayama Castle

Kii Province was now completely under the rule of Takatora's master, Hashiba Hidenaga, and in 1585 Hidenaga appointed the then 29-year-old Takatora to the position of *shin-bugyo* (magistrate) in charge of construction of the new Wakayama Castle. Wakayama would hold a special place in Takatora's heart and over the course of his lifetime, he would return to update and improve this castle on numerous occasions. For now, the task at hand was the construction. Wakayama was to be built across two mountains on the ruins of the smaller former Ota Castle, captured by Toyotomi forces earlier that year. Wakayama's basic ground plan or *nawabari* is believed by some researchers to have been decided by Toyotomi Hideyoshi, with the construction work left to Todo Takatora, Haneda Nagato and Yokohama Ichian, who was married to Takatora's sixth adopted daughter. The most common theory is that Hidenaga simply built the castle on the orders of his brother Hideyoshi. Either way it is recorded that Todo Takatora was in charge of the construction work.

Takatora walked around the site numerous times to get the lay of the land. He considered the shape and heights of the mountains, and their natural defences. He would have made design sketches of the castle and a large mud model of the mountain in order to show the various work-gang foremen what he wanted the workers to do. Many thousands of metres of rope were ordered, and the rope was stretched out between wooden pegs hammered into the ground as a guide. This is known as *nawabari*, or literally 'rope stretching', although it also refers to the layout of a castle. Once the layout was complete, Takatora gathered over 10,000 workers and during the course of around a year, finished the large-scale project. At that time the important *honmaru* and *ni-no-maru* in particular were determined, and the lord's mansion was constructed at the base of the northern mountain. At the base of the southern mountain was the castle's main entrance with a protective *masugata koguchi* gate system.

Hidenaga had only recently completed his new base, the impressive Yamato Koriyama Castle, with the help of Takatora, and now the equally impressive Wakayama was finished. Hidenaga's close retainer Kuwayama Shigeharu (1524–1 November 1606) was appointed as castellan. Under Kuwayama, the name of the area, Wakayama remained the same, but the characters, 若山城, literally 'Young Mountain Castle' were changed to the current *kanji,* 和歌山城, the more poetic 'Harmonious Song Mountain Castle'. Incidentally, the castle's other name was Torafusa Castle, or 'Sleeping Tiger Castle', as the hill on which is built was said to have resembled a sleeping tiger.

In 1596 Kuwayama retired, and his grandson Kazuharu took the reins. At Sekigahara in 1600, Kuwayama Kazuharu fought on the victorious Tokugawa side, and in 1601 was provided with a new domain at Fuse in Yamato Province's Katsuge area, becoming first lord of the Yamato Shinjo domain. In his place, Asano Yukinaga was awarded Wakayama Castle, and he too made some minor changes to the castle's design. Tokugawa Ieyasu's tenth son, Tokugawa Yorinobu (28 April 1602–19 February 1671), received Wakayama on 27 August 1619, forming the Kii branch of the Tokugawa clan and two years later he too called on the skills of Todo Takatora to again enlarge and strengthen the castle's *minami-no-maru* and *suna-no-maru* enclaves.

Because Wakayama Castle underwent multiple reconstruction phases over the years, the *ishigaki* stonework is of particular interest, as many different types of stone piling work can be found in its walls, ranging from the older rustic *nozura-zumi* techniques, through to the cleaner, closer-fitting stones of the more modern *kirikomi-zumi* style, differing not only as techniques changed, but the times too. Wakayama Castle survived the feudal period and the demolition of many castles in the Meiji Period, but was unfortunately destroyed by fire bombing during the air raids of 1945. The keep and main enceinte enclosures were reconstructed in concrete in 1958.

Pleased with Takatora's efforts in the speedy construction of Wakayama, Hidenaga further rewarded him with a promotion to the position of *Karo,* literally 'House Elder' of the Hashiba. The *Karo* were one of the few highly ranked samurai officials and direct close advisors to the *daimyo* such as Lord Hidenaga, however, in Takatora's case, he already enjoyed such a privilege. With the promotion came an increase in stipend, bringing Takatora to 10,000 *koku*, establishing him as a *daimyo*. He was just 30 years old.

Saruokayama Castle

Along with the promotion and raise, Takatora was awarded his own domain and a castle, Saruokayama, also known as Kokawa Castle, in Kii Province (modern-day Kokawa, Kinokawa City, Wakayama Prefecture). The Kokawa-dera Temple, which, along with the aforementioned Negoro-ji Temple, held a great deal of influence in the Kinokawa basin area, had been built on Mount Saruoka (currently known as Mount Akiba). In order to restrain the powers of the Kokawa-dera, after the conquest of Kishu in 1585 Todo Takatora entered the temple grounds and rebuilt it as a fortification.

The castle proper was built on the mountaintop of Mount Saruoka (currently known as Mount Akiba). Its main bailey measured around 20m x 60m while the *ni-no-maru* second bailey to the south was 60m x 25m in size. The flatlands on the western side of the castle were allocated for the construction of the castle's residential and administrative buildings, with land surrounding that set aside for the living quarters of Takatora's vassals. Along the south-western edge of the castle, below the steep slopes of the mountain flowed the Nakatsu River forming a protective moat. Very little remains of the castle now, but the site of the castle's main bailey is maintained as Akiba Park, a known local lookout spot providing a fine view of the area and is marked by a stone monument and signs explaining the castle's details and history.

Takatora had a comfortable residence built especially for his father at Saruokayama, and called on him to act as the castellan as he himself was often absent. Control of the castle, the fief, all political affairs and regional power was now entrusted to his father, Torataka. One of the reasons Takatora had requested his father take control over the castle was because his own overlord, Hidenaga's brother Toyotomi Hideyoshi, was still consolidating his control over the nation and continuing his push for unification. Takatora's role in helping to establish Toyotomi authority was ever increasing, particularly as his immediate master, Hidenaga, was finding himself often unwell, and was relying on the ever-efficient Takatora to take his place

West of Saruokayama Castle was another *yamajiro,* Yagura Castle. Both fortresses overlooked the Awaji Kaido, a major route running between them. While Saruokayama was Takatora's main castle, one of his vassals was made the commander of Yagura. Yagura's *honmaru* was 20m wide east to west, ran 25m north south, and was surrounded by an *obi-kuruwa,* a narrow strip of bailey. To the north and south of the main enclosure were two very deep *hori-kiri* trenches which remain to this day. Unfortunately, Yagura Castle's ruins lie on private property and are off limits to the general public.

Around the time that Takatora was the lord of Kokawa, there was a regional drought, and the farmers were desperate for rain. Takatora called in forty to fifty shamanistic *yamabushi,* mountain ascetics, to the area and asked that they pray for rainfall. Although records exist of the *yamabushi* being called in, no records of their success survive. Takatora also revived one of the local annual harvest festivals, donating funds to have a *mikoshi,* a shrine-shaped portable festival float, built. Around this time Todo Yoemon adopted the official name by which he is now best remembered, Takatora.

Takatora was making a name for himself as a leading designer and architect. In around November 1586, Toyotomi Hideyoshi decided that Kyoto needed a *Daibutsu,* a Great Buddha, and temple to rival that of Nara's famed Great Buddha. Typical of Hideyoshi, in announcing the forging of a giant statue of the Buddha and an equally large hall at the Hoko-ji Temple in which to house it, he boasted that the project would take three years, whereas the Great Buddha of Nara complex was said to have taken ten years to complete.[5] The architects would be Nakai Masakiyo, later to find fame as the lead carpenter for the biggest castle keep in Japanese history at Nagoya, and Heinouchi Yoshimasa. Takatora was tasked with procuring timber from the Kumano districts in Wakayama and southern Mie.

---

5. The Hoko-ji's Great Buddha and hall was completed in three years, but the great structure and the bronze image of the Buddha were destroyed in a major earthquake on 14 August 1596. Reconstruction of the temple and the Buddha commenced, but were halted a month later with the death of Toyotomi Hideyoshi. His son Hideyori would attempt to complete his father's project around 1610, and initially had a large bronze bell cast. The inscription on the bell would be interpreted by the Tokugawa as a direct slur (see Chapter 4), and provided reason enough to launch a full-scale attack on Osaka in 1614 and 1615 which would ultimately destroy the Toyotomi.

Insurrection and Akagi Castle

Timber was a precious commodity in Japan at this time. Contrary to popular belief, and scenes in samurai movies, Old Japan was not a richly forested land. Most of the mountains had been denuded and forests destroyed by warlords desperate for funds. Rice was a form of currency, and so trees were cut down and land developed to increase rice yields. The need for wood for the building of houses, temples, shrines and castles meant larger lumber was in short supply. Wood was the major fuel source for heating and cooking, and it was a major component of most household items. During the years of civil war, wood was also needed in great quantities for the smelting of steel for armour and weapons. One area that had maintained old-growth forest and was enjoying prosperity through the sales of timber was the mountainous Kumano area on the south-eastern coast of the Kii Peninsula. Various small-time warlords, long isolated and resistant to the central and even local Kii (Wakayama) and Ise (Mie Prefecture) provincial governments, continued to control the lands and the lucrative agriculture, forestry and timber trade. They also controlled the seas with their pirate-like *suigun* naval forces along the island-dotted coasts.

In early March 1585, Toyotomi Hideyoshi commenced his campaign to subjugate the Kii Peninsula. By the end of the month the Toyotomi forces had captured the modern-day Wakayama region, and had advanced as far south-west as areas such as Arida. There, the Yukawa, a minor yet relatively strong provincial clan, made repeated attempts to resist the Toyotomi but despite fiercely struggling to maintain independence, were forced to surrender after just six months.

The Toyotomi army continued its advance into the sacred Kumano area. The Horiuchi clan, masters of a large naval force based at Shingu Castle on the south-eastern coast of the peninsula, had supported Hideyoshi at the Battle of Yamazaki against Akechi Mitsuhide in 1582, and again in bowing to his authority were permitted to retain their territories. Other minor lords across the Kii Peninsula slowly came under Toyotomi control. Hideyoshi then awarded Kii to his younger brother, Hidenaga, along with Yamato Province, being modern-day Nara Prefecture.

Having had their lands forcibly conquered, the local warlords and people of the region remained averse to coming under the strict rule of a central government and repeatedly rebelled against the authority of the Toyotomi. In 1586, a large revolt, remembered as the Kitayama Ikki, occurred, staged by a band of local warriors leading thousands of commoners. In response, Hidenaga's thorough oppression quelled this rebellion by 1589.

Having suppressed the rebellion, Hidenaga placed his now most trusted general, Todo Takatora, in charge of the region. It was not to be an easy task. Takatora had only a small army with which to control a very large area with a very belligerent population. Maintaining control and authority was made even more difficult as Takatora was often absent because of his duties, leading and participating in Hidenaga's military campaigns. To provide a means of control and regional peace Takatora conceived and built a small but secure castle using the latest techniques and a great deal of ingenuity. He named it Akagi Castle.

Akagi Castle is located in Kumano City, Mie Prefecture, along part of the ancient stone-paved Ise-ji route of the now World Heritage listed Kumano-Kaido, a pilgrimage route to the sacred Kumano Hongu Shrine from Ise Province on the south-eastern coast of the Kii Peninsula. Akagi was built on a mountain around 50m high, and in the middle of a narrow basin encircled by taller mountains. At certain times of the year and when conditions are right, the basin will fill with a thick fog, leaving just the hilltop ruins of Akagi Castle poking out like an island floating in a sea of cloud, and as such has gained fame as one of Japan's top three 'Floating Castles in the Clouds'.

The castle itself covered an area around 200m long and 100m wide. Its central area was a 40m-wide square at the top of the hill, with a complex gate system built towards the south-eastern edge. Two ridges spread from the hilltop towards the south-eastern and south-western compounds, with terraces constructed along these two ridges. The edges of these terraces were shored up and guarded by *ishigaki* stone walls, and accessed by cunningly designed paths, all fully exposed to the defenders' missiles from the upper terraces.

Within that area was the main central *honmaru*, a raised square-shaped enceinte around 27m x 32m in size and surrounded by a narrow strip of land known as an *obi-kuruwa* or *koshi-kuruwa*, more akin to an *inubashiri*, and encircled by 4m-high stone walls allowing defending warriors to work their way around the castle via these narrow baileys in times of attack. The actual *honmaru* itself was rather small, yet it was guarded by a large and striking *masugata* gate system.

Obi-kuruwa, or *koshi-kuruwa*, are narrow bailey-like strips of land running around the edges of a mountain castle. Very narrow *obi-kuruwa* are often termed *inubashiri*, literally 'dog runs'. While these elements often act as constricted baileys or pathways for defenders to move quickly around castle sites, they are more often than not the result of having sections of the hillside slope cut back to increase the degree of incline at important defensive positions in order to make it harder for attackers to infiltrate. The cut sections are known as *kirigishi*, or literally 'cut cliffs'. The flattened areas at the base of these shaved sections become small baileys and tracks. *Inubashiri* became an often-used feature of Takatora's designs, and they can be seen at Koriyama, Imabari, Tamba Sasayama, and many other Takatora-related castles.

A larger bailey was situated to the north of the *honmaru*, another to the south-east, and yet another to the south. Each of these was constructed by shaving the ridges and hilltops flat to make space for watchtowers, barracks, stables and other facilities. The edges of these terraces too were protected by sturdy, steep stone walls, and the paths below remained exposed to defensive attack from the fortified upper terraces. While the *honmaru*'s walls stood 4m high, the other baileys were surrounded by walls of roughly piled drystone *nozura-zumi ishigaki* averaging around 3m in height. The south-eastern bailey had three *koguchi* gates, while the main *honmaru* bailey was designed with an indented U-shaped *uchi-masugata* gate, offering protection from three sides. The stone walls around the *honmaru* were cleverly designed with *yokoya*, flank ports on the north-eastern and south-western corners, providing defenders with an opportunity to shoot lengthways along the walls from a 90-degree angled port. These design features were seen as one of Takatora's specialties, and would be seen in other castles too. Takatora alone was responsible for the layout of this fine castle, and it became the basic design template for many of his following constructions, including Imabari, Tamba Sasayama, and Tsu. Indeed, compared with many other castles that conscientiously followed the styles of Nobunaga and Hideyoshi, this was new.

When Takatora's Akagi Castle was completed and put into commission in 1589, a public event was staged as part of the opening ceremonies. Over 500 people, including many of those known to have been involved in the earlier uprisings and civil disobedience against Hideyoshi and his *daimyo*, were invited. As the castle was dedicated, Takatora ordered the trouble-makers to be quickly rounded up and publicly executed in front of the new castle gates.[6] Authority had been firmly established.

Takatora remained nominally in charge of the Akagi area for around 11 years until 1595 when he was appointed as commander of Uwajima Castle (Ehime Prefecture), although during much of the time he was away fighting under Hidenaga's command. After the decisive Battle of Sekigahara of 1600 in which the nation was split into two factions, East and West, fighting for supremacy, and the victor Tokugawa Ieyasu being appointed Shogun, the Asano clan were made the governors of Kii, and ordered their retainers to maintain tight control over the region. In 1614, the local lords of the Kitayama area again revolted against the Asano while they were absent at the Siege of Osaka Castle. Once the siege had ended, the Asano returned to quash this rebellion and return the lands to their control. Asano Nagaakira, former lord of Wakayama Castle, is said to have used Akagi Castle from 1614, but was to be stationed here for only a year. Akagi was abandoned and demolished the following year in 1615 as part of the Tokugawa Shogunate's One Castle Per Province edict. Many hundreds of castles across Japan were also abandoned and demolished because of this law, enacted to maintain peace across the nation.

Recent archaeological excavations and maintenance has seen the stone walls restored, and other details of the castle researched. No *kawara*, fired clay rooftiles, were discovered during the excavations, suggesting that instead of tiles, the roofs of Akagi Castle's structures, keep, *yagura* watchtowers, official and residential buildings were all topped with wooden shingles instead. In 2017, Akagi was designated by the Japan Castle Association as one of the Extended Top 100 Japanese Castle sites. The remote location of Akagi Castle means it is infrequently visited and remains a rare yet valuable example of a small Todo Takatora-designed Toyotomi period castle. Nearby is another local attraction, the ancient Maruyama Senmaida, a mountainside with over 1,000 terraced rice fields cut into the sloping sides.

About this time, Hashiba Hidenaga's brother, Toyotomi Hideyoshi, was coming close to cementing his control over the nation. As Hideyoshi

---

6. The site of the executions is now a National Historical Site. In 1955, nearby roadworks accidentally uncovered many sets of human bones in shallow graves.

made his final push for unification, he banned the farmers from leaving the land, and in effect locked the population into four classes, being, from the top, the warrior elite, who ruled and protected the lands, followed by the farmers as they were responsible for the important and laborious work that went into feeding the nation. Next were the craftsmen who made the necessities of daily life including clothing, houses, tools, and items. Finally, at the bottom rung of society were the merchant class, who profited from the efforts of the other classes. Being unable to cross the class boundaries restricted the numbers of people willing to leave the land and serve as *ashigaru*, thus reducing the numbers of potential armies.

The Invasion of Shikoku

In the 1570s the warlord Chosokabe Motochika embarked on a plan to unify Shikoku under his control. By 1583, he had captured the island's four provinces to become the ruling warlord. Having mostly conquered Japan's largest island of Honshu, Hideyoshi now wanted the smallest of the four main islands, Shikoku, and so the invasion commenced in June 1585 and saw Hideyoshi's army of over 113,000 troops shipped across the Seto Inland Sea to Shikoku in 600 large ships and 103 smaller vessels.

Hideyoshi's forces were divided into three armies. The third division consisted of 30,000 men lead by Kikkawa Motoharu and Kobayakawa Takakage against Iyo Province. The second force of 23,000 under Ukita Hideie attacked Sanuki Province. Todo Takatora was in the front line of the main force, of 60,000 samurai commanded by Hashiba Hidenaga which assaulted Awa and Tosa provinces. In response to this huge Toyotomi force, the Chosokabe were able to raise just 40,000 troops.

Hidenaga's forces first attacked Kizu Castle, a geographically important base for the Chosokabe, held by Motochika's younger brother Chikayasu, and castellan Tojo Sekinobei. Kizu Castle, now a Tokushima Prefecture, Naruto City designated Historic Site,[7] was built around 1558

---

7. During the Pacific War, the Tokushima Air Corps' Special Attack Unit was based here, and dug a series of tunnels and shelters, some of which damaged the actual castle site. In 1958 a reservoir was built on the mountaintop, further damaging the remains. Kizu Castle's ruins were designated as a Naruto City Historic Site in 1963, and excavation projects and park development commenced in 2004, leading to the opening of the Kizu Shiroyama Park around 2009.

on a 60m-high hill. The castle covered an area measuring 170m north
to south and 270m east to west. Large-scale castle reconstruction is said
to have been hurriedly carried out by Tojo Sekinobei in preparation for
the Toyotomi invasion. The castle was defended by an estimated 500
Chosokabe samurai. Tojo Sekinobei managed to escape, fleeing to Tosa,
but was later captured and forced to commit *seppuku*.

Hashiba Hidenaga's forces then advanced around 23km south to
Ichinomiya Castle. First established in 1338, Ichinomiya Castle is one
of the largest mountain castles in Tokushima Prefecture. Designated
a historic site by Tokushima Prefecture in 1954, and listed among the
Extended Top 100 Japanese Castles, Ichinomiya was in fact two castles
combined into one, the *Kita-jo* or North Castle, in which the main
honmaru bailey can be found, and the *Nan-jo*, or South Castle. Together
they featured six main compounds and as many as thirteen smaller baileys
covering an area 800m east to west and 500m north to south. Only the
uppermost main *honmaru* enclosure, at an altitude of 144m and measuring
around 36m by 23m in size, has stone walls around it. It is unknown if the
castle ever sported a keep, or simply an equivalent *yagura* in its place, but
certainly there would have been some form of large defensive structure
built there. Being divided into North and South Castles, Ichinomiya had
Emura Chikatoshi as master of the northern fortress and Tani Tadasumi
as commander of the southern one. Emura had 5,000 samurai under his
command and Tani was master to around 4,000 men, and so some 10,000
samurai were said to have been inside Ichinomiya Castle at the time of
the joint Hideyoshi/Hidenaga-led Toyotomi clan attack.

Ichinomiya was the site of many a bloody battle. The first was in 1340,
and over the following years it was attacked more than six times before
Hidenaga's samurai forces finally brought it down, but not before tragedy
almost struck. Early in the attack, the ever-inquisitive Todo Takatora
wanted to know the layout, defences and the conditions inside the castle,
and so he and fellow samurai Hattori Takasuke undertook a night-time
reconnaissance mission, quietly crossing the multiple *karabori* dry moats,
dorui earthen embankments and barricades, checking for possible weak
points at the same time. The daring sortie seemed to go well at first
with both men being only lightly armoured so as to move quickly and
quietly. As they drew closer to the castle itself, they were spotted and the
defenders launched a massive barrage of matchlock fire and arrows. There

was no warning, and no cover available. Takatora was hit in the chest by a shot from a matchlock and fell, bleeding profusely. Hattori Takasuke quickly and bravely managed to drag the 110kg giant of a man back across the moats to safety, all the while under a hail of hot lead and arrows. Ichinomiya Castle remained under siege for eight days until the castle's water supply was disrupted and it finally capitulated.[8]

In an effort to sue for peace, Chosokabe Motochika sent his son, Chikatada, as a hostage and surrendered the castle. Chosokabe then travelled to Osaka to pay his respects to – and beg the forgiveness of – Toyotomi Hideyoshi. It was the badly injured Todo Takatora, now swathed in thick bandages under his heavy armour, who escorted Chosokabe Motochika to Sakae in Osaka for the arranged meeting. The talks went to plan, and the Chosokabe clan were now subservient to the mighty Toyotomi. Following this, Takatora was then tasked with returning Chosokabe's son to his father. Chosokabe was most appreciative of Takatora's considerable hospitality en route to Osaka, and particularly regarding the care with which his son was returned. Takatora had indeed taken very good care of Chikatada, and over time the two became close friends. This friendship, however, would prove to be fatal to Chikatada.

Chikatada's eldest brother, Nobuchika, was killed in action at the Battle of Hetsugigawa on 20 January 1587, while fighting alongside his father. The loss of the Chosokabe heir caused a competition amongst the remaining brothers. However, Chikatada's father Motochika would bluntly tell his son that he would not be considered eligible for the position, as he had become too close to Todo Takatora during his time as a hostage. His own father no longer trusted him, despite his having risked his son's life sending him as a hostage to ensure the survival of the clan. The year after Hideyoshi's passing, Chosokabe Motochika also died of an illness, and so Motochika's fourth son, Morichika, claimed the role of clan head over Chikatada. Chosokabe Morichika would remember his father's connection to Tokugawa Ieyasu, and chose to side with the future Shogun the very next year at the Battle of Sekigahara. However, his family connections to the Western forces prevented this from happening, and the Chosokabe found themselves as one of the armies on Mount Nangu

---

8. Ichinomiya Castle was only abandoned in 1615 on the orders of the Tokugawa's One Castle Per Province rule. Today, various baileys, stone walls and gates still remain.

to the east of the Sekigahara battlefield under Mori control. Once the Western forces had been defeated, Chikatada had sought the assistance of Takatora to apologise to Lord Ieyasu for his family having sided against him, and in an appeal for leniency for his brother, even offered his own territories to the Tokugawa.

Despite Chikatada's best efforts to protect his brother and the family name, two weeks after the Battle of Sekigahara in November 1600, Takatora was saddened to hear of the death of his friend. The then 28-year-old Chikatada had been forced to commit *seppuku* by the order of his brother on the grounds that he had dared to question Morichika's right to claim the role of clan leader. This news greatly angered Tokugawa Ieyasu too, who then ordered a reorganisation of the Chosokabe family.

The Jurakutei

In February 1586, the man who had begun life as a lowly foot soldier was appointed to the exalted position of *Kampaku*, an ancient Heian period (794–1185) title equivalent to 'Grand Counsellor to the Imperial Throne', second within the realm only to the Emperor himself. To celebrate, Toyotomi Hideyoshi commenced construction of a most sumptuous castle-like residence and administrative headquarters in the heart of Kyoto, on the very same spot as the original Heian-period Imperial Palace. This sumptuous new palace, the Jurakutei (also known as the Jurakudai), was completed within a year and a half, in September 1587. The proportions were magnificent. The complex itself consisted of four large compounds surrounded by wide moats and high walls. The Jurakutei was on a scale equal to that of the contemporary Imperial Palace but was decorated even more lavishly. Todo Takatora was appointed as the building construction manager for the project and is known to have used his own money to construct a very fine gate that he presented to Hideyoshi. A much pleased Hideyoshi thanked him personally with a finely-forged razor-sharp *katana* for his excellent work and highly-appreciated gift.

Tokugawa Ieyasu and the leading *daimyo* from across Japan were invited (read ordered!) to visit Kyoto, ostensibly to pay their respects to the Emperor, but more importantly also to Hideyoshi at his sumptuous new palace.

The Emperor Go-Yozei himself was to inspect Hideyoshi's new palace and administrative centre and had even been invited to stay there. For the five days that the Emperor and his entourage were to be there, so too were the *daimyo*. Hideyoshi used this opportunity of entertaining the Emperor to flaunt his power, financial and political, to the *daimyo*. Not only did he have the ear of the monarch, but with Oda Nobukatsu, second son of Nobunaga, ordered to appear amongst the *daimyo*, he showed one and all that he now held a position of supreme power eclipsing even that of the great Nobunaga himself.

For his part, Hideyoshi had ordered Hidenaga to construct a worthy *yashiki* mansion within the grounds of the Jurakutei complex for Tokugawa Ieyasu. Hidenaga and Ieyasu were on good terms. In fact they were brothers-in-law, Ieyasu being to Hidenaga's younger sister, Asahi. It was a marriage organised by Hideyoshi to ensure the Toyotomi and Tokugawa remained close, and appears to have worked, as Hidenaga and Ieyasu often corresponded, and Hidenaga would usually choose Takatora to be the messenger. Although Takatora towered above him, had been amongst his enemies at the Battle of Anegawa, and had opposed him at the Battle of Komaki Nagakute too, Ieyasu seemed to feel at ease with the tall warrior, and would read the letters while in Takatora's presence, and often talk with him about the contents of the messages before penning a reply for Takatora to take home to his master. Coming into Ieyasu's presence in this way and being able to talk with the future Shogun formed a certain friendship and trust between Takatora and Ieyasu. For this important construction job, once again Hidenaga called upon his most trusted and most skilled retainer, Todo Takatora, as the *sakuji-bugyo*, overall structural works project commissioner.[9] Incidentally the similar role of *fushin-bugyo* was responsible for the construction of the moats, *ishigaki* stone walls and other earthworks.

When presented with the initial designs already approved by Hideyoshi and Ieyasu, Takatora is said to have discovered a major defensive design fault. The layout of the grounds and also the *yashiki* which was to have

---

9. A letter in the possession of the Tokyo University's Former Todo Clan Collection (藤堂家旧蔵 *Todoke Kyusoku*), sent from Ieyasu to Takatora, dated the 10th month, 8th day (18 November 1586) and signed with Ieyasu's personal *kao* signature confirms that Hidenaga had constructed the Jurakutei on the orders of Hideyoshi, and mentions that Takatora was the structural works commissioner.

housed Ieyasu, were deemed by Takatora as 'difficult to defend'. Takatora then redesigned it all at his own expense. Later, when Ieyasu saw the residence, he was surprised, and asked why the plans had been changed. Takatora is said to have answered 'Lord Ieyasu is an important man, if you should come under attack, the original plan would have made defence difficult, and put your life at risk. My master, Hidenaga would be held responsible, and his master, Lord Hideyoshi too would be angered. If you are unhappy with the alterations I made, then you may cut me down, or, order it so and I shall cut myself open immediately.' There was something in Takatora's sincerity and consideration for the old warlord that touched the usually cautious Ieyasu. Much moved, he presented Takatora with a sword in appreciation, and an even stronger bond was forged between the two, one that would only increase in the years to come.

Hideyoshi would retire from his position as *Kampaku* in 1591, and hand the reins of power and his magnificent Jurakutei to his nephew and heir, Toyotomi Hidetsugu. Emperor Go-Yozei would make a second visit to the Jurakutei that year and was hosted by Hidetsugu. Meanwhile, Hideyoshi had commenced construction of an even more luxurious and opulent castle at Fushimi in the southern districts of Kyoto, and upon completion, relocated there. When a son and direct heir was finally born to Hideyoshi, and he no longer had need for his nephew Hidetsugu, the man was ordered to cut himself open. The entire Jurakutei was demolished, with various parts recycled or reconstructed at Fushimi Castle and various temples.

The Kyushu Campaign

There would be little time for Takatora to recuperate from his gunshot wounds and other injuries suffered in the attacks on Kizu and Ichinomiya Castles, as the following year Hideyoshi commenced work on the Jurakutei, and also demanded that as Shikoku had been brought under his control, the remaining territories of the south-western island of Kyushu should next be subjugated. While the Toyotomi had been active in taking Shikoku the previous year, the regional rulers of southern Kyushu, the Shimazu clan then under the command of the brilliant 16th clan head, Shimazu Yoshihisa (9 February 1533–5 March 1611), had made a push for complete control of the island, attacking the rival Otomo clan, and seizing their base, Funai Castle. In doing so they gained supremacy over Kyushu.

During 1586 and 1587, Hideyoshi had concentrated his efforts on obtaining the remaining lands yet to fall into his grasp. He himself would lead a force landing on the north-western coast of Kyushu at Chikuzen Province, in 1587. His brother, Hidenaga, and a 90,000-strong army which included some of the most noted warriors of the Sengoku period, besides Todo Takatora, such as the commanders Fukushima Masanori, Kato Kiyomasa and Kuroda (Yoshitaka) Kanbei, had arrived simultaneously on the north-eastern coast of Kyushu at Bungo, now known as Oita, and with Takatora in the lead of Hidenaga's troops, slowly, the 200,000-man Toyotomi army worked their way across Kyushu.

Takatora and his front-line samurai were next to see action in the Battle of Takajo, also known as the Battle of Takashiro, in which Taka Castle was quickly surrounded by Hidenaga's troops. Taka Castle in the township of Takagi, southern Hyuga (Miyazaki Prefecture), was known as one of the *Hyuga Sankojo*, the Three High Castles of Hyuga, and one of the forty-eight castles of Ito. This main castle was known as the Shinnoin Taka Castle. Nearby was the Sanmatain Taka Castle also known as Gassan Hiwa Castle. The ruins of both are now located in Takagi township, while the third castle, Atsuhisa, is in neighbouring Takaoka Town, Miyazaki City. Taka Castle had been in use since the year 701 and was only abandoned in 1615 under the Tokugawa-enforced One Castle Per Province laws. The area itself is surrounded by ancient battlefields, castles and fortress sites.

Taka Castle was defended by a garrison of around 300 samurai under the command of the Shimazu clan's *Karo*, or House Elder, Yamada Arinobu (1544–15 June 1609). Taka Castle was not a large fortification, but it was well-positioned, built on the edge of a plateau at an altitude of about 60m with at least five concentric rings of dry moat, and sandwiched between the Taniseto River (currently called the Kiribaru River) to the north and the Takashiro River (now known as the Komaru River) in the south, making it a difficult to attack stronghold.

Instead of storming the castle and taking it by force, Hidenaga opted to surround Taka and sever its supply lines. Once surrounded, Hidenaga anticipated the Shimazu would send reinforcements in support of Taka Castle, and so he quickly constructed a counter defensive fortress, Nejirozaka Castle, on a steep sloping hill to the south of Taka Castle overlooking the route that the Shimazu army would have to take in order to assist Taka Castle. The Tendai sect Buddhist monk, administrator and renowed warrior Miyabe Keijun (1528–20 April 1599) was the samurai left in charge of this new Nejirozaka Castle and had shrewdly reinforced their position with rows of wooden log palisades in front of and behind the multiple dry moats.

The Shimazu troops were either lured to come to the aid of Taka Castle or were compelled to do so in a bid to counter the Toyotomi attacks. Either way, on the evening of 24 May 1587, Shimazu Iehisa secretly moved his army into position, and at around midnight launched a sudden night attack against Nejirozaka. Three thousand Shimazu troops attacked with fire arrows and matchlocks but failed to climb the slopes and break through the rudimentary yet strong defences of the Toyotomi-held fortress, and the battle quickly became a stalemate. At dawn, a large division under Hidenaga arrived as reinforcements, but having assessed the situation, Hidenaga's tactical advisor, Bito Tomonobu, determined that it would be too risky to approach or even make an attempt at rescuing Miyabe and his samurai trapped in Nejirozaka, and recommended Hidenaga refrain from attacking the considerable Shimazu forces. Hidenaga complied with this counsel and believing this to be a no-win situation, suspended his army's efforts to assist.

While Hidenaga's main force held back, a small unit of 500 samurai led by Todo Takatora saw an opportunity and followed by a larger unit of around 1,000 troops under the command of Ukita Hideie's retainer, Togawa Michiyasu, suddenly advanced towards the fortress to assist Miyabe Keijun. As they approached, they made every effort to give the appearance of being a larger force and seemingly cutting off the Shimazus' escape route, caused the numerically superior Shimazu army to panic. Fierce fighting broke out on the lower slopes of the hillside, until the Shimazu began to disengage. Todo Takatora's actions against the Shimazu had given the nearby Kobayakawa and Kuroda forces enough time to reinforce Hidenaga's units and organise a pincer attack that nearly wiped out the retreating Shimazu forces. Shimazu Tadachika and Saruwatari Nobumitsu were killed in the fighting. What looked like a potential early defeat had become a complete Toyotomi victory, thanks mostly to Takatora's initial brave actions. For having suggested that attacking the Shimazu was risky, and in doing so missing a decisive opportunity to

destroy the Shimazu clan, the military advisor Bito Tomonobu had his
domains confiscated and he was dismissed from service.

The siege of Taka Castle continued, but not for long. There was to be
no final last stand. The determined Yamada Arinobu was refusing to yield
Taka Castle, but ten days after the fighting at Nejirozaka, he did just that.
The castle surrendered meekly when Yamada Arinobu capitulated on the
advice of his lord, Shimazu Yoshihisa, offering his son as a hostage and
leaving the Toyotomi brothers to turn their attentions to the last of the
major warlords to offer resistance, the Hojo clan of Odawara.

The grateful Hidenaga later thanked Takatora with a 10,000-*koku*
reward, and Toyotomi Hideyoshi himself, having heard of Takatora's fine
efforts, further rewarded him with the title 従五位下 *Jugoishita* (Lower
Jugoi) *Sado no Kami*, or Protector of Sado for his brave actions. Those
ranked *Jugoi* or above were considered among the aristocracy. The title
meant that Takatora was now considered to be of the nobility, and to have
been awarded such a rank was indeed a high honour.

Todo Takatora never forgot a debt of gratitude. With the extra 10,000
koku he was awarded by Hashiba Hidenaga, Takatora improved not his
own comfort and well-being, but in the true spirit of a samurai, used the
money to improve his services to his lord. Takatora quickly sought out
former vassals of the now-destroyed Azai and Asakura clans, men he had
served with in the past, and employed them directly to form a special corps
of retainers. Many of these men had been left as *ronin*, masterless samurai,
following the defeat and collapse of the former clans, and welcomed the
opportunity to once again take up the sword with pride and be of service.

One man he was particularly indebted to was a samurai named
Yamaguchi Shigezaemon, who had treated the young Takatora kindly
during his time in the employ of the Azai clan. Never forgetting the man's
goodwill and decency, Takatora reciprocated by welcoming him first as a
guest to his home, and then by offering Yamaguchi a fine position worth
300 *koku*. The equally grateful Yamaguchi quickly accepted and became a
trusted asset to the Todo army.

While Takatora and his master Hidenaga had been engaged with the
attack on Taka Castle, Hideyoshi's army had been fighting in the northern
Kyushu Chikuzen Province against the Akizuki clan's Ganjaku Castle.
As the castle fell, Shimazu-allied *daimyo* Akizuki Tanezane (1548–16
November 1596) managed to escape and fled to his main castle, the

namesake Akizuki Castle. The story goes that having captured Ganjaku Castle, Hideyoshi ordered all the walls of the castle be covered in sheets of strong traditional washi paper, making it appear that Hideyoshi was powerful enough to be able to renovate and replaster the entire castle overnight. Falling for the ruse, Akizuki Tanezane soon bowed in awe before the might of Hideyoshi.

Not long after the successes at Takajo and Ganjaku, the half-brothers Hideyoshi and Hidenaga, along with their allied generals' forces, arrived together to form a 170,000-strong army ready to lay siege to the home of the mighty Shimazu of Satsuma, Kagoshima Castle. On the night of 6 June, a 5,000-warrior Shimazu detachment under Niiro Tadamoto made a surprise attack on the Toyotomi forces camped by the Sendai River. The section they chose to attack was where Kato Kiyomasa's troops were bivouacked, and according to legend, Niiro himself faced the great warrior Kato Kiyomasa in hand-to-hand combat before retreating back to the safety of Kagoshima Castle under cover of darkness. This short, sharp skirmish is remembered as the Battle of Sendaigawa.

Days later, the Shimazu clan would find the Toyotomi troops on their doorstep. Toyotomi Hideyoshi, Hashiba Hidenaga and the men under Kuroda Yoshitaka, Fukushima Masanori and Kato Kiyomasa had surrounded the Kagoshima stronghold. Shimazu Yoshihisa is said to have decided to surrender to avoid an all-out battle which would have caused trouble for the people of his domain. Yoshihisa capitulated to Hideyoshi through the mediation and negotiations of the court noble, Konoe Sakihisa (1536–7 June 1612),[10] and of the seven Kyushu provinces the clan had taken control of, Hideyoshi reduced their lands to Satsuma, Osumi and half of Hyuga Provinces. This was still seen as a generous offer, and because of this the Shimazu a remained powerful and respected clan throughout the Edo period.

Not long after Oda Nobunaga's death in 1582, Hashiba Hidenaga had adopted the Toyotomi general Niwa Nagahide's third son, the then four-year-old Senmaru. Such adoptions and often marriages too between warrior families were usually undertaken in an effort to strengthen ties

---

10. In 1585, Konoe Sakihisa had adopted Toyotomi Hideyoshi, providing Hideyoshi with Fujiwara legitimacy, allowing for his appointment as *Kampaku*. Tokugawa Ieyasu would do something similar in having his family tree researched and a Minamoto clan member discovered among its branches, clearing the way for his appointment as Shogun.

between the clans, as well as to ensure the survival of a family name. In this case, it was to ensure the Niwa clan would serve the Toyotomi.

In 1588, Toyotomi Hideyoshi ordered his brother Hashiba Hidenaga to adopt Nabemaru, the younger brother of Hideyoshi's nephew and appointed heir Toyotomi Hidetsugu, but Hidenaga refused the order on the grounds that he had already adopted another boy, Senmaru. The refusal greatly angered Hideyoshi and put a strain on their relationship. In an effort to repair any ongoing animosity between Hideyoshi and Hidenaga, Todo Takatora, unable to have any children of his own because of his wife's condition, then offered to adopt Senmaru as his own son, allowing Hidenaga to obey Hideyoshi's command. The plan was accepted by both Hidenaga and by Hideyoshi, who then offered Senmaru a 10,000-*koku* incentive to be adopted by Takatora, and so Senmaru, then nine years old, became Todo Takayoshi.

The Master of Castle Design

Serving Hidenaga to the best of his ability was without a doubt Takatora's prime objective. Indeed, coming under the command of Hidenaga, having been entrusted with the leading of troops in battle and of construction teams when receiving commissions to construct fortifications, and being called on as a negotiator and envoy had changed Takatora's younger wilder ways for the better, and at the same time allowed him to make a name for himself not just as a fine soldier, but as a statesman and an expert in castle design and construction. Having pride and confidence were considered fine traits. Takatora had both, but he concealed them to ensure that he did not stand out any more than his 190cm frame already forced him to. No doubt he had a strong desire to improve his own position in life, but only so as to be of greater value to his master. Thanks to Hidenaga's patronage, Takatora soon became noted across the realm for his well thought-out maps, plans and designs for military installations and battle formations.

Hideyoshi and Hidenaga had both been born in near poverty. As their positions and wealth increased, Hideyoshi in particular surrounded himself with the trappings of success, luxuries and people of culture. Hidenaga was less flamboyant but sought out people with political understanding and creative design skills. Through Hidenaga's connections, Takatora too was drawn into this cultural world, forming friendships with luminaries such as the celebrated tea master Sen no Rikyu and his multi-talented disciple, the warrior, tea master and potter Furuta Oribe (1544–6 July 1615). Kuwayama Shigeharu (1524–1 November 1606), another famed aristocratic statesman and *daimyo* hailing from Owari Province, and the respected warrior and scholar Kobori Masakatsu (1540–29 April 1604) were all regular guests in Hidenaga's court. Hidenaga encouraged his men to improve themselves through cultural activities, intelligent communication, and political conversation. In this way, Hidenaga no doubt played a positive role, inspiring Takatora to develop his strong legislative and creative characteristics.

Similarly, with Hidenaga's money and influence at his disposal, Takatora was able to call upon the top contractors from across the country. He could access the best, hire them and study their methods and techniques, all the while developing some of the finest castles and defensive works Japan had ever seen. In this way, Takatora found himself in the company of some truly gifted men, such as the master carpenter Nakai Masakiyo and the artist, tea master, garden designer and warrior Kobori Enshu – men who would go on to make their own marks in history, and with whom Todo Takatora would come to associate with time and again.

Under Hidenaga, Takatora was awarded outstanding opportunities to test his skills and abilities, such as when Oda Nobunaga commenced construction of his magnificent and most innovative Azuchi Castle. Hideyoshi, and in turn Hidenaga were ordered to oversee the work on certain sections, and so Takatora was able to be involved in the construction.

Through such endeavours, Takatora would come into contact with the renowned Koura Daiku 甲良大工, carpenters and general contractors of Takatora's homeland of Omi who were particularly skilled in their trade, and whose work may well have influenced Takatora's later designs and innovations, such as the *sotogata tenshu* keep design.[11] Same too with the famed stonemasons of Anoshu, also based in western Omi, who had been called upon to complete the stone walls of castles such as Azuchi. These experiences undoubtedly taught Takatora the importance of castles, and instilled in him the importance of the skills of the stonemasons

---

11. *Sotogata tenshu* was an innovative construction style and method for building large, strong castle tower keeps quickly and cost effectively. See below.

and carpenters, and gave him an insight into their techniques. The introduction of firearms, particularly those of Omi's Kunitomo gunsmiths, to the samurai arsenal changed warfare. It also changed the design and construction of samurai castles. The addition of extensive *ishigaki*, dry stone walls, and even strong fired-clay *kawara* roofing tiles had already made great differences in castle design. These changes Takatora took in his stride, further developing new ways to fortify areas, confound the enemy and defend the castles.

Takatora began to develop his particular style of simple but effective castle layouts, with high, straight-edged stone walls and wide, water-filled moats. He made use of the strong, effective *masugata* type gate systems, and ensured that large, impressive *sumi yagura* corner watchtowers graced the ridgetops of the stone walls.

Gates are major defensive elements of a castle, and while Japanese castles have numerous types and names of gates depending on their design and positioning, the basic structure and function remains the same. Preventing a view, and more importantly, preventing direct access into the castle and its compounds.

Basic gates leading to the various baileys within a castle are known as *koguchi* in Japanese and are written with the characters 虎口 or 'tiger mouth', and gives you an idea of their function, being a way in and out, yet as dangerous as the jaws of a tiger. (Incidentally, Takatora's name, 高虎 means 'High Tiger'.)

The samurai castle's ultimate defensive gate system was the *masugata* gate. A *masu* was a small lidless wooden box, used to measure rice portions, and even smaller wooden *masu* were used for the serving of saké. A *masugata*, or *masu*-shaped gate system featured an outer gate, known as the *ichi-no-mon*, and the inner gate or *ni-no-mon*. The addition of the outer gate was a later Takatora innovation.

Basically, should the enemy breach the first outer gate, they would then enter a courtyard enclosure surrounded on all sides by either earthen embankments or stone walls topped with *tamon yagura* or clay walls, then have to turn 90 degrees — usually to the right – to be confronted by an even larger, stronger *ni-no-mon* gate, usually a *yagura-mon*, being a type of gatehouse with a protective turret-like structure built above it.

The enemy would be trapped within this enclosure, and then be fired upon by the defenders from multiple directions. Another way of remembering the *masugata* is by referring to it as a 'Death Box'. Any enemy entering this box-shaped courtyard would be killed.

The reason the majority of these *masugata* gate systems have the second, or *ni-no-mon* gate positioned to the right on entry are both psychological and physical. Most samurai weapons are used with the left side of the body facing forward. Archers carry the bow in the left hand, while the right hand notches and draws the arrows. Same too with the spear, and the matchlock. In both instances, the left hand is forward, and the right hand is to the rear of the weapon meaning that the body is slightly angled facing to the right, with the left foot forward. Having entered the *masugata* gate system, and having the next, highly defended gate on the right side – and therefore being most open to attack – is both physically and psychologically damaging. Add to this, the samurai understanding of human physics. The samurai understood that turning to the left is physically easier than turning to the right. Hold this book at arms-length in front of you. Twist your body left, . . . then right, . . . you will find it is easier and more natural to turn to your left. The same reason why athletic running tracks turn left, why racecars go anticlockwise around circuits and aircraft make left hand approaches to airports. Your heart is on the left, and the body naturally wants to protect that. The liver, being on the right side of your body, makes right-hand turning difficult and uncomfortable. It is of interest to note that the Kuroda clan, also recognised for their castle-building skills, seemed to prefer *masugata* gates that turned left upon entry, lessening their effect to a degree. The reason why they chose to build them like this remains a mystery.

Along the tops of the walls between the watchtowers ran *tamon yagura*. These are long, corridor-like structures built atop *ishigaki*, stone walls or embankments between, or adjoining, corner turrets. Classified as a type of *yagura* watchtower, some *tamon yagura* were two or three-story structures, but the majority were single-storey corridors. *Tamon yagura* usually had white plastered walls and were topped with tiled roofs. The outer walls featured armoured windows and loopholes along their length for the shooting of matchlock guns and arrows.

The *tamon* served as storage for armour, weapons, food and provisions. In times of attack, they provided protection from enemy fire, allowing defenders to remain hidden from besiegers, yet maintain full view of the enemy. Defenders could move about the castle within the *tamon* undetected by the enemy while remaining under cover from the elements such as sun, rain and wind that might also affect weapons such as matchlocks.

The first basic *tamon yagura* are believed to have been developed by the infamous warlord Matsunaga Hisahide (1508–19 November 1577) at his Tamon Castle in Nara, from where the structures get their name. While Takatora didn't invent them, employing *tamon yagura* around the vitally important gates and along the walls of castle compounds became a characteristic of Takatora designed castles.

The wide, open baileys within Takatora's castles were, when possible, usually square in shape. This allowed plenty of room for spacious *goten*, palaces that served as both administrative offices as well as residences for the castle's lord. Larger enclosures also allowed room for large bodies of troops to assemble in times of attack. Other features, include the strong *umadashi* – the Japanese term *umadashi*, literally 'horse opening', implies a place for cavalry to muster and exit – a semi-circular or square barbican-like defence consisting of an extra fortified earthen wall and moat positioned immediately outside of the main gates and across the moat were also further developed. Takatora would incorporate some of the nation's biggest and most impressive *umadashi* in his castle designs.

The International Negotiator

Todo Takatora was now living in a stately *yashiki* residence within the inner enclosures of Yamato Koriyama Castle and had been awarded an extra 10,000 *koku*, raising his stipend to 20,000 *koku*. His importance as a retainer to Hidenaga had risen greatly too. Also on the rise by 1587 were the numbers of foreign missionaries coming to Japan and now making conspicuous inroads by converting many peasants and townsfolk. In fact, Japanese Christians are said to have numbered around 300,000 by the late sixteenth century.

Of greater concern was the increasing number of prominent *daimyo* and samurai also falling under the spell of the foreigners. Some were beginning to find their new religion and adherence to the missionaries' teachings posing a conflict of interest with their duties and Hideyoshi's orders. This potential challenge to his authority provided Hideyoshi with sufficient reason for immediate action. He had kindly granted certain privileges and exemptions to the Christian priests, but in the summer of 1587 appears to have suddenly become suspicious of the foreigners and wanted them gone. Indeed, Nagasaki now appeared to be increasingly under foreign control. Hideyoshi wanted the missionaries' powers curtailed – but without interfering with the supply of weapons, gunpowder and other trade he was otherwise enjoying, of course. He arranged to have Takatora go to Nagasaki and negotiate with the foreign priests.

Through his envoy Takatora, Hideyoshi accused the Jesuits of various offences, including inciting uprisings, encouraging the *daimyo* and their people to abandon their traditional religions, trading Japanese slaves in China, Korea and other parts of Asia, slaughtering animals such as horses and cattle for food, and destroying Buddhist and Shinto effigies and structures. Hideyoshi promptly banned Christianity and ordered the Jesuit priests to leave the country within 20 days. The expulsion order, dated 25 July 1587, shocked the missionaries and their converts. While the priests were now recognised as undesirables, foreign merchants on the other hand were declared free to come and go for purposes of trade providing they did not engage in religious activities. Nagasaki would remain under the influence of the Jesuits until 1590, when Hideyoshi brought it firmly under his authority.

Takatora saw this as a fine opportunity to improve his negotiating skills, knowledge and experience in other areas. It was not his first experience in such dealings. Hidenaga had sent Takatora to negotiate with the Imperial Court in Kyoto on various occasions, proving that he was not just highly trusted by Hidenaga and Hideyoshi, but was considered cultured, clever and graceful enough to be able enter the realm of the aristocracy and was able to converse with them on various political topics. This also suggests that Takatora's roots were of higher ancestry than the simple landowning samurai we have been led to believe, as he had obviously been educated in the dignified and haughty manners of the court. The experiences at the Imperial Court and the connections he made would help Takatora to better serve another future master in his bid to have this lord's granddaughter marry into the Imperial family. Meanwhile, his success in ensuring that Hideyoshi's goals were met, simply increased his value to the ruler of Japan.

Toyotomi Control

Toyotomi Hideyoshi's desire for total control in the name of peace led to locking the population into the four traditional main classes, the warrior elite, the farmers, the craftsmen and finally the merchant class. The next step was to issue laws banning the farmers from leaving the land. Until now, farmers had been able to drop their tools and join the armies of the local warlords as foot soldiers, suddenly swelling army numbers and providing extra income for the conscripts. In preventing the field workers from becoming warriors, Hideyoshi prevented large armies from forming. He then attempted to disarm the population through his *Katana-gari*, 'Sword Hunt', project, whereby swords and weapons were collected up. This was not a forced confiscation and disarmament, but typical of Hideyoshi. By telling the populace the weapons would be melted down to create Buddhist statues of peace, the pious gladly donated their weapons.

He then ordered the undertaking of the *Taiko kenchi*, the surveying of the land, so as to know the exact size and rice-production value of each of the *daimyo*'s domains, and in doing so revealed the true political and military strength of the various *daimyo*. This also helped him distribute the *kokudaka* stipend system better, and more importantly, to determine the land taxes. Hideyoshi's laws and methods of control were seen as draconian by some of the lower classes, and so *Ikko Ikki* peasant uprisings and insurrections led by militant monks were not uncommon, particularly in regions such as Ise Province (modern-day Mie Prefecture).

Old Yodo Castle

In early 1589 Toyotomi Hideyoshi ordered a fortress, Yodoko, also known as Yodo Castle, to be constructed in which his wife, Chacha, could safely give birth to their first child. Lady Chacha is generally remembered as either Lady Yodo or Yodogimi and was so named because of this particular castle. Hideyoshi turned to his brother, Hidenaga, to take control of the project, and naturally he would have turned to the man he knew to be the most skilled at such projects, who had completed works on Wakayama Castle, Yamato Koriyama Castle, the *yashiki* residence for Tokugawa Ieyasu at Hideyoshi's Jurakutei and others – Todo Takatora.

The original Yodo Castle was located in Nosokitashirobori, in Kyoto's southern Fushimi district, and had been in service since 1504. The castle was a natural fortress surrounded by rivers on three sides and built on the northern bank at the point where the Kizu, Katsura and Uji Rivers meet. Yodo Castle and nearby Makishima Castle were the area's two major military bases. Yodo was also a key commercial area and an important land and water transportation point. Yamazaki Castle was located nearby on the opposite bank.

Akechi Mitsuhide had renovated Yodo around the time of the Honno-ji Incident of June 1582, and it played a part in the Battle of Yamazaki fought between Hideyoshi and Mitsuhide. Although no surviving records provide any proof that Takatora designed this new castle, it is generally believed by researchers that because of its conventional square-shaped layout, the wide moats, the manner in which the *ishigaki* stone walls are constructed and the positioning of the gates, that it is most probably Takatora's work. Certainly, considering the new Yodo Castle's importance to Hideyoshi, no other contemporary castle designer would have been more trusted, nor have the technical skills to come up with such a simple yet effective design. In July 1598, Hideyoshi's son, Tsurumatsu, was not only born at Yodo Castle but sadly died there three years later. With the death of the child, Hideyoshi's nephew, Toyotomi Hidetsugu, was then named as his heir. Hidetsugu appointed his vassal, Kimura Sadamitsu, as commander of the castle, which was finally abandoned in 1595 when Hideyoshi's second son, Hideyori, was born. To ensure this child was free from rivals, the now superfluous heir Hidetsugu and his family were forced by Hideyoshi to commit *seppuku*, and to extinguish the languishing memories, Yodo Castle was abandoned.

Todo Takatora would return to the Yodo area in 1623 to construct yet another castle. The original site has now been mostly consumed by residential development and an elementary school. A stone monument can be found at the nearby Myokyo-ji Temple.

The Siege of Odawara

By 1590, Toyotomi Hideyoshi had subjugated most of Japan. One of the last major warlord clans still refusing to submit to his authority were the long-established and rightfully proud Hojo of Odawara. In an effort to bring the only major threat to his power and peace under his control, Hideyoshi ordered the Siege of Odawara.

Odawara Castle was first established in the late fifteenth century as a stronghold built by the Omori Clan. Hojo Soun conquered the area in 1495, and as the Hojo clan gained power, he and his descendants gradually expanded the castle. At the height of their power, the Hojo controlled much of the Kanto area with support castles on the fringes as far away as modern-day Chiba, Ibaraki, Saitama and Kanagawa Prefectures. Odawara Castle faced three major attacks; the first siege was staged in 1561 by the warlord Uesugi Kenshin. It lasted two months with 110,000 Uesugi troops against 15,000 Hojo defenders. The siege was abandoned when the Uesugi clan's traditional rivals, the Takeda, threatened Uesugi territories forcing them to reconsider the siege, and through lack of adequate supplies. In 1569 Takeda Shingen too conducted a short three-day siege with 50,000 samurai. The castle's town was burned down by the Takeda before they left.

The third was this siege, lasting from May to 4 August 1590. Some 82,000 Hojo warriors were ensconced within Odawara while some 220,000 samurai from across Japan completely surrounded the fortress. Approximately 20,000 of these warriors belonged to the extensive naval flotilla watching Odawara along the Pacific coast.

In the lead-up to the siege, the various generals converged on and conquered the many surrounding Hojo castles and strongholds on their way to Odawara to prevent any possible attack from their rear. Despite the massive forces, the actual Siege of Odawara Castle itself saw very little fighting, and has been called 'the most unconventional siege in samurai history', as Hideyoshi staged huge tea ceremonies with the tea master Sen no Rikyu, and entertained the samurai with musicians, dancers, prostitutes and theatrical performances. It has been likened to an extravagant party rather than a military operation. The ongoing sound of the lively parties also infuriated the Hojo samurai trapped within Odawara.

At the time Hashiba Hidenaga was too ill to participate, and so he remained in Osaka protecting his stepbrother's castle. In his stead, it would be Takatora who would lead Hidenaga's army in first attacking Nirayama Castle, an extremely strong fortress, along with Yamanaka, Ashigara, Tengatake and a number of smaller castles and fortifications protecting Odawara's western flank. It was vital that these castles be taken or at least contained before the siege of Odawara Castle proper could begin. Originally built around 1493, Nirayama Castle had four supporting forts built atop surrounding mountains making for a 3,600-man garrison, which held out for 100 days – longer than any of their other allies – against the 40,000 troops headed by Takatora, but ostensibly under the joint command of Oda Nobukatsu and Tokugawa Ieyasu to whom the castle would finally be surrendered, but only after Odawara's capitulation. Once again, Takatora was to distinguish himself, bringing honour to his family name.

The Hojo of Odawara Castle only surrendered because of some of the most brilliant psychological warfare ever conducted in samurai history. Seemingly overnight, Toyotomi Hideyoshi built a large and impressive castle on a nearby mountain overlooking Odawara! One evening, after the noise of the partying and incessant firing of guns around the castle had become more than infuriating, the Hojo were alerted to work commencing on a mountain to their south-west by large bonfires being lit there. The next morning the Hojo samurai woke up, looked to the south-western hills, and there, overnight, the powerful Hideyoshi had completed a large and sturdy castle! The Hojo were shocked! Not only had Hideyoshi surrounded them, but now, a castle, with *ishigaki* stone walls lining the shaved sides of the mountain, complete with an impressive tower keep, multiple turrets, walls and gates, stood watching over them. A castle! Hideyoshi's might was indeed incredible! How could the Hojo hope to defeat such an enemy?

Known as Ishigakiyama Ichiya Castle, or the 'Overnight Castle', over 40,000 labourers had been employed working almost around the clock for 80 days and nights, cutting into the mountain to create baileys, and constructing the first stone castle walls in the mid-eastern Kanto region – something the majority of Hojo samurai had never seen[12] – and something that would have been most psychologically damaging. As Takatora was playing an important role leading Hidenaga's army and was engaged at Nirayama, Hideyoshi appears to have called upon the Kuroda clan to build this fine castle. A large five-storey *tenshu* keep, multiple *yagura*

---

12. The Hojo had basic *ishigaki* stone-wall technology and had used it at their remote mountaintop Hachioji Castle, the ruins of which lie in the far western suburbs of Tokyo but preferred the older earthen-based castle construction as Kanto loam becomes very slippery when wet, making it very difficult to climb during attacks.

turrets and gates were all constructed in secret behind a thick canopy of tall trees. Once all the construction work had been completed, that night large bonfires were lit around the mountain, alerting the Hojo to work being undertaken there and attracting their attention. Overnight, the surrounding curtain of trees was cut down, revealing the fortress in the morning light, and giving the impression that Hideyoshi had indeed built it overnight. It was a castle made as a show of authority and having seen this demonstration of the might of the Toyotomi, the disconcerted Hojo capitulated some days later. Toyotomi Hideyoshi now controlled Japan completely.

Incidentally, with the surrender of the Hojo, Ishigakiyama Ichiya Castle was no longer required, and so it was dismantled and abandoned. It had taken only 11 weeks to construct, and was operated, decommissioned and demolished in less time than it had taken to construct. Odawara Castle was handed over as a spoil of war to the *daimyo* Tokugawa Ieyasu, who was offered the Kanto region around the fishing town of Edo.

The Death of Hidenaga

In the cold days of mid-February 1591, the powerful *daimyo* who had seen great potential in the giant of a man, and had brought so many positive changes to Takatora's life over the last 15 years, the highly respected Hashiba Hidenaga, died a month and a half before turning 52. Just prior to his death, the ailing Hidenaga had appointed his 13-year-old nephew Hideyasu as his heir and successor, and in doing so requested Takatora care for and serve the boy with the same devotion he had served Hidenaga with. At first Takatora reluctantly refused, saying he could not possibly serve another, but finally relented as a last service to his dying master. It would see Takatora take on the role of statesman, handling political engagements and administrative duties in place of his new youthful master.

Hidenaga was buried in the Daiko-in Temple not far from Yamato Koriyama Castle, however, Takatora had his former master's remains relocated to the Daitoku-ji Temple in Kyoto in 1599. The reason for this was that the Mashita clan now ruled the Yamato area and visiting Hidenaga's grave became difficult. By moving the grave to Kyoto, Takatora was able to visit freely and more regularly. Here, Takatora would continue to show his gratitude and respect to his former master on many occasions. Indeed, he staged ornate memorial services in 1607, on the 17th anniversary of Hidenaga's death, as per Buddhist rites, and again in 1623 for the 33rd anniversary. Two years later, Takatora would donate a Shoin reception hall to the temple, and the following year, accompanied by Takatsugu and Takashige, he would again pay his respects at Hidenaga's grave. The Daiko-in would be destroyed by fire in 1816, and Takatora's Todo clan descendants would volunteer funds and workers for its rebuilding between 1818 and 1830.

The tea master Sen no Rikyu was ordered by Hideyoshi to commit *seppuku* not long after the death of Hidenaga, further depriving Hideyoshi of council. Rikyu, like Hidenaga, had been one of Hideyoshi's closest advisors. Whether Rikyu had had a difference of opinion, or had taken advantage of his position, or simply because he remained independent may never be known, but a rift emerged between Hideyoshi and Rikyu, leading to Rikyu's death on 21 April 1591, aged 70. Hideyoshi, it appears, later regretted ordering Rikyu to cut himself open. In the vacuum, Ishida Mitsunari, Uesugi Kagekatsu, Mashita Nagamori, Satake Yoshishige and other *daimyo* rose to fill their places.

New Horizons – The Korean Invasion

With the end of the Siege of Odawara and the capitulation of the Hojo clan, Hideyoshi had brought Japan's *daimyo* under his control and achieved what his own master, Oda Nobunaga, had set out to do – the unification of Japan. With the nation at peace, and with hundreds of thousands of battle-hardened samurai now sitting idle, Hideyoshi hit upon the audacious plan of subjugating China. Japan had long considered China to be the historical and cultural centre of the world, and now the aggressively ambitious Hideyoshi wanted to eclipse even that. Stage one of this plan was the annexation of Korea, Japan's gateway to China. In 1591, Hideyoshi ordered the construction of Hizen-Nagoya Castle in Karatsu City, Saga Prefecture, Kyushu. Kuroda Kanbei was in charge of the project's *nawabari* layout, with Kuroda Nagamasa, Kato Kiyomasa and Terasawa Hirotaka acting as *fushin-bugyo*, in charge of public works. Asano Nagamasa was general superintendent, with various Kyushu *daimyo* tasked with the construction of various sections.

Hizen-Nagoya Castle was a *hirayama* castle constructed on a 90m-high bluff on the wide Higashi-Matsuura Peninsula near Karatsu, modern-day Saga Prefecture. Nagoya Castle including the various outlying defences covered 17 hectares.[13] Nagoya was completed very quickly, starting in 1591 and finishing by March 1592. It was a very large castle, and it had to be, as this was to be the starting point for Hideyoshi's fleet to carry his thousands of samurai across the straits to what is now Busan in South Korea. The central *honmaru* compound featured a huge *tenshudai*, a stone-clad keep base, with a large five-storey keep soaring proudly above it in the north-western corner. The *honmaru* was positioned with the *ni-no-maru* and another two baileys to the west, to the east was the *san-no-maru* and another compound, the *Higashi Demaru Kuruwa*. Hideyoshi's mother was on her deathbed by the time the castle was nearing completion, and as Hideyoshi returned to Osaka, Toyotomi Hideyasu and Todo Takatora stayed on at Hizen-Nagoya.

Within a 3km radius of this enormous castle were *jinya*, fortified residences beloning to about 120 vassals, which became the temporary private living quarters of the various *daimyo*. Toyotomi Hideyasu's *jinya*, located south-west of the main Hizen-Nagoya Castle, was one of the larger of these, measuring 60m x 45m in size. It was surrounded by 2–2.5m high *ishigaki*, with a large 18m by 18m *masugata* gate on the northern face. A two-storey *yagura* watchtower overlooked this *jinya* and the centrally located traditional samurai-preferred *shoin* style *yashiki* living quarters. As Hideyasu was only 14 years old at the time, it was left to Takatora to design and construct his master's *jinya*, the layout of which was loosely based on Takatora's earlier Akagi Castle, only slightly bigger. This particular *jinya* can be seen on the surviving Hizen-Nagoya Castle *byobu* folding screen depicting the castle and its surroundings. The high stone and earth walls Takatora erected for this *jinya* remain standing to this day.

April 1592 saw Todo Takatora leading Lord Hideyasu and a large contingent of 15,000 samurai from Koriyama Castle to Hizen-Nagoya Castle before being dispatched to Korea. Todo Takatora, Kuki Yoshitaka, Wakisaka Yoshiharu and Kato Yoshiaki had been given the task of

---

13. This Nagoya Castle 名護屋城 is not to be confused with the similar Nagoya Castle 名古屋城 of Aichi Prefecture.

coordinating the shipping of samurai across to the Korean Peninsula. Takatora's navy consisted of around 2,000 men. They arrived in Busan that May, and immediately commenced operations against the Korean fleet along the southern coast.

The Battle of Okpo

On 16 June 1592, the first naval battle of the Korean campaign took place when a fleet of fifty transport ships under Takatora's command was attacked by a fleet commanded by Korea's brilliant Admiral Yi Sun-sin.

The Korean invasion had begun only weeks before, when Konishi Yukinaga had prematurely led 18,700 men in 400 transports to the Korean Peninsula, laying siege to Busan from 23 May. Over the following weeks an invasion force of 158,000 arrived in Busan and deployed northwards. By 16 June they had successfully captured the Korean city of Hanseong, modern-day Seoul. The roads throughout Korea were notoriously poor, making the overland transport of provisions difficult. To overcome the logistics issue, Takatora's transport ships prepared to sail the western coasts of the peninsula in support.

The sight of the Japanese ships put the Korean forces into a panic. Fearing the Japanese would easily take his fleet, and well before engaging in battle, naval commander Bak Hong scuttled his 100 warships, destroying his weapons and equipment in the process. Meanwhile his counterpart, Admiral Won Gyun, commenced his retreat to Hansando in South Gyeongsang Province, and in mistaking a flotilla of fishing vessels for the Japanese armada, also scuttled his own considerable fleet leaving just four ships afloat, and only the urging of his subordinates to remain at his post prevented him from deserting. He then called on Admiral Yi Sun-sin for assistance. The two admirals sailed to an area near Geoje Island having been alerted to the presence of Japanese ships anchored at Okpo Port.

Yi's fleet of twenty-four large oar and sail-powered ships, fifteen smaller ships and forty-six open boats was followed into the harbour by the cowardly Won Gyun's few remaining ships. As per their intelligence reports, they discovered Takatora's fifty mostly empty Japanese transports there, the occupants and crews having already disembarked. Todo Takatora's men were only alerted to the enemy fleet's arrival when the

Koreans commenced firing their cannons on the empty ships. Takatora had been caught off guard. Fearing being trapped in the port, he quickly ordered his men back to their ships in an attempt to escape. As the Korean fleet encircled the Japanese, Takatora had his men shoot back at the Korean ships, but their matchlocks had little effect on the thick wooden hulls of the enemy warships. Twenty-six Japanese transports were destroyed, and the samurai were forced to dump their armour and weapons overboard, abandon their ships and swim to the shore as Korean cannon shot and fire arrows rained down upon them.

The crew of one of Admiral Yi's ships managed to capture one of Takatora's ships, and when coming out of the harbour with their prize were fired upon by Won Gyun, who has mistaken them for the enemy. The attack had been a great success for the Korean navy, and morale soared. Admiral Yi was wise enough not to pursue the samurai on land, knowing them to be better fighters on land than they were at sea. For Takatora, it was a bitter defeat.

There was no time to wallow in self-pity. Orders from Hideyoshi in Japan were for Jinju Fortress to be captured and destroyed. Takatora lead his men inland and into action against a garrison of Korean troops stationed there. The Koreans had experienced one of their greatest victories over the invading samurai a year earlier at Jinju, but now the samurai were back, and this time with 90,000 men, 20,000 more than the defending Korean troops and militia behind the high walls and strong gates. Arriving on 20 July, the samurai forces first drained the moats around Jinju. Protected by *taketate*, strong yet lightweight shields made from large bundles of bamboo, great hordes of samurai advanced in unison, only to be repulsed by Korean bows and arrows, gunfire and cannon, even explosive shells from mortar-like weapons, killing hundreds. Once again in the thick of the action, not just Takatora but his 15-year-old adopted son, Takayoshi, also distinguished himself and received praise from his father as a true member of the Todo clan for his bravery. On 24 July, the samurai brought up some mobile shelters, under which sappers successfully undermined a section of the outer wall. Made from frames of bamboo and timber and covered in rawhide to protect them from gunfire, arrows and rocks, the shields had carved masks of an angry, devilish-looking cow fitted to the front. These 'tortoise shell carts' as the siege devices have been called, would become the basis for the Uwajima Ushi-Oni (devil cow) Festival.

The Korean defenders had hindered the samurai by dropping flaming torches onto the armoured carts, and setting the brush below the walls on fire, but heavy rains put an end to this, and the walls were compromised.

On 27 July, Japanese sappers managed to dislodge the foundations of the now-vulnerable walls, made even more unsound by a rainstorm, and the walls tumbled. Hordes of samurai attacked with renewed efforts against the weary Koreans. The fortress fell soon after. The samurai recorded the taking of 20,000 heads, while Korean records state three times that amount, as the samurai are said to have massacred not just the defending garrison, but civilians in the surrounding towns too. The battle appears to have been little more than a symbolic show of authority. The Japanese forces, Takatora and his men, would then return to Busan on the coast rather than use the victory as a stepping-stone northward.

On 23 August, a week after another Japanese fleet under Wakisaka Yasuharu and supported by Kuki Yoshitaka and Kato Yoshiaki had been defeated at the Battle of Hansan Island, Takatora would receive orders directly from Toyotomi Hideyoshi to halt naval operations around Busan and concentrate on reinforcing operations within the peninsula. Takatora would also see action in the Battle of Busan Bay on 5 October 1592, in which Admiral Yi launched a surprise attack on the Japanese fleet in an effort to recapture Busan and cut off the samurais' supply lines. Only one officer, Admiral Yi's trusted Chong Woon and six Korean fighters were killed with another 25 wounded, while over 128 ships belonging to Wakisaka Yasuharu, Kuki Yoshitaka, Kato Yoshiaki and Todo Takatora were lost in the attack. Even then, it failed to dislodge the samurai.

That December Takatora and his son Takayoshi sailed home to Japan. After reporting to Hideyoshi directly, and receiving 10,000 *koku* and Ukena County worth an extra 80,000 *koku* as a reward, Takatora returned to Lord Hideyasu's service at Yamato Koriyama Castle.

Hideyasu's Death

Todo Takatora's sixth liege lord, Toyotomi Hideyasu, died aged just 17 on 24 May 1595 from what is believed to have been measles. Takatora had only agreed to serve Hideyasu on the urging of his previous lord, Hideyasu's uncle Hidenaga on his deathbed. Hideyasu had no successor and so the clan officially ceased to exist. Takatora, now aged 39, once again found himself masterless. Hideyasu's premature death so soon after that of the much respected Hidenaga, and the extra role he had assumed running the domain in his young master's name had caused Takatora great stress, and so in a state of near exhaustion and in great pain from the loss, he retreated to the famed hot springs of Totsugawa in Nara's Yoshino District to consider his future. Takatora had greatly admired and respected Hidenaga, and had taken on the role as a guardian and mentor to Hideyasu as a final act of loyalty. Takatora felt that he could serve no other, and so in mourning both Hidenaga and Hideyasu, he climbed holy Mount Koya, and entering a monastery, went into a self-imposed retirement.

Takatora's retirement was not to last long. In fact, he was only to spend around two months on Mount Koya before the most important person in Japan besides the Emperor himself, Toyotomi Hideyoshi, was to call him down again. Hideyoshi was well aware of what a fine warrior and skilled castle architect Takatora was, and of the value he had been to both Hideyoshi's brother Hidenaga and his nephew Hideyasu. Hideyoshi wanted such a man, and so he sent a message inviting Takatora to serve him directly. Takatora's prompt reply was that although he was deeply gratified, he could not bring himself to serve another lord. To show his determination and that he had indeed retired to a quiet monastic life, he cut off his topknot and sending it as proof of his conviction, remained on Mount Koya. This only served to convince Hideyoshi he was a man worth pursuing, and so the nation's leader ordered his vassal and a close friend of Takatora, Ikoma Chikamasa, to make a direct offer to Takatora. Again Takatora refused, and so Ikoma was sent again, and again, until Takatora finally relented and coming down from the mountain paid his respects to Hideyoshi at Fushimi Castle in late July. Delighted, Hideyoshi presented Takatora with a 70,000-*koku* stipend and offered him lands in Awa Province, currently Tokushima Prefecture on the easternmost coastline of Shikoku.

Todo Takatora had a new master. His seventh.

Chapter 3

Retainer of the *Taiko*

Toyotomi Hideyoshi was most pleased and proud to have a man of Takatora's standing among his men, and not only offered him a handsome stipend and domains, but also the use of the *Kiri Mon*, the admired paulownia crest of the mighty Toyotomi clan.

The elite *Kiri Mon*, the Paulownia Crest.

To be offered even part of a *daimyo*'s name, such as a *kanji* character, or to be offered his family crest was a very high honour indeed. There are over 140 variations of the *Kiri Mon*, being basically three leaves supporting three florets, the main types being a three, five and three flower-bearing *Kiri Mon* and the even more elite five, seven and five flower-bearing crest. The *Kiri Mon* represented several branches of the Imperial family and the previous Ashikaga Shogunate had also used it. Even now in modern-day Japan the *Kiri Mon* is held in the highest esteem. Along with the Imperial *Kiku Mon*, the Chrysanthemum Crest, it has been used since the Meiji period as a symbol of the National Government. Today it remains the official crest of the Office of the Prime Minister of Japan, his cabinet and the ministries. It can be seen on the decoration of government stationery, supplies and documents, including passports and visas, even on the face of the current ¥500 coin. At the time the *Goshichigiri Mon* (as the five-seven-five flowered version of the crest is officially known) was offered to Takatora, it could be seen stamped onto the large oval-shaped gold coins known as *koban*, and was a visual symbol of supreme Toyotomi power.

Takatora refused the honour.

A humble man such as Takatora considered himself unworthy of such a high distinction, and bowing deeply before his new master, Hideyoshi, told him so. Although a large man physically, and therefore someone who would literally stand out in a crowd, Takatora never sought to be the focus of attention, unlike many men who would no doubt have relished such an honour and taken advantage of the many opportunities having such a crest would offer. Rather, this sincere, hardworking man saw himself as a samurai first and foremost. The origins of the word 'samurai' mean 'One who serves'. That was Takatora's role, as a samurai, one who serves and supports his lord to the best of his ability, with little need nor desire for reward nor recognition. His heartfelt righteousness in refusing the honour simply elevated him yet again in the eyes of his new master.

In late August 1595, Takatora entered the medieval Itajima Marugushi Castle in Uwa, Iyo-gun, then known as Itajima.[1] The previous master

---

1. According to Uwajima Board of Education, the regional name of Itajima was changed to Uwajima for unknown reasons during the Date clan's rule of what is now Uwajima City.

of Takatora's new fief, the warlord Toda Katsutaka, had died from an illness eight months earlier on 4 December 1594, while aboard a ship returning from serving in Korea. Toda Katsutaka had first been employed by Oda Nobunaga and was among Hideyoshi's oldest vassals. The veteran warrior had seen battle time and again, and Katsutaka had been with Todo Takatora during the Shikoku campaign at the Siege of Kizu Castle.

Toda Katsutaka and his clansman Toda Yozaemon had not governed the Uwajima region well, leaving the villages and province in disarray. As there had been no heir designated by Katsutaka to carry on the governorship, the Toda clan were dismissed and the vacant domain was offered to Takatora. The Todo clan replaced the Toda clan.

Upon Takatora's transfer to Shikoku, he was shocked to discover the extent of the hardships suffered by the people of the region. The Toda clan had been overly zealous in their handling of the strict rules set by Toyotomi Hideyoshi in regards to the 1588 *katana-gari* disarming of the peasantry, as well as with the *Taiko Kenchi* land surveys, so much so that they had overtaxed and severely impoverished the area. A set of thirty books known as the *Seiryo-ki*, 清良記, remains the best source of records, explaining how during a cold winter, many had died due to the mismanagement of the Toda clan. It also states that around 800 people had been crucified, and another 2,000 townsfolk had simply been killed or executed outright by the Toda for having taken part in protest riots or for other offenses real or imagined.

Realising the strategic importance of the area, Takatora had wanted to commence building a castle as quickly as possible. However, seeing the sorry state of the people and villages across the province due to the Toda's misgovernance, he decided that rather than build the castle, it would benefit all if he were to concentrate on improving the conditions of the townsfolk first. The people of the area had lost trust in the Toyotomi administration, and so rebuilding that trust was the first task Takatora set for himself.

Four months later, he released a document outlining his plans and promises to improve the plight of the people and to better govern the area. Unlike many of the *daimyo* who ruled through fear and intimidation, the forward-thinking Takatora's approach was a more humane one, in which he considered the people of his domain first.

Takatora met with the villagers and where none was available, appointed a headman from each village. With their input and assistance, he helped pinpoint problems and develop the villages to improve living standards. Takatora then relieved the heavy tax burden on the residents, giving them a year's grace from having to pay any taxes. He also announced that executions for all but the most inexcusable of crimes were to stop. He then set about repairing and rebuilding all the Shinto shrines in his domain, such as constructing and donating the Haiden Hall of the Mishima Jinja Shrine of modern-day Seiyo City in the summer of 1596, where a 1m long, 20cm-wide wooden plaque handwritten by Takatora remains. In 1601 he decreed 20 bushels of rice be gifted annually to the area's leading Mishima Daimyo-Jin Shrine. In 1607, Takatora oversaw construction of the Ibuki Hachiman Jinja's Shaden Hall. These shrine improvements appeased not only the people of Takatora's domain, but the gods as well, and this would bode well for all.

Later having improved the province's circumstances, Takatora set his sights on protecting the area and establishing his authority with a new castle. He was eager to undertake such works knowing that building a military installation such as this new castle would also bring economic and cultural benefits to the region. Part of this low-cost, high-speed approach to the construction of Uwajima included the recycling of parts salvaged from other regional castles. The *san-no-maru* bailey's squat looking two-storey *Tsukimi Yagura*, or Moon Viewing Turret, for example, had been dismantled and brought from nearby Kagomori Castle.

Kagomori Castle

Chosokabe Motochika had defeated many lesser rivals over the preceding years to establish himself by 1584 as the premier warlord of Shikoku, only to lose the bulk of his domains the following year to Toyotomi Hideyoshi in his push to subjugate the southern island. The lands of Iyo Province were given to Hideyoshi's talented retainer Kobayakawa Takakage. Under the Kobayakawa, Kagomori Castle, a small but vital outpost on the border of Iyo, Kochi and Tosa Provinces (southern Ehime and Kochi Prefectures), became the property of his vassal, Toda Katsutaka (?–1594). When Katsutaka died of a sudden illness without a successor, Kagomori Castle was offered to Takatora in 1595. Takatora then installed one of his trusted vassals as castellan. The castle had been built in the late fourteenth or early fifteenth century by the Watanabe clan on a 50m-high horseshoe-shaped hill surrounded by the Hiromi River and overlooking the important Matsuyama Highway at Tomioka Matsuno Town. Both the Hiromi River and Matsuyama Highway were vital trade and communications routes between Iyo and Tosa. Kagomori Castle was relatively well established when Takatora took command, and so little work was needed to bring it up to contemporary standards, although Takatora's innovations made Kagomori a formidable fortress. The redesigned ground plan was a confusing one for attackers, and featured three *horikiri*, deep 'V'-shaped trenches, the widest 5m and the narrowest 3m, cutting off access to the various baileys.

Takatora reconfigured and strengthened the main central *honmaru* bailey, cutting into the outer slopes, making them steeper while encircling the *honmaru* with a *koshi-guruwa*, a narrow strip of surrounding land. The most visible and modern of improvements was the construction of a small keep for the castle's new role as a border stronghold against the threat of the neighbouring lords of Tosa Domain, the Chosokabe clan. This small keep, which was in reality little more than a two-storey *yagura*, was most probably called the *Honmaru Yagura* rather than a *tenshu* at the time. When building his castle at Uwajima, Takatora would dismantle his small tower keep structure at Kagomori, and taking the pieces with him, would reconstruct it at Uwajima as the *Tsukimi Yagura*, the Moon Viewing Turret, in the *san-no-maru* compound. Takatora would also cleverly strengthen the castle by developing a *tanima*, a rainwater collection point, as only limited water sources were available at the castle.

In a direct exchange of fiefs, Todo Takatora would be transferred from Uwajima to Tsu Castle in Ise in 1608, while Tsu's Tomita Nobutaka of Ise was transferred to Uwajima, and part of his new domain included Kagomori Castle. The Tomita were later replaced by Date Hidemune, son of the great warlord Date Masamune of Sendai, and while the Date were based in Uwajima, Kagomori Castle came under the command of their retainer Kori Kageyori for a year before being decommissioned in 1614 and demolished around 1615 following the Tokugawa Shogunate's issuing of the *Ikkoku Ichijo Rei*, the One Province One Castle decree. The ruins of Kagomori Castle are now a registered National Historic Spot and is listed among the Extended Top 100 Castles of Japan.

Uwajima Castle

Uwajima was originally built by the poet and nobleman Saionji Kintsune (1171–1244), as Itashima Marukushi Castle in 1203 on a 77m-high hill along the south-western coast of Shikoku at Ehime. Uwajima was captured when Hideyoshi's forces attacked Shikoku in 1585, and the lands were then awarded to the *daimyo* and 14th head of the Kobayakawa clan, Kobayakawa Takakage (1533–26 July 1597), who installed his close vassal, Mochida Ukyo, as caretaker castellan. Kobayakawa was transferred in 1587 and replaced with the Toda clan. The master of Otsu Castle, Toda Katsutaka, decided to remain at Otsu, and so he installed his vassal, Toda Yozaemon, as castellan.

When Takatora entered Uwajima, he was accompanied by his adopted son Takayoshi. During their time in Uwajima, Takayoshi would become betrothed to one of the five daughters of the prominent *daimyo* of Echigo Province's Shibata Domain, Lord Mizoguchi Hidekatsu (1548 – 13 November 1610), but they soon divorced. Takayoshi would however keep one of his ex-wife's handmaidens as his concubine. Takatora's grandchild would be born to them. Takayoshi would remain in Imabari Castle as castellan after his father was transferred.

Takatora's Uwajima Castle was a pentagonal shape, with the sea on the northern and western sides. It had the *honmaru* at the top of the mountain on the seaward side, and the *ni-no-maru* beside that. The *Fujibei-maru* was located to the north, the *Daiemon-maru* one level below that to the west side. The *Nagato-maru* was positioned with the *Ido-maru* on the east side, and the *Sanno-maru* on the north-east side at the foot of the mountain. Takatora's higher ranked vassals were provided with the flat area around the bottom of the mountain in which to build their *yashiki* residences. This area was surrounded by a wide protective moat. The castle was accessed by four main gates, the main Otemon, and the Etsumon gates faced inland and the Kuromon and Yakemon gates opening directly towards the sea.

Its pentagonal shape is difficult to see now because of landfill and urban development, however looking at road maps, and following National Route 56 and connecting roads which were built on top of the filled in moats, one can still make out the original five-sided shape of the old castle. This was seen as an interesting development, as any attacking force would usually be prepared to attack a castle from four sides, but as Uwajima had five, any attackers would have to quickly reform their ranks.

The mountain chosen by Takatora was shaved flat at the top to form the main *honmaru* bailey. Those of this castle was not square as were most of Takatora's castles, but long and narrow as it conformed to the shape of the mountain, being made in the manner of *yamajiro* mountain castles of the Middle Ages. The sides of the mountain below the baileys were carved to increase the degree of incline at important defensive positions making it harder to infiltrate. These sculpted slope features are known as *kirigishi*,[2] literally 'cut cliffs' and when carved from around the outer slopes, form a narrow bailey at their base known as a *koshiguruwa* or 'waist bailey'.

Ishigaki measuring up to 13m high – the highest ever for those times – were built around the *honmaru* and the northern facing sections to further increase the strength and image of the castle, with the various defensive structures built on top of them. These walls were built in the standard way, angled inwards from bottom to top, yet were mostly straight, with very little curvature as per Takatora's preferred style. Other parts of the castle's outer walls were left as earthen-faced *kirigishi*. There were eight small *yagura* watchtowers surrounding the edges and corners of the *honmaru*, with the small three-storey *tenshu* keep located in the centre of the *honmaru* bailey. Why these *yagura* were not connected by *tamon yagura* remains a mystery, but this may have been because although the design and construction was done by Todo Takatora, it was built to specifications demanded by Toyotomi Hideyoshi himself. It is known that Oda Nobunaga and Toyotomi Hideyoshi would only give their permission for their *daimyo* to build castles after having seen the plans first, and usually after having some say in how they were to be constructed. Much of this castle's *ishigaki* and the *tenshu* were built in the older Toyotomi style, as commanded by Hideyoshi. Despite it being a medieval style of castle construction and one of Takatora's earlier works, it bore the marks of an innovative *kinsei*, or early modern *hirayama*, hill and plains castle.

Uwajima Castle was not just a *yamajiro*, mountaintop castle, but was also recognised as one of the country's top three *umijiro* – sea castles. At

---

2. *Kirigishi* are also known as *doi* or *dode*.

the time of its construction, Uwajima was located on a hill surrounded by the sea. Today, land reclamation projects have positioned the castle some distance inland. These rare *umijiro* actually allowed for the entry of ships and boats into the castle confines. In fact, there are remaining Meiji-period photographs of Uwajima's two-storey corner *Kuromon Yagura* watchtower, and what appears to be a *tamon yagura* connected to that, with boats moored around it.

The warrior scholar Hosokawa Yusai, his son Tadaoki and Todo Takatora are recognised as pioneers of sea castles and of seawater moat systems. Takatora had gained experience in building a castle by the ocean complete with harbours and sea access while in Korea, and used a similar style to construct Uwajima. As such, Uwajima was the most contemporary of *umijiro* at the time of its construction. Kuki Yoshitaka, master of Toba Castle in Mie Prefecture, and Todo Takatora both made fine use of *suigun* naval forces. Takatora's keen mind quickly grasped the importance of a navy, and the experience gleaned from forming and organising his own navy at Uwajima would serve him greatly in the years to come as Hideyoshi, having brought the nation under his control, would later make moves to annex the Korean Peninsula, and Takatora's waterborne forces would play a major part in the transportation of troops, and the securing of ports and waters along the southern coasts of Korea.

The small keep was originally built on a natural rock base at the top of the mountain. The current *tenshudai*, the stone base on which the keep sits, was added in the late Edo period, and was simply fitted around the original natural stone base, hence adding an approximately 1m wide *inubashiri*, or literally 'dog's run' space between the walls of the keeps and the stone base's outer edge. If one was to remove the outer layer of stonework, the original natural rock would be visible below. Uwajima was one of the first *tenshu* keeps to have been built directly on rock, which was chipped and shaved to make a flat top, upon which the carpenters and builders erected the tower. Almost all *borogata* keeps until now had been basically rectangular in shape, yet the ever-original Takatora built Uwajima's keep as one of the first completely square-shaped *tenshu*, and this appears to have been an early inspiration for the future *sotogata*-type keeps developed by him.

The original architectural plans of Takatora's *tenshu* keep remain, as does a Date clan folding screen depicting the castle and dated 1622. Unfortunately, the Date clan's folding screen wasn't very well painted, and so little reliable information can be gleaned from this, however a much better sketch remains and shows the original *borogata*-style *tenshu* was three storeys high, with a small *tsuke-yagura*, an annex, adjoined to the front through which entry could be made. The keep had *shitami ita bari* wood panelling protecting the outer walls around the keep's first floor. Takatora's original *tenshu* was much better designed than the current keep which stands on the same location as Takatora's original.

According to reports submitted to the Shogunate in 1662, it appears that the entire building had become structurally unstable just over half a century after its construction. The report mentions eight pillars and ten beams on the first floor, and three pillars and seven beams on the second floor as having decayed. An attached drawing detailing the repairs required show around half of the pillars had succumbed to wood rot, but there were no records of any large-scale repair work being carried out in its 61 years. It is believed that this problem was due to the use of old timbers being recycled from sources such as a local temple and other old castle structures built prior to Takatora's assignment at the time of the tower's construction.

The extant castle tower that remains to this day was reconstructed in 1666 by Date Munetoshi but was based on the size and principal design of Takatora's original keep. Major renovations were carried out in 1860 following damage from an earthquake three years earlier. This castle keep remains the only example of the older design style in which traditional *washi* paper-lined sliding *shoji* doors remain inside along the corridors, and there are high thresholds, suggesting tatami mats having been once fitted. In Edo period castle structures, these thresholds were often simplified, however Uwajima's new keep interior was based on an older design from the Azuchi-Momoyama period. Despite the old Warring States design, the keep's outer walls are not to battle standard, nor do they feature the supposed *ishi-otoshi* 'stone dropping' chutes common in other castle structures. The windows do have the common vertical pillars allowing for visibility as well as some protection for the defenders. There are matchlock gun and match hooks on the walls below the windows, believed to have been designed to allow defenders to shoot directly from the windows, and another interesting feature shared only with Himeji Castle are the long narrow windows along the upper walls just below the ceiling. These are for allowing the smoke from matchlocks fired inside the keep to clear. Unfortunately, the emphasis on decoration, such as the triangular roofing devices known as *hafu*, and the extended roof over the entrance way have lessened the effectiveness of the keeps' defensive capabilities by partially obstructing the field of fire.

Besides the small keep, on the south side of Uwajima Castle is the extant Nobori Tachi-mon Gate, believed to be Japan's largest remaining *yakuimon* gate. (*Yakuimon* are simple, single-storey castle gates. Seen from the side, the single gabled roof appears to be off centre from the four support pillars.) Scientific chronological analysis of the pillars revealed that the logging was done between 1430–1530, and so the structure is believed to have been founded around the Todo renovation period (1596–1601). The gate is an Uwajima City-designated Tangible Cultural Property. The northern entrance to the castle is via the mid-Edo period Kuwaori Nagayamon Gate. This relocated Nagayamon Gate belonged to the estate of the Kuwaori family, the chief retainers of the Uwajima domain during the feudal era. Most of the left side was cut off, meaning much of its original shape is lost, even then it is also a city-designated Tangible Cultural Property. The final remaining part of Uwajima Castle is the Yamazato Warehouse, originally an armoury built in the *san-no-maru* precinct in 1845 and relocated to its present location in 1966 where it serves as the Shiroyama Folk Museum. This current keep is one of only twelve remaining *tenshu* in original condition of the 170 or so castles in commission during the Edo period.

As has been mentioned, Uwajima Castle's Tsukimi Yagura was originally the tower keep of nearby former Chosokabe-held Kagomori Castle on the border of Ehime and Kochi Prefectures. Todo Takatora received 70,000 *koku* when he accepted Uwajima Castle and as Takatora's mother had since died, he invited his father Torataka and his new stepmother, Jozai no Fujin, to come and live at Uwajima. Following the Battle of Sekigahara in 1600, he was offered half of Iyo Province, and permission to build Imabari Castle along the Seto Naikai Inland Sea, a much more convenient and strategically important site, more so than Uwajima, which was considered inconvenient. Even today, Uwajima Castle is relatively difficult to reach, and therefore a rarely visited castle. Uwajima is listed as an Important Cultural Property by the national government, and one of the Top 100 Castles of Japan.

Amasaki Castle

Seen from the air, Amasaki was a gourd-shaped castle, and another owned by Takatora. In 1608, Takatora was given Iga Ueno in Ise, and in his place the Tomita clan, formerly of Anotsu Castle (also known as Tsu Castle), would enter Uwajima. Tomita Nobutaka had received Uwajima because of his service to the Tokugawa in the Battle of Sekigahara eight years earlier, but in 1613, he would be dismissed.[3] In his place, Todo Takatora would be provided with his lands. In lieu of Takatora, Todo Yoshikatsu would remain at Uwajima as the caretaker castellan.

Fushimi Castle

Toyotomi Hideyoshi had given his Kyoto-built Jurakutei to his heir Hidetsugu in 1591, and in its place commenced work on the very lavish Fushimi Castle some 9km south of the capital. Takatora had been employed early on the project as the developer and architect. Besides supervising construction of the large, authoritative keep and various structures, Takatora also sourced, gathered and supplied a large amount of stone to be used in the walls that he also directed the construction of.

---

3. Tomita Nobutaka was dismissed from service due to a rather complex incident involving his brother-in-law, head of the Tsuwano Domain of Iwami, one Sakazaki Naomori. Naomori had discovered his nephew, Ukita Samon, was having an affair with one of Naomori's female servants. Naomori had a retainer kill the servant, executing her with his sword. In revenge, Samon then slayed the retainer who had been ordered to kill the servant. Naomori's father, Ukita Tadaie, concerned for Samon's safety, ordered him into the protection of his son-in-law, Tomita Nobutaka. Naomori soon went in search of Samon, traveling to Nobutaka's Tsu Castle. Upset at having been told that Samon was not at Tsu, but at Fushimi Castle, Naomori planned to kill Nobutaka in his anger, but was prevented from doing so by his retainers. Instead, he took some of Nobutaka's men as hostages. Seeking justice, Naomori finally took his complaints to Ieyasu, accusing Nobutaka of concealing a criminal. Ieyasu had already retired, so he instructed Naomori to appeal to the *Bakufu*. In the meantime, Tomita Nobutaka was transferred to Uwajima Domain. This complicated incident escalated, and owing to his complicity in the matter, Tomita Nobutaka and even his younger brother, the Lord of Sano Domain, who was also involved, were dismissed some years later. Nobutaka was then confined to Iwaki Village in Mutsu Province. Samon was executed.

A violent earthquake in 1596 badly damaged the castle, and so the *tenshu* and various *yagura* from nearby Yodoko Castle, also believed designed and built for the Toyotomi by Takatora, were dismantled and rebuilt at Fushimi to replace the damaged parts.

Fushimi Castle was also known as Momoyama Castle, and part reason for the late Sengoku era of 1568–1600 being also known as the Azuchi-Momoyama Period was because of Oda Nobunaga's Azuchi and this visually and strategically monumental castle.

Toyotomi Hideyoshi died within the sumptuous Fushimi Castle in 1598, and the following year his young son, Hideyori, relocated, making Osaka Castle his official residence. On his deathbed, Hideyoshi had called for Tokugawa Ieyasu and requested that because of his wisdom and experience, he serve as the young Hideyori's guardian, and that Ieyasu treat the boy as a grandson. This Ieyasu agreed to – and appears to have interpreted literally. Maeda Toshiie, another of the *Go-Tairo*, the Five Regents, and the only one strong enough to keep Ieyasu in check died in 1599 and so the now unopposed leader of the five Regents, Tokugawa Ieyasu, entered Fushimi Castle, adopting it as his own.

Besides having claimed Fushimi, he also took a modest plot of land within Osaka Castle to build himself a small fortified residence, a move that also greatly upset his antagonists who further accused him of plotting to overthrow the Toyotomi. Ieyasu then ordered the bulk of the samurai and staff of Fushimi to relocate their residences to Osaka. That left Fushimi with very few samurai with which to man it, and the once-gorgeous castle, a symbol of the great Toyotomi Hideyoshi, soon went into decline. Although a more detailed explanation will be forthcoming, basically, by mid-1600, the nation began to split into two factions, East, being a Tokugawa-led coalition, and the Western forces, those loyal to the Toyotomi clan. Prior to moving his troops north to the Siege of Aizu, Tokugawa Ieyasu, knowing full well Fushimi Castle would be among the first castles attacked by the pro-Western armies, he installed a much-trusted vassal as castellan.

As expected, in the late summer of 1600, as a precursor to the Battle of Sekigahara, over 40,000 Western-allied samurai laid siege to an undermanned Fushimi. The once-splendid castle at Fushimi was ordered rebuilt in 1601 with Todo Takatora playing an important role in improving the fortress, employed as the designer in charge of the new layout. The castle was reconfigured and rebuilt and extant structures repaired. In 1604, Ieyasu ordered the development of the Mizu Kuruwa enclosure, and again Takatora was selected to work on the layout and oversee various stages of its fabrication. The site of the actual Fushimi Castle would later be chosen as the site of Emperor Meiji's tomb.

Korea Revisited

Ongoing peace talks between Japan and China's Ming Dynasty had broken down, and so in anger Hideyoshi had ordered a second invasion force be launched against Korea. Once again, in 1597, thousands of samurai sailed from Hizen Nagoya Castle for the Korean Peninsula.

The seventh day of the seventh month by the lunar calendar is the traditional date for the Tanabata Festival, in which the legendary star-crossed lovers, Princess Ori and her beloved cow herder, Hikoboshi, exiled to the heavens by her angry deity father, are allowed their single annual rendezvous as their stars come together in the Milky Way.

On that date, 19 August by the Gregorian calendar, Takatora again departed for the Korean Peninsula. Once again, he led the Iyo Suigun naval forces and arrived off Busan nine days later, where he played a major role in the defeat of the Korean Navy off the coast of Hanyang Island, about 40km south west of Busan. This victory made it almost impossible for the Koreans to block the sea routes, allowing more Japanese troops as well as supplies to make it safely to the peninsula. The orders from Hideyoshi had been to capture territories, and then build castles to hold those territories.

A week later, the now 41-year-old Todo Takatora received a letter from Toyotomi Hideyoshi himself, dated the 7th month, 16th day (28 August). In the extant letter, Hideyoshi encouraged Takatora to take control of the waters south of the Korean Peninsula and mentions that although Takatora has had minimal experience in naval battles, he (Hideyoshi) believed Takatora would do well.

Takatora did better than well. He excelled himself. A single engagement with the Korean Navy would lead to its near-complete annihilation.

The Battle of Chilcheollyang, Geoje Island

The first Korean campaign of 1592–3 had proven the Korean navy superior under Admiral Yi Sun-sin. The experiences against this formidable force had dealt the Japanese a savage blow. By the time of this second campaign, the Japanese navy had improved dramatically, and was now more than ready. Over the previous five years, court politics encouraged by Japanese spies had brought the Korean fleet under the command of the incompetent and unpopular Admiral Won Gyun (12 February 1540–27 August 1597). The Korean leaders had intercepted intelligence suggesting that Kato Kiyomasa was encouraging the Japanese troops to continue their efforts, and that he was about to make another crossing of the Tsushima Straits between the two countries. Admiral Yi was ordered to capture Kato Kiyomasa at sea but was aware that the intelligence had been planted by Japan's Konishi Yukinaga as a ruse. Unfortunately, he had no proof, and as such, he repeatedly refused his orders on tactical grounds, but his refusal was seen as insubordination, and he was demoted and imprisoned.

His rival, Admiral Won Gyun, had been most vocal against his predecessor, and had played an active role in Yi's demotion. Won Gyun now relished his position as the new commander of the remaining Korean navy and set sail for Busan on 17 August with the entire fleet of around 200 ships, arriving three days later.

Todo Takatora was leading an armada of 500 to 1,000 ships flying the flags of Kato Yoshiaki, Wakisaka Yasuharu, Konishi Yukinaga, Shimazu Yoshihiro and Kuki Yoshitaka, carrying some 140,000 men. Takatora invited the other fleet commanders to convene for a war council on 22 August to plan a joint assault on the Koreans. As a result, Shimazu Yoshihiro sent 3,000 of his men to Goeje Island, setting up camp high on the north-west coast, overlooking the Korean fleet in the waters below.

A week later, on the night of 27 August 1597, Todo Takatora's armada entered the straits around Goeje, where the 57-year-old Won Gyun's fleet had anchored and engaged the 200 Korean ships in the Battle of Chilcheollyang.[4] Surprised by the assault, Admiral Won Gyun ordered a general attack on the Japanese and fired cannon at them. Takatora initially

---

4. Also known as the Battle of Goeje Island, and in Japanese as the Shissen Ryou Kaisen, 漆川梁海戰.

turned the fleet back, encouraging the Koreans to pursue. Takatora's ships soon turned again, forcing the confused Won Gyun and his smaller fleet to halt and consider turning back themselves. Again Takatora feigned retreat, drawing the Koreans after them yet again. After a few such exchanges, the Japanese ships promptly turned and fired en masse, outmanoeuvring and destroying thirty Korean ships and scattering the fleet. Won Gyun soon discovered both his own failings as a naval commander, and the degree to which the Japanese navy had improved. The sea battle had quickly turned in favour of the Todo, Kato and Wakisaka fleet. Four hundred surviving Korean sailors broke away from the battle and fled to the supposed safety of nearby Goeje Island, where however they were promptly ambushed and cut down by the Shimazu garrison of 3,000 samurai stationed there. Their captured vessels were burned and sent to the bottom of the sea.

By dawn, over 160 Korean ships had been either destroyed or disabled. The majority of their leading captains had been killed in action. Prior to the battle, Korean captain Bae Seol had sailed twelve ships to an inlet farther down the strait to near Hansando – possibly in fear of the Japanese – and therefore managed to escape the carnage. Later, knowing the Japanese were closing in, Bae Seol burned down the camps at Hansando and sailed westwards, escaping with the Korean navy's final twelve remaining ships. In losing his first and only naval engagement as commander, Won Gyun also lost his life.

The rest of the Korean fleet was either captured or sunk by Konishi Yukinaga's fleet, and this allowed the Japanese to advance with little hinderance onto the Korean Peninsula and towards Jeolla Province. Todo Takatora together with Kato Kiyomasa and Konishi Yukinaga then planned the joint land and sea attack on Hanyang (modern-day Seoul). However, Japan's advances were crushed, and Todo Takatora would suffer severely with the return of Admiral Yi Sun-sin at the Battle of Myeongnyang.

Weeks later, Todo Takatora and his son Takayoshi were again on the front lines during the Siege of Namwon. Fought from 23 to 26 September 1597, the Japanese forces under the leadership of Ukita Hideie attacked and captured Namwon Castle, almost 100km inland from their landing point. In dealing an earlier devastating blow to the Korean ships that July, Takatora's fleet had allowed troops to land safely en masse. The Japanese forces were then divided into two forces, the Left and the Right Armies. The Japanese navy would fight as part of the Left Army.

Namwon Castle and Hanyang Castle were located on the border between Gyeongsang Province and Jeolla Province. Japan's Right Army marched on Hanyang, while the Left Army together with the fleet contingent, a total of 56,800 men, stormed Namwon Castle. The Ming general, Yang Yuan had been dispatched to secure Namwon Castle, and on arrival had hurriedly strengthened the castle's defences, extending the walls and digging deeper, wider moats. He ordered crenelated battlements be installed, had earthen mounds built around the castle, and had three cannons installed above the castle gate. That was still not enough to calm the fears of its defenders. When the news broke that the Japanese troops were about to attack, the bulk of the Chinese and Korean troops in the castle panicked and fled, leaving Yang Yuan and 3,000 cavalry to defend it. There are said to have been some 6,000 Korean civilians sheltering from the samurai in the castle at the time too.

The siege began as soon as the Japanese troops arrived at Namwon on 23 September. The commander Ukita Hideie, together with Todo Takatora and Ota Kazuyoshi, quickly deployed his troops and command post along the southern edge of the fortress. Kato Yoshiaki and Shimazu Yoshihiro took positions to the north of Namwon. To the east were Hachisuka Iemasa, Mori Yoshinari and Ikoma Kazumasa, while the western front was held by Konishi Yukinaga, Sou Yoshitoshi, Wakisaka Yasuharu, and Takenaka Shigetoshi.

The battle began with small groups of Japanese troops approaching the castle and firing off round after round of matchlocks, and while the Japanese matchlocks often hit their Korean targets, the Korean soldiers responding with their primitive firearms failed to make much of an impact. The next day the Japanese troops filled the moats with straw woven sacks of soil, and bundles of dampened rice straw were piled against the castle walls. On the third day of the siege, the Japanese forces offered the defenders a chance to capitulate. The offer to surrender was refused as the defenders of Namwon were waiting, having requested help from the 3,000 Ming troops in Jeonju, but as none were forthcoming, on the evening of 26 September, the samurai attacked. First the castle was heavily fired upon, and then hordes of samurai rushed the castle walls, using the bales of straw as a ramp. The defenders attempted to ignite the straw bales with fire arrows, but as they had been dampened, the straw failed to burn. Once again samurai close-combat matchlock, spear and sword tactics proved superior to the skills of the Chinese and Korean soldiers. In such cases, the Japanese fought with a swarming ant-like mentality. The first few facing the enemy might lose their lives, but there would be many more following. Helpless against the samurai onslaught, Namwon Castle soon fell with the loss of over 5,000 lives.

The few remaining Ming and Korean forces tried to escape, but as the castle was already under heavy siege they were quickly defeated, cut down savagely one after another as they attempted to flee. Yang Yuan and around 100 of his remaining men managed to break through the Japanese barricades and fled to Jeonju only to find the city deserted. The Ming commander, Chen Youyuan, had not only ignored Yang Yuan's repeated request for reinforcements, but had abandoned the city on hearing news of Namwon's defeat. While Yang Yuan would later be executed by his masters for his failure, Todo Takatora, and particularly his son Takayoshi, were praised and rewarded by Hideyoshi for their fine efforts.

At the time Japan's Left Army and the navy had captured Namwon Castle, the Right Army had successfully taken Hanyang Castle. Both battalions then advanced toward Jeonju. The Ming-Korean army units there abandoned the city in panic, and defences collapsed. The samurai forces soon occupied the entire state. From there the samurai forces again split and began to take the neighbouring Jeolla-do and Chungcheong-do areas in their attempt on the capital. A month later, Takatora's fine work would come unravelled, and the Koreans would get their revenge.

The Battle of Myeongnyang

The naval Battle of Myeongnyang is often regarded as one of the most tactically brilliant victories in the history of warfare. Fought in the Myeongnyang Straits, off Jindo Island, on the south-western corner of the Korean Peninsula on 26 October 1597, this was to prove a humiliating defeat for Todo Takatora personally, and for the Japanese fleet in general. Admiral Yi Sun-sin had been forgiven by the Korean high command and was reinstated at the head of the navy, or what was left of it. Despite having barely a handful of ships remaining after Admiral Won Gyun's disastrous defeat at the Battle of Chilcheollyang, Admiral Yi would both shame and fluster the Japanese forces.

Takatora's fleet were making their way northwards along the western coast to support the ground forces' advance towards the capital of Hanyang. Yi Sun-sin's small fleet blocked their route, and fully intended holding firm. The Japanese flotilla heavily outnumbered Admiral Yi's fleet at a ratio of at least ten to one. Although actual numbers are unclear, Takatora was in command of around 120 warships and 200 smaller non-combat supply, support and troop transport vessels. Yi Sun-sin's small fleet consisted of around thirteen ships. It was a David and Goliath-like situation, with Yi refusing to yield, and treating this as a do or die last-ditch effort to stop the Japanese. In this desperate attempt, the Koreans gave it their all.

As the Japanese ships neared, Admiral Yi fired well-aimed salvo after salvo towards the invaders. In the short but ferocious sea battle, thirty Japanese warships were sunk or crippled. Attempting to come alongside and board the Korean warships, fleet commander Todo Takatora was badly wounded in action, and over half of his subordinate officers were killed, drowned or were also wounded. Victory went to Admiral Yi, but because of the overwhelming numbers of Japanese watercraft remaining, he quickly withdrew to the Yellow Sea to resupply his ships, allowing Takatora and the remainder of his navy to limp their way to coastal Yeonggwang Province.

One incident regarding the Korean campaign worth remembering is that Toyotomi Hideyoshi had personally paired Todo Takatora and Kato Yoshiaki together to effect the smooth operations of shipping samurai to Busan, and to coordinate sea and land military action against the Ming and Korean defenders. The contemporary Christian missionary Charlevoix had mentioned in his journals and dispatches that 'The Koreans could not stand before the Japanese on land, but they are superior on the sea as they have the better ships'. Indeed, the Japanese navy consisted of not only former pirates, but mostly of sailors who had worked on cargo ships and had little to no experience in warfare. At the same time, these men were at a disadvantage having little understanding of the currents, tides or waters around the Korean Peninsula. Kato Yoshiaki had built up a substantial naval force, and since Takatora had accepted Uwajima Castle as his domain, he too had formed his own. There was friendship between Takatora and Yoshiaki, yet a fierce rivalry also coursed through their veins.

Despite the Koreans' perceived advantage at sea, Takatora had shown great promise, particularly in naval battles, where he and his men would bring their ships alongside those of the enemy vessels and board them to bring the fight directly to the Korean sailors. A variety of steel grappling hooks attached to chains and poles were used to catch the enemy vessels and hold them when boarding. Once on board, the samurai fighting skills far outweighed those of the Korean sailors and many heads were collected. Through this method, Takatora begun to enjoy considerable success, and outshine the efforts of the proud Kato Yoshiaki who had considered the boarding of Korean ships far too risky, and this difference in tactical styles – and possible jealousy of Takatora's achievements – led to increased and highly vocal disagreements which caused a rift between the two able warriors, one that would only deepen when Hideyoshi later appointed Takatora the Vice Admiral of the Sea, and made him commander of the great Toyotomi warship, the *Nippon Maru*, flying the *Taiko*'s own *Akane* red sail. That deep rift would simmer for many years to come.

Suncheon Castle, Korea

It appears native Korean castles were not well suited to either the needs nor the tastes of the invading samurai forces, and so rather than simply take over Korean castles, the Japanese built their own in their native style. The majority of similarly designed castles built in Japan around this time, and particularly during the 1575–1615 castle construction boom period would never actually see action, and so they were never truly tested as such. In Korea, however, these castles would see repeated fierce attacks and were able to withstand and repel them, showing that the Japanese designs were indeed particularly effective, even against the siege engines used by the Chinese and Korean troops that were new to the Japanese. In fact, one of the last battles during Hideyoshi's invasion of the Korean Peninsula would take place between mid-October and early November of 1597 when allied Korean and Chinese Ming troops attempted but failed to take an under-manned Suncheon Castle, just weeks before the Japanese were set to withdraw from Korea.

Because most samurai castles from the Nobunaga and Hideyoshi periods were overhauled, changed or destroyed over the years, these *Wajo*[5] as they are called, are very important for the study of samurai castle design and evolution, as the majority remain unchanged, although in ruins. Over thirty Japanese-style castles were built between Suncheon in the far west and Kato Kiyomasa's Ulsan Castle in the east.

Commanded by Konishi Yukinaga, Suncheon Castle, also known as Junten Castle, was a large and imposing strategically positioned castle constructed by Todo Takatora, Konishi Yukinaga and Ukita Hideie within two months between September and November 1597 and while fighting the previously mentioned Chilcheollyang and Myeongnyang naval engagements. It was the westernmost bastion of Japanese castles lining up along the southern coast of the Korean Peninsula. Along with Ulsan and Seosaengpo Castles, it is considered one of the top three *Wajo* in Korea.

Typical of Takatora's designs, Suncheon was not just a defensive castle, but one built for offensive purposes too. It was designed to secure and protect the two harbours below it, allowing supplies and samurai to be brought in, as well as provide a secure base from which the samurai armies could commence rolling across Korea.

Suncheon Castle covered an area of 18.8 hectares. The outer areas covered 12 hectares, and the main mountaintop sections covered 2,502m². A garrison of 14,000 Konishi troops were stationed here during Japan's final year of occupation. It was built on a prominent 60m-high bluff, part of a rocky cliff-faced peninsula with three sides overlooking the sea, and the harbours at its base. As with castles in Japan, the engineers levelled and sculpted the summit of the hill into a plateau, with the sides encased in impressive walls of masonry.

A long, narrow main *honmaru* bailey was built on the uppermost area of the mountain overlooking the sea, while the landward side featured an array of earthworks, moats and gatehouses as defences. According to a contemporary Ming painting of the fortress, Suncheon had a three-storey tower keep in the northern part of the *honmaru*, although other inscriptions claim it stood five storeys high. It had twelve gates and at least three *yagura* watchtowers around the main bailey which was

---

5. 'Wa' was the ancient term used by China when referring to Japan. 'Jo' means castle.

protected by an *uchi-masugata mon* gate system. *Uchi-masugata* gates were a basic yet effective form of protective gate, consisting of a gated enclosure built into a section of the bailey, and surrounded on three sides by defensive features. Enemy would have to enter the well-defended compound to reach the main access gate to the bailey. On entering the enclosure, they could be contained and shot with matchlock guns and arrows. The castle proper was surrounded by a 30m-wide *karabori*, dry moat, with a double dry moat along the western edge. The outermost border of the fortress was surrounded by both earthen and stone walls. The defences such as *horikiri*, trenches etcetera, had not been seen in Korea, the designs were 100 per cent Japanese, and the size, scale and speed at which they were constructed would have been most intimidating to the Korean people.

A wide moat between the lower levels of Suncheon Castle's main and outer walls was probably fed by seawater, suggestive of Todo Takatora's design elements. Indeed, the Korean signage at the site also suggests the moats were filled with seawater, solidly fortifying the castle. The large gates were typical Japanese *yagura mon* with battlements. The surrounding thick wattle and daub mud walls were pocked with upright rectangular holes or *ya-zama* for the shooting of arrows, and round, square and triangular *teppo-sama* gunports.

At one stage the shallow waters around the base of Suncheon were deemed hazardous for the troop and supply ships coming and going from Korea, but the shallow waters proved to be an asset at one point when the Korean navy accidentally ran their ships aground at low tide as they prepared for an attack.

The designs of these castles were unmistakably Japanese. Not just the *nawabari*, ground plans, but the *ishigaki* and the structures too were of Japanese origin. On a research tour of the *Wajo* in mid-2019, the author personally discovered evidence at Angolpo Castle of these *Wajo* being topped with Japanese fired roof tiles, suggesting that many of the castle structures and fittings may have been pre-fabricated in Japan, shipped to Korea along with the troops and supplies, then used to quickly erect the by now *de rigeur* large and impressive Japanese keeps and *yagura* watchtowers. Indeed, the speed by which these fortresses were constructed, and the high probability of problems and delays with in-country production, suggests such a possibility, with only the stone for the bases sourced locally. Interestingly, the Japanese did adopt one local design feature in their castles, and these were Korean-styled roof tile edges. Known as *tekisui-gawara*, these tiles featured round-edged flanges facing 45° down at the end of the tiles. Instead of rain gushing off the ends of the roof, the flange channelled rainwater into a neat stream. Similar tiles were used at Kumamoto Castle by Kato Kiyomasa and Ikeda Terumasa's Himeji Castle.

The Siege of Ulsan

The Siege of Ulsan, from 26 January to 19 February 1598, was an unsuccessful attempt by Korean and allied Ming Chinese forces to capture Ulsan from the Japanese. Kato Kiyomasa and Asano Yukinaga (also known as Yoshinaga, 1576–9 October 1613) were still working on constructing Ulsan when they were attacked by an army of 50,000 to 60,000 led by China's General Yang Hao. Yang Hao regarded Kato Kiyomasa as the strongest of the Japanese warlords and believed that if he could capture or kill him, the morale of the samurai would collapse, and the entire Japanese army could be defeated. The attack on Ulsan started with the allies surging forward, followed by a false retreat designed to lure the Japanese out of the fortress. The ruse succeeded and over 500 samurai were killed, and the large garrison were forced to retreat to the castle's protective Fort Tosan. The Korean and Chinese troops launched another offensive on 30 January, capturing the outer sections of Tosan, forcing the samurai to retreat further into Ulsan's innermost defences, abandoning much of their rations and supplies. The attackers pushed on, storming the inner fortress situated higher up the small mountain, but the samurai fought back with vigour, and the Korean and Chinese forces suffered heavy casualties, leading to the assault being aborted, and a siege began. Another attack was also repelled by the Japanese on 19 February, before samurai reinforcements arrived. Mori Hidemoto, Nabeshima Naoshige, Kuroda Nagamasa and Hachisuka Iemasa's army approached, and General Yang Hao found himself sandwiched between the recent arrivals and the men of Ulsan. He ordered a quick retreat. In the panic, many Korean and Chinese soldiers were killed by Japanese matchlock fire and blades.

1. 1907 copy of an Edo-period portrait of Todo Takatora. The original was lost to an air raid in 1945, while this copy is kept in the Kansho-in Temple in Tsu.

2. The armour worn by Todo Takatora during the Battle of Osaka, now part of the Osaka Castle collection.

3. This distinctive *Tokan Kabuto* (Chinese cap-shaped) helmet was presented to Todo Takatora by Toyotomi Hideyoshi just prior to Hideyoshi's death in 1598. The helmet was later given to a relative, who wore it in the 1615 Summer Siege of Osaka. This helmet is now on display in the Iga Ueno Castle Museum.

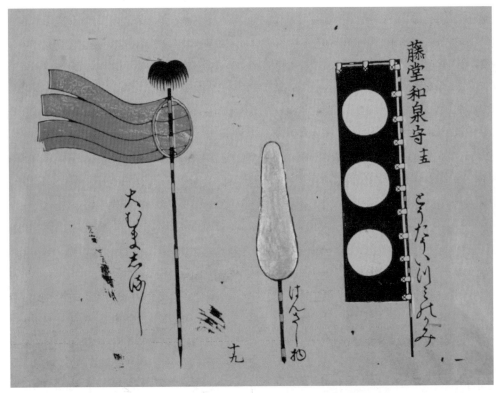

4. Todo Takatora's *umajirushi* battle standards as recorded in Edo-period books of samurai heraldry, and the Todo clan Sekigahara battle flag of white *mochi* on a black background.

5. Koriyama Castle ruins in Nara Prefectures' Yamato Koriyama City.

6. Wakayama Castle, designed and continually improved over a number of years by Todo Takatora.

7. The ruins of Akagi Castle's central precincts carved from a 50m-high mountain and shored up by thick walls of piled natural stone.

8. Looking across the site of Akagi Castle's front gates to the main *honmaru* enceinte at the top.

渡櫓

9. A *masugata* gate system, showing a smaller gate leading to the courtyard and requiring a right-hand turn to the *yagura-mon* gatehouse, surrounded by connecting corridor-like *tamon yagura*. Illustration from an original copy of the *Gunshi no Maki* (軍詞之巻) dated 1716, collection of the author.

10. Form and function – Imabari Castle's graceful and elegant lines mask its military strengths.

11. Wide moats, high, straight stone walls with *inubashiri* at the base, square outline with corner watchtowers, *tamon yagura* and thick clay walls surrounding it, and a towering keep. Imabari is one of Takatora's masterpieces.

12. The wide moats and stone-walled ruins of Takatora's excellent Tsu Castle.

13. Tsu Castle's reconstructed tower.

14. Strong, square and sturdy Sasayama Castle ruins.

15. Wide *inubashiri* can be seen skirting the base of Sasayama's high stone walls.

16. Iga Castle's impressive stone walls stand 27m high above the moats, about the height of a modern-day ten-storey building. Until Osaka was redeveloped by Takatora in the 1620s, Iga Ueno's walls were Japan's highest.

17. Iga Ueno Castle's 1935 reconstructed *tenshu* keep.

18. At 30m, Osaka Castle lays claim to having the highest stone walls of any samurai castle. Todo Takatora was responsible for the overall design and wall construction techniques.

19. The staggered wall sections of Osaka Castle provide coverage at all angles.

20. Kyoto's largest Sanmon Gate belongs to the ancient Nanzen-ji Temple, and was donated and constructed by Todo Takatora. The upper section, not open to the public, houses a statue of Tokugawa Ieyasu, with Todo Takatora to his right. The Buddhist memorial tablets of seventy-one of Takatora's closest vassals and family members killed in battle at Osaka are also kept here.

21. Wooden effigy of Todo Takatora, housed in the upper section of the Nanzen-ji Temple's Sanmon Gate. Taken with the permission of the Nanzen-ji Temple.

22. The typical straight, clean, squared lines of a Takatora-designed castle are evident at Suncheon Castle in South Korea. The *tenshu* tower keep base can be seen upper center.

23. Ozu Castle in Ehime Prefecture, Shikoku, was owned by numerous warlords, with Todo Takatora being the major contributor to the overall outline of the current structure.

24. Flanked by the original wings, Ozu Castle's soaring tower keep was reconstructed using authentic techniques and traditional craftsmanship.

25. Inner walls of Tamba Kameyama Castle, Kyoto, originally owned by Akechi Mitsuhide, the general who turned against Oda Nobunaga, and later redeveloped and strengthened by Todo Takatora.

26. Photo dated 1872 showing Kameyama Castle's *tenshu* tower keep, the first Todo Takatora developed *sotogata*-type keep, originally used at Imabari Castle, later dismantled and rebuilt at Tamba Kameyama.

27. The wide moats and high outer walls around Edo Castle's *honmaru*, central enceinte, are built like a traditional folding screen to increase protective coverage. Each corner had a multi-level *sumi yagura* watchtower protecting it, and corridor-like *tamon yagura* running along the tops of the walls between them.

28. The walls of Edo Castle in central Tokyo, between the *ni-no-maru* and *honmaru* baileys were designed and worked on by Todo Takatora at the request of the Shogun.

29. Small but sturdy Uwajima Castle's *tenshu* keep is one of just twelve remaining in original condition. Although the keep itself is based on the size and design of Todo Takatora's original keep, this extant *tenshu* was rebuilt by the Date clan. The actual stone walls and general layout of the castle were the work of Takatora.

30. The body of Todo Takatora was laid to rest directly beneath this unusually shaped 4m-high gravestone. His concubine, O-Matsu, was laid to rest to his right below an equally large and flamboyant gravestone. The similarly designed graves and memorial stones of thirteen of his descendants surround Takatora's burial site. The grave, in Tokyo's Ueno Park, is off limits to the public. (With thanks to the Kansho-in Temple)

Of the 10,000 samurai garrisoned at Ulsan,[6] less than 1,000 survived the siege. Because of the great loss of life, Kiyomasa's superior – and nemesis – Ishida Mitsunari, in concentrating on the negative aspects, deliberately failed to report Kiyomasa's fine actions and bravery during the siege of Ulsan to Hideyoshi. General Yang Hao who led the attacks would later be called back to Beijing to explain his failure at Ulsan.

Angolpo Castle

Todo Takatora and his troops would also spend some time as the guardians of Angolpo Castle, about 25km west of Busan. Angolpo was initially three separate castles built on the ridge of a large hill by Kuki Yoshitaka, Kato Yoshiaki, and Wakisaka Yasuhiro. forming one huge and vitally important castle, serving as one of the main bases for the samurai forces.

The main bailey of this particular castle was 100m long and 60m wide with walls of piled stone 3m high. The south-eastern corner featured a large *tenshudai*, stone base, for a keep. Much of the technology and skills developed building strong, effective castles in Korea was later used in castle construction in Japan. Kato Yoshiaki's Iyo Matsuyama Castle and the Ii clan's now National Treasure designated Hikone Castle would utilise many of the techniques and ideas refined at Angolpo Castle.

The Passing of the *Taiko*

Realising his end was near, and that his son Hideyori, being just five years old, was far too young to rule a nation, Hideyoshi had organised five of the top *daimyo* to form a council, the *Go-Tairo*, to rule in place of Hideyori until he came of age. Its members were the warlords Uesugi Kagekatsu, Ukita Hideie, Mori Terumoto, Maeda Toshiie and, at the head of the five, Tokugawa Ieyasu.

On his deathbed Hideyoshi, having ruled for nearly 15 years and having finally unified the nation, called for the then 56-year-old Ieyasu. Hideyoshi who had worked tirelessly to unify and stabilise Japan was now entrusting the most powerful of the *daimyo* to lead the council of regents who would attend to his five-year-old son and designated heir

6. Some sources put the numbers at Ulsan at 20,000 to 23,000.

Hideyori. Hideyoshi begged him to care for Hideyori like a grandson. Ieyasu accepted the position.

When Toyotomi Hideyoshi died on 18 September 1598, the majority of his samurai were still fighting in Korea. In October they were recalled to Japan. Tokugawa Ieyasu had chosen Todo Takatora to deliver the news to the men in the field that Toyotomi Hideyoshi had died, but the Takatora-designed Suncheon Castle was under siege and surrounded by overwhelming numbers of enemy and the samurai inside were unable to extract themselves from the siege. Shimazu Yoshihiro and Tachibana Muneshige came to their rescue with 500 ships and enough samurai reinforcements to allow them to escape. That the castle held was due to Takatora's fine design work that allowed the defenders to prevent Suncheon from falling.

Takatora arrived home and set foot again on politically changed Japanese soil in late 1598. On his return, as part of his reward, Takatora was offered an extra 10,000 *koku* and Ozu Castle in modern-day Ehime Prefecture, taking him to 80,000 *koku* total.

Ozu Castle

Also known as Jizogadake Castle after the small hill on which it was built, Ozu Castle in Ozu City, Ehime Prefecture was built on a slight rise overlooking the wide, fast flowing Hiji River that doubled as a natural protective moat. A small fortress surrounded by rudimentary barricades had been erected on the site by the warlord Utsunomiya Toyofusa around 1331, but the castle's current layout was not formulated as such until the later Sengoku period, when unification under the Toyotomi was carried out.

Between 1585 and 1617, Ozu came under the control of a number of commanders. Kobayakawa Takakage held Ozu from 1585 until the castle came into the hands of Todo Takatora in 1595. Wakisaka Yasuharu, well known to Takatora from their early days in Omi Province, was master of Ozu from 1609 following Takatora's transfer to Iga Ueno and Tsu. Wakisaka was moved to Iida in Nagano Prefecture, and so Kato Sadayasu was next to be awarded Ozu Domain in 1617. Thirteen successive generations of the Kato clan then maintained the castle and lands until the end of the Edo period in 1868, remaining there until 1871, 540 years after fortifications had first been constructed.

A *hirayama* castle, Ozu was once guarded by as many as eighteen protective turrets. The main *honmaru* bailey was surrounded by the *ni-no-maru* and *san-no-maru* baileys to the south, and further protected by a *nakabori*, central and *sotobori*, outer moat system. By the time he was awarded Ozu Castle, Takatora had come to prefer simple but effective squared designs for his castle layouts, but, having been built on a small hilltop and surrounded by a flowing river, Ozu Castle's grounds and baileys were irregularly shaped, and remained unchanged.

The straight lines of the streets of modern-day Ozu City centre were designed by Todo Takatora to facilitate better trade and commerce for the townsfolk. In late 1601, Takatora's vassal Watanabe Kanbei built a fortified mansion on a small rise near the castle. The residence had a moat around it, and a spiralling pathway lead to the central sections. Kanbei's own samurai lived within the confines of the hill fortress. The Kato clan, masters of Ozu after Takatora, would maintain this residence as an emergency castle. The area around it is still known as Kanbeiyashiki to this day.

Once the Edo period had passed and Ozu Castle had been abandoned, typhoons, heavy rains and a general lack of maintenance allowed deterioration of the keep, so much so that it was in danger of collapse. Unable to afford the maintenance, the local government ordered the demolition of the keep in 1888, leaving the keep's side-flanking Koran and Daidokoro *yagura* standing. These two Edo-period *yagura* and two other surviving corner turrets, the Owata and Minami-sumi yagura were designated National Important Cultural Properties and were slated for preservation from 1957. In 2004, Ozu Castle's 19.15m high, four-storey keep was authentically reconstructed using old photographs, maps and with the discovery of an old design model. Original materials and techniques were used by traditional craftsmen and carpenters to once again restore the keep above the original flagstones. The properly restored castle is now listed as one of the Top 100 Castles of Japan.

The Changing of the Guard

On the passing of Toyotomi Hideyoshi, Tokugawa Ieyasu, as the head of the *Go-Tairo*, began to show signs of an attempt at a takeover of power. He gave a number of recently-returned *daimyo* leave to visit their lands, without consulting the other regents, he took over Fushimi Castle, and built a fortified residence for himself within Osaka Castle. Ieyasu deliberately flouted the rules, marrying his children to various personages, forming cliques, and generally upsetting his political antagonists. Machiavellian marriages had been banned by Hideyoshi as he considered them politically dangerous to the peace and stability he had worked so hard to create. Ieyasu arranged the marriage of his sixth son, Tadateru, to the daughter of Date Masamune, the powerful *daimyo* of the north. He wed his adopted daughter to Fukushima Masanori, the lord of Kiyosu Castle, and two of his granddaughters were married to other suitably ranked nobles. These moves were part of a plan hatched by Ieyasu to discover who was against him, and who might be relied upon in the Tokugawa master plan. His actions naturally concerned a number of Toyotomi loyalists, especially the Toyotomi commissioner, Ishida Mitsunari, whose once-elevated position was now in jeopardy without Hideyoshi.

Ishida Mitsunari was born in Omi Province (Shiga Prefecture) in 1560. He was a high-ranking samurai within the Toyotomi administration. Although a gifted mathematician and a most able administrator, his elevated position was not awarded on his martial merit, nor on his having performed heroic deeds or services which gained him the attention of Hideyoshi, but his ability in the tea ceremony.

Hideyoshi had come across the teenage Ishida Mitsunari in the summer of 1573 during troop manoeuvres not far from Nagahama Castle, where Mitsunari made three cups of tea for the thirsty lord. The first was in a big *chawan* teacup, the large amount and warm temperature were just right to slake Hideyoshi's thirst, and he drank it all at once. The second cup was served in the same *chawan*, but a bit hotter than the last and only about half as much. Now relaxed, Hideyoshi could take his time over this one. Finally, a third smaller serving in a smaller bowl, but much hotter than the previous two cups was offered. Hideyoshi, now totally composed, could enjoy this cup. Recognising the 13-year-old tea server's intellect, he appointed Mitsunari to his staff. Mitsunari would serve the Toyotomi loyally and would be rewarded as such.

The foreign missionaries of the time had written that Ishida Mitsunari, Maeda Toshiie, Kuroda Nagamasa and Konishi Yukinaga were the most politically astute men surrounding the Hideyoshi. As he rose in the ranks, he came to be in charge of Hideyoshi's famed 'sword hunt' to disarm the non-military classes and preserve peace. Mitsunari had been allocated a stipend of 186,000 *koku* and the castle of Sawayama in Omi, and although a *daimyo*, his land, wealth and power was just a fifth of that of Ieyasu. During the Korean campaign, Ishida Mitsunari was made a commissioner, writing reports directly back to Hideyoshi. Many of these reports contained negative comments regarding a number of Hideyoshi's generals and their supposed reckless action and disregard for authority. Those that the bureaucratic Mitsunari complained about for these real or imagined breaches of conduct were reprimanded or punished by Hideyoshi, and so Mitsunari soon found himself very unpopular amongst the warrior class samurai.

After the Korean campaign, he would return to find that his position as a senior retainer was now powerless upon the creation of the *Go-Tairo*. Ieyasu even had the gall to suggest the pencil-pusher Mitsunari retire now that his services were no longer required. Mitsunari soon realised that besides his own position, the power of his lord, the young Hideyori, was now being potentially usurped by the Tokugawa in just the same way as Hideyoshi had usurped the power of the Oda. Mitsunari wanted Tokugawa Ieyasu out of the way!

He found his opportunity six months later, when one of the key figures in the *Go-Tairo*, Maeda Toshiie, fell ill. It was 4km from Ieyasu's *yashiki* mansion north-west of Osaka Castle to Maeda Toshiie's residence in the south. Knowing that Ieyasu would be visiting Toshiie to pay his respects, Ishida Mitsunari devised a plan to set a trap along the route and assassinate Ieyasu.

Todo Takatora was aware of the plan. Through his work under both Hashiba Hidenaga and Toyotomi Hideyoshi, Todo Takatora had come to know Tokugawa Ieyasu well, and a rapport, a mutual trust, had been established between the two men. Takatora now found himself in a quandary. Should he warn Ieyasu, or should he stay quiet and see how things worked out?

Takatora was among the elite in the Toyotomi forces. His service to Hidenaga, Hidenaga's heir and then his brother Hideyoshi had been exemplary. If he decided to warn Ieyasu, he would be turning against the Toyotomi loyalist cause fronted by Ishida Mitsunari, whose rising power had already come to the attention of many. He would risk losing the trust and support of the Toyotomi clan, their many *daimyo* and warrior supporters, and being branded a traitor. His reputation would be ruined. He might even be forced to commit *seppuku*.

On the other hand, Takatora had pledged his allegiance not to the Toyotomi as such, but to Hideyoshi directly, and now Hideyoshi, the great leader, was dead. Takatora would well have understood that without a strong leader in control, Japan would again quickly erupt into the violence of a prolonged civil war. In Takatora's eyes, the only *daimyo* politically and militarily capable of maintaining the peace and operating a central government was Tokugawa Ieyasu. The ever-resourceful Takatora came up with a brilliant plan. One that would alter the course of history.

Chapter 4

Servant of the Tokugawa

Tokugawa Ieyasu was born Matsudaira Takechiyo to the minor *daimyo* of Mikawa Province and the Lord of Okazaki, Matsudaira Hirotada on 31 January 1543 at Okazaki Castle, in modern-day Aichi Prefecture. The Matsudaira family lands had long been hemmed in by rivals; the Imagawa clan to the north-east, the Oda clan to the west, and they faced invasion from the Takeda of the north. To their south were the waters of Mikawa Bay.

To secure his hold on Mikawa against invasion by the Oda or Takeda, Matsudaira Hirotada decided to form an alliance with the influential warlord to his north-east, Imagawa Yoshimoto, and so he sent his six-year-old son, Ieyasu, as a hostage to the Imagawa clan in Sumpu, Totomi Province (now Shizuoka). En route to his captors' castle at Suruga, the convoy was detoured by the maverick Matsudaira vassal entrusted to deliver the boy to the Imagawa, and instead, he was taken to Oda Nobuhide. The conditions for peace offered by Oda Nobuhide to the Matsudaira were so unacceptable that Hirotada was forced to refuse even at the risk of his young son's life. Ieyasu was then confined to Nagoya Castle, where it is believed he first came into contact with Nobuhide's son, Oda Nobunaga. Some three years later, Imagawa Yoshimoto's samurai attacked Anjo Castle, capturing Nobuhide's other son, Nobuhiro, and offered him in exchange for Ieyasu. Now aged nine, Ieyasu was traded, and would spend the following ten years under the control of the Imagawa.

The word 'hostage' has negative connotations of a captive being held against their will and with a loss of freedom. The samurai understood that hostage-taking was a political move and a way of forming close familial bonds. As a hostage under both the Oda and the Imagawa, Ieyasu was treated as a family member, well cared for and properly educated with the expectation that he – and in turn the Matsudaira/Tokugawa clan – would be a future close ally of the Imagawa. In a way, this bears comparison to a form of Stockholm Syndrome, a condition in which hostages develop a psychological bond with their captors during captivity. As a long-term hostage, Ieyasu took part in the 1560 battle between the Imagawa and the Oda at Okehazama in the invading Imagawa forces. In this battle, 25,000 Imagawa soldiers were defeated in a surprise attack by an estimated 2,500 Oda samurai. Luckily, Ieyasu had been leading a supply mission to nearby Odaka Castle when the Oda attacked. With the death of Imagawa Yoshimoto, Ieyasu was at last free. Upon his return home to Okazaki Castle he soon allied himself with Oda Nobunaga, who had indirectly brought about his freedom.

Ieyasu later took over parts of the former Imagawa domains of Totomi, and had relocated to Hamamatsu Castle when he faced near-total defeat in 1573 against the much-feared Takeda clan in the Battle of Mikatagahara. Two years later, and with the assistance of Oda Nobunaga, he would get his revenge, near-on decimating the Takeda forces as they attempted yet again to invade Mikawa, at the Battle of Nagashino.

Following the death of Oda Nobunaga, Ieyasu would face off against Hideyoshi at the Battle of Komaki Nagakute in 1584, although relations between the powerful warlords would later improve. Ieyasu would continue to expand his political influence, playing an important role supporting Hideyoshi in the 1590 Siege of Odawara. During the conflict, Hideyoshi had offered him the Kanto region, and so Ieyasu had reluctantly given up his ancestral lands in Mikawa and his spoils of war, Totomi Province, to accept the offer, basing himself in Edo. Ieyasu, with 2,500,000 *koku* at his disposal, was now the second most powerful of the warlords, after Hideyoshi himself. When Hideyoshi sent the bulk of his forces to conquer Korea and China in the 1590s, Ieyasu managed to avoid having to go.

Tokugawa Ieyasu had been made the leader of the five-member *Go-Tairo* in August 1598, and once the members of this council of regents was in place, Hideyoshi was able to pass away in peace. Maeda Toshiie, the only man who could have opposed Ieyasu and hold him in check, now too lay on his deathbed. Ieyasu envisaged his role as a preserver of the peace, the potential new leader of the nation, and made moves to cement that position. These upset a number of *daimyo*, in particular Ishida Mitsunari and others loyal to the Toyotomi clan.

Mitsunari, in claiming loyalty to the young Toyotomi Hideyori, audaciously denounced Ieyasu and demanded his resignation. With the support of the ailing Maeda Toshiie, Ishida Mitsunari penned a series of letters he had delivered to the nation's warlords in which he openly accused Ieyasu of seizing power for himself. Mitsunari's grievances focused on Ieyasu having taken over the late Hideyoshi's residence at Fushimi, and having arranged marriages between his and strategically important families, something Hideyoshi had banned in fear of the forming of cliques. Despite a ban on all castle building and maintenance, Ieyasu's building of and then residing in a small tower keep within the *nishi-no-maru* grounds of Osaka Castle also came under scrutiny. Ieyasu was further accused of having made offers of strategic lands and titles without the consent of the Council of Regents in an effort to gain followers. He was, as Mitsunari claimed, taking on too much responsibility. As the accusations flew, troops gathered around the capital, Kyoto, and the situation became volatile.

Mitsunari found himself in a difficult situation. Openly opposing Ieyasu could be misconstrued as an attempt to appropriate power for himself – the scoundrel hiding his true intentions by proclaiming his devotion to the Toyotomi – and as the *daimyo* supporting Ieyasu were too powerful, he wisely refrained from waging an open war. Instead, he planned to rid the world of Ieyasu through assassination. Todo Takatora became aware of the plan, and knew what he had to do and why.

In mid-April 1599, Ieyasu arrived by ship at Hachikenya-hama, a pier close to Osaka Castle. When his ship docked, there was a palanquin waiting for him, but there was no one around it. This made Ieyasu and his party nervous. Obviously something was afoot. There was talk of remaining on the ship for safety and preparing to set sail again when a familiar figure, a giant of a man, strode onto the landing followed by a small unit of samurai. The giant himself was about to take an equally giant risk. Todo Takatora approached the cautious Ieyasu and standing on the water's edge at Osaka, outlined to him Ishida Mitsunari's plan to assassinate Ieyasu in an ambush somewhere along the 4km route between his estate north-west of Osaka Castle and Maeda Toshiie's property directly south of the castle. He also suggested a plan in which he, Takatora, would offer to ride in Ieyasu's palanquin acting as a decoy. If the palanquin was attacked as expected, Takatora would be killed, not Ieyasu. The future Shogun would be able to follow some time later in safety. Takatora was willing to risk his reputation, his position within the Toyotomi administration and even his own life to save that of Tokugawa Ieyasu, an offer a touched Ieyasu gratefully accepted. That he was willing to risk his own life to save that of Ieyasu speaks not only of Takatora's bravery, but his desire for peace and his sense of righteousness. For this, he also firmly cemented the trust of Tokugawa Ieyasu. Not long afterwards, Todo Takatora would formally change his allegiance yet again to his eighth master, Tokugawa Ieyasu.[1] Ieyasu changed his plans to go directly to the Maeda mansion, denying Mitsunari the opportunity to kill him, instead going to Fushimi Castle. Not long after, an intriguing role-reversal unfolded.

Barely weeks later, in late April, Ishida Mitsunari again travelled to the great castle in Osaka to pay his respects to the dying Maeda Toshiie. An association of *daimyo*, including Ikeda Terumasa, Kato Kiyomasa, Kuroda Nagamasa, Fukushima Masanori, Hosokawa Tadaoki, Kato Yoshiaki and Asano Yoshinaga,[2] all long loyal to the Toyotomi clan, and who had learned of Mitsunari's assassination plot against Ieyasu, decided instead to do away with the troublesome Mitsunari once and for all.

Together this group planned a counter-attempt on Mitsunari's life but the much-despised Mitsunari somehow learned of the plan and escaped Osaka by dressing as a woman and riding in an enclosed noblewoman's litter. Surprisingly enough, he went straight to Fushimi Castle and begged the man he was trying to kill – Tokugawa Ieyasu – for asylum.

Ieyasu hid the frightened Mitsunari away in Fushimi for a few days before sending him home to Sawayama Castle in Omi Province with one of Ieyasu's sons as escort. Despite being aware of Mitsunari's original plot against him, Ieyasu had a brilliant rationale for providing refuge to his adversary. Many of the *daimyo* disliked the bureaucratic Mitsunari for his haughty attitude, his meddling in affairs during the Korean invasions, and for the negative reports he wrote back to Hideyoshi regarding these *daimyo*. As long as the unpopular Mitsunari remained the leader of the pro-Toyotomi loyalist cause, Ieyasu could use him to complicate future opposition.

---

1. It is important to remember that while we are led to believe that the samurai were loyal to one master, and one master only, this was basically an Edo period, and later a particularly Meiji period concept, a form of propaganda concocted to control the populace. During the Sengoku period, the changing of one's masters was not so unusual, and was done in order to improve one's position, as well as for self-preservation.
2. Some contemporary reports claim that Takatora too was possibly involved in the plot against Mitsunari's life, but this is not certain.

O-Matsu

It was during this time in Osaka that the then 44-year-old Takatora came across a 20-year-old woman named O-Matsu. O-Matsu's late husband, Miyabe Keijun, was known to Takatora, in fact he had been saved by Takatora's brave actions in 1587 when Keijun was in charge of Nejirozaka Castle, and it had come under attack by the Shimazu clan during the previously explained Battle of Takajo. The Buddhist monk, administrator, and warrior Miyabe Keijun had died on 20 April that year (1599), and now five months later, his widow had become acquainted with her husband's former saviour. O-Matsu was a great beauty and an intelligent woman. Her father happened to be from the same village as Takatora's wife, O-Ku, and so she was known to O-Ku. Takatora had married O-Ku some 19 years earlier and loved her deeply, and even though she was unable to bear him children, he had so far refused the common custom of taking a concubine in order to produce heirs. Having heard the sad tale of O-Matsu's life, and with the consent of his wife, Takatora took O-Matsu as his concubine. Three children would be born from this arrangement, including the second generation of the Todo clan.

Not long after, O-Matsu's younger sister would be adopted, becoming the daughter of Takatora and O-Ku. That adopted daughter would later marry Hidenaga's top vassal, Takatora's friend, Yokohama Ichiyan. One of their children, a daughter, would go on to become the concubine of the *daimyo*, Kobori Masatsugu, father of Kobori (Masakazu) Enshu, who had become Takatora's son-in-law in 1597.

In the Service of the Tokugawa

Despite the potential for accusations of opportunism, and for disdain and rebuke from the warrior class, Takatora's decision to follow Ieyasu appears to have been an easy one to make. Hideyoshi was no more. While changing lords was not uncommon, a greater sense of loyalty and perseverance was still seen as a positive attribute. However, because he had experienced the uncertainty of being a *ronin*, and as he had already changed masters in the past, Takatora felt little in the way of stigma attached to change.

So why would Takatora, a *tozama daimyo*, one not traditionally allied with the Tokugawa clan work so hard to support them? It could be speculated that Takatora wanted to fill the role played by Hidenaga in

Hideyoshi's organisation for Ieyasu. Like Hidenaga, Takatora was not one to seek fame and glory for himself, but desired to better himself and to serve.

Takatora was also well aware of the strong bond between Hidenaga and Ieyasu. Hidenaga's younger sister, Asahi, was married to Ieyasu. It was a marriage organised by Hideyoshi to ensure the Toyotomi and Tokugawa families remained close, and appears to have worked, as Hidenaga and Ieyasu often corresponded, and Hidenaga would usually choose Takatora to be the messenger.

In 1582 when Oda Nobunaga had been killed in the Honno-ji Incident, Ieyasu had been in Sakai near Osaka. Hidenaga is believed to have assisted Ieyasu in making his escape via Iga, guided by the Iga ninja Hattori Hanzo and his team. When Hidenaga fell ill, Ieyasu had come to visit him often. Takatora was usually at his master's side during these much-appreciated visits, and no doubt came to respect Ieyasu even more because of it. Takatora may well have seen other similarities between Hidenaga and Ieyasu, in the way they acted, their political skills, their ways of thinking and their desire for national unity.

Takatora had witnessed first-hand how the respected Lord Hidenaga worked, acting as the right-hand man behind the scenes in support of his brother Hideyoshi, helping him to reach his zenith and realise peace. Now the brother-in-law of his former master was in need of such support, and Takatora, seeing his role mapped out before him, was willing to offer that assistance. Takatora now served his eighth master, Tokugawa Ieyasu. Not long after having found a new master, Takatora lost another respected figure in his life. Later that year, on the fifth day of December, 1599, Takatora's father Todo Torataka died aged 84 at Uwajima Castle in Iyo Province where he had been serving as caretaker for his son's estate.

1600

Tensions began rising across the country in the early months of 1600. *Daimyo* were hurriedly preparing for war. The questions on everybody's lips were less will it happen as much as *when* will it happen, *where* will it happen, and more importantly, *which* side to support? Many chose to support the Western forces through loyalty to the Toyotomi clan in memory of Hideyoshi and to support Hideyori. Some saw Western leader

Ishida Mitsunari as an arrogant, self-serving bureaucrat and refused to fight under his name, and so begrudgingly looked to the East. There were even clans who, unable to decide, sent one member of the family to fight for the West, and another to fight for the East to ensure that a family member would be among the winners whatever the outcome. There were others, like Takatora, who believed the future lay with the Tokugawa.

In February 1600, Ieyasu learned that Uesugi Kagekatsu, one of his fellow *Go-Tairo* and a *daimyo* whose affluence was surpassed only by his own, had begun preparing for war. Some 80,000 men were employed to build a castle at Kazashigahara in Aizu on the plains of Wakamatsu, and the strengthening of seven strategic positions around his domain. In a letter, Uesugi Kagekatsu was accused of making preparations for war, and it was demanded that he face the chief counsellor, Ieyasu, in Kyoto to explain himself. The belligerent Kagekatsu made excuses not to go. Instead, he had his senior minister, Naoe Kanetsugu, send written communications claiming these supposedly banned strategic works were being undertaken 'through necessity', since his master had taken over the lands at Aizu only recently, and that they should be of no cause for alarm. In closing he quite rudely pointed out that, 'It must be remembered, country samurai collect weapons just as city samurai collect tea ceremony implements.'

Soon after, Uesugi troops began intruding on Tokugawa-held territories. Ishida Mitsunari had persuaded Uesugi Kagekatsu to wage a campaign against the Tokugawa, and as Ieyasu had correctly suspected, this was a trap to lure him out of Osaka. On 16 June 1600, Ieyasu finally left Osaka Castle and slowly, over a two-week period, made his way east along the great Tokaido Highway towards his own magnificent castle in Edo, arriving on 2 July.

To assist Ieyasu in the planned siege of the Uesugi clan at Aizu, Todo Takatora had left Osaka for the Kanto region the day before Ieyasu's departure, and arrived in Utsunomiya (Tochigi Prefecture) on 17 August.

Takatora was with Ieyasu for around a month before the Oyama War Conference took place, in which Ieyasu gathered his supporters together and laid out his plans to face Ishida Mitsunari and the growing numbers of Toyotomi loyalists. Those in a position to remain by Ieyasu's side soon pledged their allegiance and received their orders. Others, such as those whose families were being held hostage, were forced to take their leave. Takatora's army was then directed to position itself within reach of the enemy. Now well aware of the Western forces' incursion into Eastern lands, on 29 September, Takatora and his army departed Utsunomiya bound for Fukushima Masanori's Kiyosu Castle in Owari (Aichi Prefecture).

The Battle of Sekigahara

As the Tokugawa allies were concentrating their efforts on defeating the Uesugi clan in the northern districts, the Western forces under Ishida Mitsunari had taken the opportunity to pass unhindered through the gap in the mountain range separating east and west Japan at a place called Sekigahara, and encroached on Eastern territory. They made their way 14km inland from Sekigahara, via the village of Tarui, eastwards to Ogaki Castle where they had scheduled their first stop. The initial plan had been to make their way deeper into Eastern-held lands castle by castle, but, on having entered Ogaki, they discovered that they would not be welcomed at Kiyosu Castle in the south-east as had been expected, nor would the gates of Inuyama Castle in the north-east be opened to them. In fact, the temporary commander of Kiyosu had quickly dispatched a letter to his master Fukushima Masanori, currently in Utsunomiya, telling him of Mitsunari's plan to take Kiyosu. Fukushima Masanori wasted no time in telling Tokugawa Ieyasu of the situation. In the time it took for the Western forces to change plans and consider alternative castles, the Tokugawa had become aware of their plans and had commenced moves to foil them.

Having reached Kiyosu Castle, Takatora and his men waited. Other *daimyo* also loyal to Ieyasu began to arrive, and soon the township was filled with warriors. The master of Kiyosu, Fukushima Masanori and his army, Kuroda Nagamasa's troops, Ikeda Terumasa and many more began to gather. Meanwhile Fukushima Masanori was growing impatient for action. All were aware that Gifu Castle could potentially threaten their rear once they attacked Mitsunari at Ogaki. It was decided by the leading *daimyo* that Gifu Castle should be made impotent before Ieyasu arrived to ensure the Eastern force's safety. On 22 August a joint attack was launched on Gifu Castle.

Takatora had teamed up with the forces of Kuroda Nagamasa and Tanaka Yoshimasa forming a combined army of 16,000 and departed for Gifu. They attempted to cross the Kiso River, the physical border between

Owari and Mino near modern-day Ichinomiya City, but were prevented from doing so by the large contingent of Western allies firmly entrenched on the opposite side. A small contingent remained to face these enemies and cover the bulk of this army that then went further south to cross the river at Higashi-Kaganoi, before attacking and defeating a small garrison of Western army troops at Takehana Castle near present-day Hashima City.

Ikeda Terumasa had also left Kiyosu Castle that morning and, heading towards Gifu, crossed the river at Koda in the Haguri district, meeting resistance from Hidenobu's matchlockmen, but even the gunners of Gifu failed to stop their advance. The Battle of Koda-Kisogawa Toko, as the skirmish is known, soon ended with the Ikeda forces overrunning the gunners. They continued to advance before further clashing with a force of 3,000 Gifu samurai at Komeno (modern-day Kasamatsu). This Battle of Komeno saw another defeat for Hidenobu, who had been watching from the nearby village of Ginan and then ordered a hasty retreat to Gifu Castle, rather than risk facing the Ikeda army on the plains. Despite his heavy losses, Hidenobu remained confident in Gifu Castle's invulnerability. He and his younger brother, Oda Hidenori, waited within the castle confines, while the remainder of his vassals' troops were dispatched to the various passes surrounding the castle for protection.

Meanwhile Todo Takatora and Kuroda Nagamasa's troops advanced westwards towards Ogaki in an attempt to block possible reinforcements from Ogaki Castle reaching Gifu. As often happens in the humid months after cool rains, the Nagara River was enveloped in a thick mist when they arrived on the eastern banks, masking their arrival. The Western units stationed there were caught off guard by the sudden appearance of the Todo and Kuroda troops on the opposite side, and overestimating the actual numbers, made a quick retreat back into the safety of Ogaki Castle.

The very next day, on 23 August, Fukushima Masanori and Ikeda Terumasa combined their armies and stormed Gifu Castle. Oda Hidenobu had already sent for reinforcements from Ogaki Castle in the west and Inuyama Castle in the east, thinking that these fresh samurai could trap the Eastern forces between them. Aware of the danger, the Eastern commanders arranged to have Yamauchi Katsutoyo, Horio Tadauji, Arima Toyouji and Togawa Tatsuyasu take positions in the villages to the south-east of Gifu, while the troops of Todo Takatora, Kuroda Nagamasa and Tanaka Yoshimasa prepared for battle in the south-western regions. However, no samurai were forthcoming from Inuyama Castle. The samurai that eventually sallied forth from Ogaki arrived too late to be of help. The highly regarded Gifu Castle had fallen in one day.

The joint Todo-Kuroda army then continued even further west to the mountains of Akasaka, just west of Ogaki, where the Eastern troops soon numbered around 40,000 men, and established command posts overlooking the castle in which the Western forces and their leader Ishida Mitsunari now found themselves effectively trapped. Ishida Mitsunari was now unable to advance further into Eastern lands, and with the Eastern forces to his west, was unable to retreat back to the safety of the Western domains on the other side of Sekigahara.

Having made camp at Akasaka, Kuroda Nagamasa had suggested attacking Ogaki Castle to the other *daimyo*, but Takatora had earlier promised Ieyasu not to commence any action until Ieyasu himself arrived, and cautiously prevented his allies from making any pre-emptive moves. Over the following days, many more Tokugawa-allied warlords and their armies began to arrive and take their positions in and around Akasaka, further upsetting the Western forces inside Ogaki Castle.

Around 17 October, Takatora left the Akasaka camp with a unit of mounted samurai and travelling south-easterly, made his way to Owari Ichinomiya, just north-west of modern-day sprawling Nagoya City, where he met and welcomed Ieyasu the following day. From Owari Ichinomiya, Takatora led the Tokugawa warlord to Kiyosu Castle where they spent the night. The following day Ieyasu rested, talking over strategy and making plans with Takatora. Early the next day, 20 October 1600, Takatora escorted his lord to a specially-prepared command post on a low hill known as Mount Maruyama just below Akasaka, arriving about midday. The entire Eastern forces had been waiting for Ieyasu, and greeted him with rousing cheers.

Ieyasu was a master of field battles. He had less confidence and even less patience with sieges and wanted to wrap this one up as quickly as possible. Various ideas had been suggested, including the damming of nearby rivers and flooding the low-lying castle out. Ieyasu had a faster and less costly idea in mind. That afternoon, with Takatora by his side, and knowing there were most likely spies present, Ieyasu openly revealed his plans, stating that he intended to turn his troops to the west, travel through Sekigahara, the gap in the central mountain range separating east and west Japan, and after first attacking and destroying Ishida Mitsunari's home fief of Sawayama Castle (well known to Takatora as he had lived there over 25 years earlier while serving Isono Kazumasa and then his successor Oda Nobuzumi), Ieyasu grandly announced that he would then continue south-west to Osaka, and capture the Toyotomi stronghold, Osaka Castle. As expected, the news soon reached Mitsunari entrenched in Ogaki Castle, and put him in a panic.

That night, cloaked by both darkness and a cold, heavy rain, the bulk of the Western troops decamped from Ogaki and raced to Sekigahara in the hopes of blocking the confined passage west and preventing the Eastern forces from passing. Shortly afterwards in the very early hours of 21 October, the Eastern troops too made their way through the rain and mud and both sides, around 160,000 troops in all, soon found themselves packed into the narrow Sekigahara basin.

The Todo clan diaries, the *Koshitsu Nempu Ryaku*, mention that Takatora would order a different helmet for each and every campaign. He was kitted out for this particular battle in a black-laced set of armour with a *tokan* type helmet, resembling an aristocrat's cap, and was mounted on a large chestnut-brown horse. Takatora chose his command post site at Sekigahara well, on the south central plains within full view of the enemy Otani and Hiratsuka bases where campfires burned bright on the hills before them. Arriving about 3 a.m., he ordered his 2,490 troops to set up the flags, standards and crested curtains to mark out their headquarters. His friend Kyogoku Takatomo and his 3,000 men set up their encampment close by.

The cold heavy overnight rains on the sun-warmed soil of the Sekigahara basin produced a thick fog that completely enveloped the area in the early morning, bringing visibility down to as little as 15m in places. Around 8 a.m. the mist began to disperse, prompting a small unit of around thirty mounted samurai and matchlockmen under the Tokugawa stalwart Ii Naomasa and his son-in-law Matsudaira Tadaoki, the fourth son of Tokugawa Ieyasu, to advance.

They didn't get far before being stopped by Fukushima Masanori's captain, Kani Saizo,[3] who reminded them that Ieyasu himself had awarded his master, Fukushima Masanori, the great honour of being the first into battle. Ii Naomasa replied that they were simply a small group on a reconnaissance mission seeking intelligence on the enemy positions. Grudgingly, Kani let them proceed. This Ii and Matsudaira expeditionary force ventured further west until they came upon the largest army in the Western line-up, Ukita Hideie's 17,000 troops. With a shout the Ii suddenly emerged from the swirling mist at speed and made a daring attack.

With the crackling of gunfire and a roar of men the small Ii group drew first blood, cutting into the Ukita front lines, robbing the Fukushima regiments of their chance to be the first into battle. Having scattered the Ukita's front lines, they quickly extracted themselves as the furious Fukushima forces rushed to catch up and into action.

Watching in surprise, the nearby Western-allied Konishi forces raised a flare seen by all across the Sekigahara battlefield signalling the start of the battle. Fukushima's troops had by now taken the lead, closely followed into action by those of Todo Takatora and Kyogoku Takatomo, and then the samurai of the Governor of Nagasaki, Terazawa Hirotaka. The greatest open field battle in samurai history, the Battle of Sekigahara, had begun!

A large company of Fukushima samurai had first formed into ranks, with the matchlockmen up front. Running some 300m towards the war camp of Otani Yoshitsugu, they stopped within effective range of around 60 to 80m of the Otani front lines, and opened fire. Although being blinded and crippled by leprosy, Otani Yoshitsugu retained a sharp mind. Expecting such action, he had sent his men down the slopes from their base on Mount Tenman to meet the enemy on flat ground. Those Otani samurai were then assailed by the massed forces of Todo Takatora and Kyogoku Takatomo, who had moved into position from behind Fukushima.

Takatora's gunners too ran forward, crouched, aimed and on the Todo gunnery captains' shouted orders of '*Utte!*', fired in unison. The Todo

---

3. Only two years older than Takatora, Kani Yoshinaga Saizo (1554–10 August 1613) took a record seventeen heads during the Battle of Sekigahara. Somewhat of a maverick, like Todo Takatora, he too changed lords a record seven times, although Takatora served ten men with his seven changes of allegiance

archers then stepped forward through the clouds of white gunsmoke and shot volleys of arrows towards the Otani, keeping them at bay while protecting their own matchlockmen. The spearmen then moved forward on order with their 4m-long spears held vertically before them, right hand above left. As they neared, the spears were brought down heavily on the heads, shoulders, arms and hands of the enemy ranks ahead of them causing concussions and broken bones before the sharpened business end of the spears were employed to slash and stab. Stepping over the bodies of their fallen comrades, the well-trained Otani troops quickly launched a counter-attack and were able to temporarily repel the Todo, Kyogoku and even the Fukushima samurai, sending them back well over 100m, before matchlock gunfire again boomed across the narrow plain. This close combat went back and forth for the next few hours with the giant Takatora – an easy target because of his great size – remaining in the front line, continually encouraging his men.

Some respite from the close and violent action came around 11:30 a.m., when Terazawa's samurai having gone some distance north then about turned, broadsiding the left flank of the Konishi, then continuing straight on into the flank of the Ukita forces. Terazawa's attack on the Ukita greatly assisted the Fukushima counter-attack, helping them regain lost ground. Terazawa again rallied his troops and drove the remaining fighting core of his 2,400 men hard at the Otani's left flank as the crippled lord's men faced Todo Takatora and Kyogoku Takatomo's samurai head on.

Otani had placed the disciplined samurai of Toda Shigemasa and Hiratsuka Tamehiro ahead of his own troops, with those of Kinoshita Yorichika and his nephew Otani Yoshikatsu on his right flank in fear of the possible turning of the Kobayakawa positioned high on Mount Matsuo to their right. These Hiratsuka and Kinoshita troops were being crushed by the combined force of Eastern samurai under the command of Todo Takatora and Kyogoku Takatomo, who were later joined by Oda Yuraku, the younger brother of the great Oda Nobunaga.

Leaving the bulk of his men facing the Otani, Todo Takatora then led a large unit north to the foot of Mount Sasao, where they engaged the remainder of Shima Sakon's Western army. Shima Sakon was positioned below Ishida Mitsunari's base and having only 1,000 samurai had faced the brunt of the Eastern forces' attack. Early in the skirmish, Sakon had already fallen to gunfire, but had re-entered the battle despite his serious wounds. Sakon's 17-year-old son, Nobukatsu, had meanwhile taken his injured father's place on the front line. The mounted Shima Nobukatsu was leading troops in the vanguard when the first wave of Takatora's samurai attacked from the south.

Takatora's nephew, Todo Gemba, was among his champion warriors and was widely recognised as a most able commander. Being among the front lines, he soon spotted Shima Nobukatsu directly ahead of him. Spurring his horse into action, he led the next charge straight at the younger samurai. The two horsemen came alongside each other, trading savage spear blows, until Nobukatsu finally succeeded in closing in on the older samurai, grappling with Gemba and gaining a grip on his armour, pulled him from his horse, but in the act, unseated himself and the two fell crashing to the earth between their mounts. The younger Nobukatsu was quickly able to regain his footing, and seeing his opportunity, thrust his spear deep between the narrow openings of Gemba's armour. While the mortally wounded Gemba was struggling to stay alive, Nobukatsu again pounced on him, slicing the dying man's head off with a short sword.

Nobukatsu stood and holding his gristly trophy in hand, looked down on the still-twitching headless body, only to be run through by a spear wielded by one of Gemba's retainers, the Todo samurai Yamamoto Heisaburo, who had seen his lord being killed, and had quickly disengaged from his own duel to come to his master's assistance. Seeing he was too late, Yamamoto had rushed his lord's killer and taken the teenager's life – and then head – in revenge. Takatora had seen violent bloodshed from an early age, time and again he had experienced battle and personally felt its horrifying results, yet even this veteran of over thirty battles was still affected by death. He was greatly shocked at the loss of his skilled nephew's life and mourned him greatly.

Todo Takatora's role in this decisive battle was more than as just one of the tens of thousands of warriors. He had played a major yet mostly unrecognised political part in the lead-up to Sekigahara. His activism and behind-the-scenes manipulation of various *daimyo* no doubt assisted in giving the Tokugawa the advantage. Long before the battle was decided, Takatora had been active in securing the services of a number of lords, especially those originating in his own home of Omi Province, for the Tokugawa cause. It was a trump card hidden up Ieyasu's armoured sleeve, slipped to him by Takatora, and one that was shortly to be called into play.

At around 10 a.m., two hours after the start of the mighty battle, Tokugawa Ieyasu was becoming impatient. He also felt that his initial command post on Mount Momokubari on the eastern edge of the Sekigahara basin was too far from the action, and so he ordered a relocation of his troops to a more central position. By midday, Ieyasu and his men had set up a new headquarters for themselves in the very middle of the valley, just 800m south of the Western force's base on Mount Sasao. Through this daring move, Ieyasu had placed himself in a precarious position. The Eastern forces were now completely surrounded. Directly ahead to their north and to their west were the main Western forces. To their south on Mount Matsuo sat the large contingent of Kobayakawa Hideaki supported by Wakisaka Yasuharu, Kutsuki Mototsuna, Ogawa Suketada and Akaza Naoyasu, making a combined force of 19,300 troops. Behind them, to the east, the 29,100-strong combined army of Mori Hideie, Kikkawa Hiroie, Ankokuji Ekei, Natsuka Masaie and Chosokabe Morichika waited on the slopes of Mount Nangu. To their north-north-east, mountains formed an impenetrable barrier. With Ieyasu now in the very centre, Ishida Mitsunari believed he had the Eastern battalions surrounded and trapped, and so he sent up flares supposed to call the forces on Mount Nangu and Mount Matsuo into action.

But no one moved. Ishida Mitsunari was enraged. Tokugawa Ieyasu was concerned, but not overly so.

Around midday, the armies of the Kobayakawa on and around Mount Matsuo finally stirred, and they started to enter the battle, but instead of attacking the Eastern forces as Mitsunari had expected, they turned on their supposed allies, attacking the Westerners, starting with the Otani! This sudden great defection turned the tide of the battle, causing the domino-like downfall of the Western contingents. Ieyasu had received the promise of the Kobayakawa forces to turn against the West days in advance of the battle.

According to the popular stories, the ultimate defection of the Kobayakawa forces was said to have been triggered by Ieyasu having sent a team of matchlockmen south towards the Kobayakawa camp high on Mount Matsuo and firing on them, spurring them into action. This episode is known by most Japanese as the *Toideppo* incident and remains a favourite story from the Battle of Sekigahara. However, the range of the matchlock guns at the time being only 200–300m at best, and Mount

Matsuo being 293m high, and the fact that the guns would have been barely noticeable amongst the cacophony of thousands of other guns being fired simultaneously in battle, makes it hard to believe that any effect was made at all. While it has been suggested by the author and others that a small cannon or *Outsu*, with a 2–4km range may have been used, yet another theory has it that the Kobayakawa were prompted to defect having seen Ieyasu's 30,000-strong force move from their initial command post at Mount Momokubari to a more central position just 800m away from the Western force's headquarters on Mount Sasao. The move is believed to have bolstered the moral of the Eastern forces' samurai greatly, while psychologically upsetting the Western forces and triggering the Kobayakawa's movements.

Yet another, and much more most plausible, reason is recorded in the Todo clan diaries. As mentioned, Takatora had acted behind the scenes on behalf of the Tokugawa, recruiting a number of potential allies, wooing them away from the Western alliance. Among them were the Kobayakawa, but just as importantly, the four armies located below the Kobayakawa base on Mount Matsuo, those of Wakisaka Yasuharu, Kutsuki Mototsuna, Ogawa Suketada and Akaza Naoyasu. These men were all from Omi Province, Takatora's home province. Takatora had been in communication with Kobayakawa Hideaki and these men for some time before the battle and had received their promises of defection. The signal to defect was, according to the remaining diaries, communicated by the waving of the large Todo clan battle flags.

The battle flags used by Takatora at Sekigahara were slightly different from his usual ones, in that they featured three large white dots on a black background instead of the usual dark blue background. This was to distinguish his troops from the Ukita clan who used a similar motif at Sekigahara. The story behind Takatora's battle flags' design began when he was a young *ronin*, before coming into the employ of Toyotomi Hidenaga.

Along the famed Tokaido highway running through Toyohashi City of modern-day Aichi Prefecture, was a small roadside store known as Kiyosuya serving pounded sticky rice cakes called *mochi*. The first owner of the shop was a man named Nakanishi Yoemon who was originally a samurai from Kiyosu in the service of Oda Nobunaga. For some reason, the samurai Nakanishi had become a *ronin*, and to sustain himself had resorted to selling sake, and later making and selling *mochi* rice cakes.

The story recorded in a diary written by Todo Takatora's vassal, Nakagawa Kurodo, tells that a young Takatora was once traveling through Toyohashi when he came across Nakanishi's stall selling *mochi*. From childhood Takatora had loved *mochi*. Being a big, strong and hungry man, he ate all the *mochi* on display, but then he revealed that had no money to pay for them. Embarrassed, he humbly apologised to the stall owner. Nakanishi, who seemed only too glad the strong, young samurai enjoyed his *mochi*, and not only forgave him, but even provided him with money for his travels. The kindness of the man touched Takatora greatly, and he never forgot his debt to the vendor. To remind himself, Takatora's battle flags carried the story. The white circles on Takatora's battle flags represented the *mochi*.

Takatora's *Shiro Mochi* battle flag also had another meaning – a pun. The words 'white' (白) and 'castle' (城) in Japanese are both pronounced as '*shiro*'. The pounded rice cakes are called '*mochi*', which also means 'to have', or 'to hold'. Because he was known to have built and owned a number of castles, he was known as a '*Shiro Mochi daimyo*', or castle owner (城持).

Some years after the *mochi*-eating incident, when Todo Takatora had become successful, he travelled to Edo together with a large retinue and taking the Tokaido, stopped at Toyohashi. While he was there, he sought out the *mochi* maker who had treated him so well all those years ago and visited his stall. Naturally, having brought a huge entourage, there were many *mochi* sold that day.

From that time on, whenever Takatora or any of the Todo clansmen traveled through Toyohashi, they would always be sure to patronise the *mochi* shop. The tradition was carried on throughout the Edo period. Indeed, the diary of the Todo clan samurai Nakagawa Masahiro, in an entry dated the 14th day of the 5th lunar month, or 24 June 1839, shows that while returning home to Tsu from *Sankin Kotai* service in Edo, the Todo entourage stopped to rest in the Yoshida-Juku post town, where many of the popular *mochi* were purchased by Nakagawa and the other Todo samurai. The Kiyosuya survived in Toyohashi until the end of the Second Wolrd War when it was unfortunately destroyed in an air raid. A grilled eel restaurant stands on the spot today.

It was these large battle flags, although the white-on-black *Ishi Mochi* version, that were waved at Sekigahara, finally signalling the Kobayakawa and their supporters into action.

Having seen and accepted the command to attack from Takatora's base camp on the plains below, the Kobayakawa troops had moved into action and quickly overcame the by now battle-weary Otani samurai. No longer able to walk on his own and blinded by his disease, Otani Yoshitsugu was aware of the Kobayakawa defection, and had suspected them all along. As they neared, he continually asked his second, Yuasa Gosuke, how close the Kobayakawa were. When Yuasa finally admitted that they were about to be overrun, the crippled lord asked to be carried about 150m across the hillside from his command post, and removing his armour, cut himself open. As is the case with *seppuku*, cutting one's stomach open is an extremely painful process, and death does not come quickly. To alleviate the excruciating pain, prevent any cry of anguish or fear and to preserve the honour of the man committing the act, a second, known as a *kaishakunin*, assists by cutting off the head in one clean cut, yet leaving a small flap of skin to stop the head from rolling away. Yuasa Gosuke performed this role admirably for his master.

Having taken Otani Yoshitsugu's head, Yuasa moved some distance away from the body and buried the head in a secret location. It remains hidden somewhere on the mountain at Sekigahara. As Yuasa was covering up the head, he was challenged by an Eastern forces captain, Takatora's nephew, Todo Nizaemon Takanori, who had been a friend of Yuasa Gosuke for many years. Now they faced each other as enemies. Takanori understood what his friend was up to and promised never to reveal where the head was hidden; however, as they were now opponents, they would have to fight to the death. Yuasa then stood, keeping his eyes on the warrior before him. Wiping the dirt from his hands, Yuasa drew his long *tachi* sword. The two men faced each other for one last time, before a short, furious duel erupted. It did not last long. Yuasa had lost his lord. His future was uncertain, and so it appears he allowed his former friend, Takanori, to take his head.

Takatora was proud of his nephew's achievements, and following the Battle of Sekigahara, Tokugawa Ieyasu, having heard of the fight, personally requested to see Yuasa's head for himself. When the hare-lipped man's head was presented to him by Todo Takanori, Ieyasu then enquired about the head of Otani Yoshitsugu. The Todo clan's reputation was only enhanced by his reply. 'I gave my word as a samurai to Yuasa not to divulge the whereabouts of Lord Yoshitsugu's head. I cannot tell even you, my lord.' Despite not getting what he wanted, Ieyasu was pleased with the reply, and rewarded Takanori with a spear and a sword.

Although it was not expected, less than two months after the Battle at Sekigahara, Todo Takatora ordered a grave be erected for the man he and his troops had fought so hard to destroy, Otani Yoshitsugu, on the site where the leper lord had committed *seppuku*. Yuasa Gosuke's descendants added a second memorial stone to the grave site some 300 years later. The graves remain to this day on the hill overlooking the battlefields.

About the same time, on the 18th day of the 11th lunar month, Todo Takatora came before his friend and master, Tokugawa Ieyasu to receive his rewards for his actions and achievements at Sekigahara. Ieyasu granted him an additional 120,000 *koku*, raising Takatora's *kokudaka* standing to 203,000 koku, and offered him domains at Imabari, in modern-day Ehime Prefecture. Incidentally, as Wakisaka Yasuharu had been the only one of the four *daimyo* at the foot of Mount Sasao to have made his pact not only with Takatora, but also directly in person with Tokugawa Ieyasu, he was properly rewarded for his efforts. The others who fought alongside him, not so. They would suffer a reduction in lands and income.

Shortly before the Battle of Sekigahara, a disturbing incident had occurred in Takatora's domain at Iyo Uwajima. A certain Mitsuse Rokubei, a descendant of the former Mitsuse clan of Wakayama, had taken advantage of both the uncertain times and Takatora's absence to ally himself with the rival Mori clan, with whom he had begun scheming to overthrow the Todo and take Uwajima Castle, possibly in the hopes of reviving his family's long-lost fortunes. When the Todo clan caretakers of the castle became aware of the plot, over 300 samurai were quickly dispatched to the Mitsuse residence and a nearby sake brewery where Mitsuse Rokubei and his band of followers had fled. A skirmish occurred resulting in the deaths of some thirty-six people from both sides. On the verge of being defeated, Rokubei put his wife and children to the sword and then took his own life. Other members of the Mitsuse clan and their associates were captured, imprisoned, executed or ordered to commit *seppuku*. The rapidly-quashed rebellion appears to have been downplayed by reports written in the Todo clan records, but was a major concern at the time. This is one of the very few occasions when the Todo clan ever faced a rebellion. Either way, it was seen as a case of opportunistic greed on behalf of the Mitsuse, rather than any form of protest or animosity against Takatora.

Zeze Castle

After Sekigahara, in 1601 Ieyasu employed Takatora to work on the construction of Zeze Castle in southern Omi (Shiga Prefecture) on the banks of the mighty Lake Biwa. Kyogoku Takatsugu (1560–4 June 1609) had been the master of Otsu Castle, but during the Sekigahara campaign, it came under an exceptionally strong attack from Western-allied Mori Terumoto and the famed warrior Tachibana Muneshige. Kyogoku and his men put up a good defence but lost and so he surrendered. He retired to holy Mount Koya on the very day the battle was fought. After that Toda Kazuaki entered Otsu, but having been badly damaged in the fighting the previous year, the castle was abandoned in 1601, and in its place the victor of Sekigahara demanded that Zeze Castle be constructed.[4] Ieyasu personally requested that Todo Takatora take charge of the castle's layout and general design, but other *daimyo*, in particular those who had opposed him by supporting the Western cause at Sekigahara, were called upon to do the construction work under what was known as the *tenka bushin* system. This was the first time Ieyasu had used this system, and he would use it from that time on in the many castles that were to be made in the following 10 to 15 years. Each time, Takatora would play a role in design or construction.

This *tenka bushin* system appears to have been very typical of the wily Ieyasu. By calling upon his former enemies to construct the castle, he not only kept them close and under careful watch, but also kept them busy. These *daimyo* were expected to supply labour for the digging of moats and the laying of the stonework, using stones sourced and transported to the site by the *daimyo*, and for carpenters to build the structures and naturally, source the timbers to be used – all at their own expense! They were not compensated by Ieyasu in any way except for being allowed to keep their lands and their heads. Basically, Ieyasu kept them unable to

---

4. While various parts of the damaged Otsu Castle would be used at Zeze Castle, other parts would be recycled by the Ii clan in the construction of the now-National Treasure listed Hikone Castle. The top three floors of Otsu's five-storey keep were disassembled and then rebuilt as Hikone's surving elegant keep.

plan or even afford the samurai, weapons and supplies required to rebel against him. It was a way of ensuring peace and at the same time building splendid castles to maintain that peace.

Considered one of Japan's top three lakeside castles, along with Takashima Castle in Nagano and Matsue Castle in Shimane Prefecture, Zeze was located on the south-eastern banks of Lake Biwa. It consisted of three main baileys, each an island. The elongated rectangular *san-no-maru* to the west was carved from the shoreline and featured three main gates, located to the north and south, with a third *chuo otemon* central main gate in the middle. The *san-no-maru* was where the samurai residences were located. To the east of that, jutting out into the waters of Lake Biwa, was the quarter-circle or quadrant-shaped main *honmaru* bailey. The *honmaru*'s northern edge was the site of a four-storey *tenshu* tower keep. The *tenshu* being four storeys high was rare, as the number four, pronounced as *shi* (四) in Japanese, is considered unlucky as it is also the word for death, *shi* (死) and so the superstitious samurai avoided such unlucky numbers whenever possible. From the *tenshu* along the curved outer edge of the main bailey were the Takatora signature *tamon yagura* forming an impenetrable protective wall. It also had two three-storey *yagura*, and numerous other two-storey ones around it.

To the south was another smaller rectangular island called the Demaru. This was connected by a bridge heading north to the *honmaru*, and by another bridge to the west, linking it to the *san-no-maru*. Also known as the *ni-no-maru*, this island housed the lord's living quarters, the Goten Palace.

Zeze Castle was severely damaged by an earthquake in May 1662. The original keep was partially toppled, and some of the *honmaru* and *ni-no-maru* turrets including their stone bases collapsed and sank into the lake. The important *honmaru* and *ni-no-maru* enceintes were hurriedly repaired, although by filling in the moat between them, merging both baileys into one.

The sight of Zeze Castle seemingly floating on the calm waters of Lake Biwa, and its walls, turrets and tower reflecting in the lake's surface was so beautiful that even today folk songs about the castle's beauty remain. Unfortunately this beautiful castle can no longer be seen. At the end of the feudal period Zeze Castle was abandoned and then completely demolished in 1870 with various gates and structures being sold off. The ruins of the *honmaru* and *ni-no-maru* citadel became the lakeside Zeze Castle Ruins

Park. Some of the original gates and an original turret still remain and can be found at local shrines. Zeze Castle's former North Otemon Gate now fronts the Shinozu Shrine. The main gate of Wakamiya Hachiman Shrine was originally the *honmaru's* Inuhashi Gate. The *honmaru's* south-facing gate, leading to the *ni-no-maru* and another smaller gate can be found on the Zeze Shrine precincts. A two-storey *yagura* from the *honmaru's* eastern side is now located in nearby Chausuyama Park, where it serves as a public meeting hall. These few remaining structures are now designated as Important National Cultural Assets.

A Son

There was great cause for celebration within the Todo household on 4 January 1602, when Takatora, then aged 46, and his concubine O-Matsu unexpectedly produced a legitimate son, whom they named Takatsugu. Not everyone was as pleased with the arrival of the child as Takatora himself, however. As Takatora had been without children, he and his first wife, O-Ku, had adopted the son of Niwa Nagahide, whom they had named Todo Takayoshi, but now a true heir had been born. The now-displaced Takayoshi would find himself being made master of a branch of the Todo clan based in distant Imabari. The newborn child would eventually grow to 190cm in height, as large as his father, and follow his father to serve as the second lord of Tsu Domain.[5] Despite the nation easing into a period of peace following the Battle of Sekigahara, it was still a time of caution. Hundreds of years of incessant warfare had left the samurai naturally nervous and overly vigilant. Realising the frailty of his position, and noting Takayoshi's apparent strengths, Takatsugu would long consider his older half-brother Takayoshi as a threat, and a growing animosity between the main Todo clan line and the Nabari Todo clan where Takayoshi was later transferred would continue until around the 1730s.

What may come as a shock is that Takatsugu was not Takatora's first son. Despite Takatora remaining seemingly faithful to O-Ku and O-Matsu, Takatora had an affair with a handmaiden, the daughter of one Takei

---

5. In 1669, Takatsugu officially retired from his posts in favour of his eldest son, Takahisa. He died aged 74, the same age as his father had, on 20 December 1676.

Chubei, resulting in a child being born in 1592. Once born, the child was sent to live with Takatora's trusted retainer Ishida Kiyobe, the *Tsukegaro* or chief elder of Iga. That child, named Ishida Saisuke Saburozaemon, would become a vassal to Takatora with a 200-*koku* income when he turned 16 in 1608, and for his fine service in the Summer Siege of Osaka, was made a captain of Iga's *ashigaru* corps in 1615. His grave can be found in Iga.

For his efforts and valour in the Battle of Sekigahara, Todo Takatora was rewarded with half of Iyo Province in what is now Shikoku's Ehime Prefecture, and a raise to 203,000 *koku*. This placed him alongside the domain of Kato Yoshiaki, master of the very fine and still extant Iyo Matsuyama Castle. It may be remembered that Kato Yoshiaki and Todo Takatora had once been friends during Toyotomi Hideyoshi's days but had had a falling-out over tactics and action during the Invasions of Korea and had remained on frosty terms since then.

Kato Yoshiaki had been one of Hideyoshi's seven most trusted and experienced generals and had been ranked higher than Takatora, however after the death of Hidenaga, and having come into the employ of Hideyoshi, Takatora's star had risen to the heights of Yoshiaki's. Because of this, Takatora and Yoshiaki had argued over exactly who was commander of the naval forces, and who would take the honour of attacking first in Korean waters. Yoshiaki had been awarded Shichi Castle in Awaji, along the Seto Inland Sea, in 1585 where he had developed a fine navy. As such, he believed he should call the shots. However, to Yoshiaki's chagrin, Takatora had won the argument and did exceptionally well in the engagement, eclipsing the actions of the Kato fleet.

In 1595 Yoshiaki was made master of Masaki Castle (Ehime Prefecture), an *umijiro* sea castle, with 60,000 *koku*. That same year, Takatora was made master of Itashima (Uwajima) Castle with 70,000 *koku*, where he organised his own naval forces, which appears to have unwittingly increased the rivalry with Yoshiaki. Not long after, Takatora had left the Toyotomi clan to support the Tokugawa. To Yoshiaki, this was unforgivable, and the bitterness increased, particularly as when Hideyoshi died, Yoshiaki found his position both stalled and at risk. Takatora's career, on the other hand, was going from strength to strength thanks to his support of Tokugawa Ieyasu. Eventually, Kato Yoshiaki too would change allegiance and come to support Ieyasu in time for the Battle of Sekigahara, and both Takatora and Yoshiaki had fought well there under the Tokugawa banners. Both had been rewarded accordingly.

Now based in Iyo with his newly-increased income, Todo Takatora approached the great warrior Watanabe Satoru Kanbei (1562–9 September 1640) and hired him with the offer of a remarkable 20,000 *koku*, equal to around 10 per cent of his own income. Takatora shared many similarities with Watanabe. Both had been born in Omi Province, and both had served Atsuji Sadayuki, with Watanabe marrying one of his lord's daughters. Like Takatora, Watanabe too was a master of the spear and had been singled out for his brave actions during the 1578 attack on Suita Castle in Setsu Province in which he had been praised by Oda Nobunaga himself. From 1582, Watanabe had served Toyotomi Hideyoshi, and along with Takatora had seen action at the Battle of Yamazaki and again at Shizugatake. In 1590, he would be under the command of Toyotomi Hideyoshi's nephew, Hidetsugu's chief retainer Nakamura Kazuuji, in the successful storming of Izu Yamanaka Castle in a forerunner to the Siege of Odawara. He was later offered a position worth 4,000 *koku* under Mashita Nagamori (1545–23 June 1615) and was assigned to hold Koriyama Castle – where Takatora had earlier lived and worked under Hashiba Hidenaga – while Mashita joined the Western cause at the time of the Sekigahara campaign, remaining in Osaka Castle. Even after the hostilities at Sekigahara had ceased, and Mashita had been banished to the temples of Mount Koya, Watanabe continued to hold Koriyama, refusing to yield to the Eastern victors, claiming that he would only open the gates on the direct orders of Lord Mashita. Nagamori would be made to write a letter telling his loyal servant to hand the castle over quietly. Having relinquished the castle, and now being of masterless status, Watanabe was not short on offers from various *daimyo* wanting such a loyal and able warrior on their staff. It was the very generous offer of 20,000 *koku* from Todo Takatora that had Watanabe relocate to Iyo Province in Shikoku. Upon hearing of Watanabe's acceptance, Takatora's former friend and now chilly neighbour Kato Yoshiaki asked incredulously, 'Why give 20,000 *koku* to one person? I could get 100 men at 200 *koku* each!' Takatora is said to have replied, 'Just hearing the name of the great Watanabe Kanbei makes 100 men tremble. That is why one hundred fools are inferior to one good man.'

Iyo Province had formerly been the domain of Tsutsui Sadatsugu. At the time, Iyo was ruled from Kofuku Castle on Mount Karako, however Takatora found Kofuku both inconvenient and poorly positioned for its role as a primary military installation and administrative facility and so in 1602, with Watanabe Kanbei employed as *fushin bugyo*, building commissioner, he abandoned Kofuku and commenced construction of a new fortress, the bigger, better, highly innovative and unique Imabari Castle.

Imabari Castle

The co-founder of the computer company Apple Inc., Steve Jobs, was once quoted as saying 'Simplicity is the ultimate sophistication'. Takatora excelled at simplicity. Other noted castle designers such as Kato Kiyomasa, Ikeda Terumasa and Kuroda Kanbei all created some very fine castles with multi-gated labyrinth-like layouts designed to confuse and confound invaders. They were complicated, with many twists and turns, and as such, they took a great deal of time and money to build and maintain, as well as needing large numbers of samurai to defend them. Takatora on the other hand perfected the art of simplicity. One such example is his early masterpiece, Imabari Castle.

Imabari is a *hirajiro*, a flat plains castle, but is also recognised as one of Japan's top three major *umijiro*, sea castles. Imabari Castle was strategically and defensively positioned along the coast of Japan's Seto Naikai Inland Sea making it a key point from which to control both marine traffic as well as the land. Maps of Imabari reveal the clean, straight lines favoured by Takatora in his castle designs.

Many castles have a square-shaped layout, but Imabari holds the honour of being the squarest of all samurai castles. Its central main *honmaru* was designed in a perfectly square shape and featured straight stone walls of *uchikomi-hagi* style construction, whereby the masonry is roughly cut and inserted, eliminating many of the gaps and the rustic appearance of the older *nozura* style of drywall construction, made using natural unprocessed stone. Typical of Todo Takatora, there was very little curvature present in the angled stone walls, which – also in typical Takatora style – were quite high at 14m and topped with corridor-like *tamon yagura* around the edges of the main precincts. All *tamon* were in turn connected to the two-storey *yagura* standing vigilant on each of the four corners. Situated in the middle of the *tamon*-enclosed bailey was the prominent keep. A strong *masugata* gate system guarded the enceinte's entrance, making this *honmaru* one of the most difficult to penetrate.

Masugata gate systems had long been in use at Japanese castles, and there are five such gates located around the precincts of Imabari Castle. Here Takatora made a slight change, an innovation that greatly enhanced the gate system as well as the castle's strength and security, leading to the formation of the first true *masugata*. *Masugata* until then had been indented sections at an entranceway, with a gate set at right angles towards the back. The three sides of the indent looked down into a courtyard, where any enemy gathering could be shot by arrows or gunfire. Takatora simply added another gate, a small yet practical *korai mon*, to the open end of the courtyard, fully enclosing it. A simple, yet most effective innovation.

These *masugata*, possibly better understood as 'Death Boxes', were approached across the wide moats via a *dobashi*,[6] an earthen bridge, and featured a simple, single-storey *korai mon*, built in a squared U-shape with its overhead and rear extended supports covered by roof tiles as the initial gate. If the enemy managed to somehow – under intense fire from the gun and arrow ports along the walls surrounding this first gate, from the turrets above the gatehouses, and from the *tamon yagura* left and right – get through this first outer *korai mon* gate and into the *tamon* surrounded courtyard – effectively the Death Box – they would be under even heavier fire while trapped within it. A right-hand turn was required to face then pass through a larger, stronger, better protected *yagura mon* gatehouse access. Most *masugata* gates would incorporate a right-hand turn, the reasons being that for an attacker, a right-hand turn is physically and psychologically difficult.

On recognising the benefits of adding the outer *korai mon* gate to the *masugata* system, many other *daimyo* followed suit, and the double-gated *masugata* system devised by Takatora would become a standard feature of the early-modern era samurai castles. This new *masugata* system of double gates proved so effective they were adopted by Nagoya, Edo and the Tokugawa Osaka Castles in that order. Imabari Castle greatly influenced the defensive composition of those three Tokugawa castles, in particular,

---

6. *Dobashi* can also be read in Japanese as *tsuchibashi* or *tsuchihashi*. They are simple bridges made of earth and/or stone spanning wet or dry moats.

Nagoya Castle. Nagoya's *masugata* are of the same design, but with the front section protruding forward, ahead of the stone walling, which in turn provided additional left and right flank defence ports along the walls. A similar design style was later employed on Ieyasu's Sumpu Castle, and even later were added to Edo Castle. The moats too are wide and straight.

As with all of Takatora's projects, he sought quality masonry for his castle walls, often sending his stonemasons some distance in search of good stone, even if the cost was higher. For Takatora, the most important thing was to build a sturdy castle. There is a story that tells of him ordering great quantities of stone from various regions for Imabari's walls, but then reporting to the stone cutters that far too much had been hewn, and he needed no more. The stone cutters, unable to sell it, then abandoned all the stone they had prepared, and Takatora later collected the unused stone left behind for free. This appears to be a smear on Takatora's reputation, as no proof of his ever having done such a dishonourable thing can be found. Takatora was a man of high principles and was ever aware of the hardships faced by the person in the street, the carpenters, stone masons, craftsmen, merchants, the peasants, and the people of his domains. His considerations lay not just in castle construction, but in ensuring that the lives of the townsfolk could be improved through his designs and management. Further, Takatora took pride in his work and management skills. When reconstructing Osaka Castle's walls in the 1620s, for example, he would have a manifest of the rocks, sizes and rough shapes compiled. He was fully aware of the the amount, size and quality of stone being brought into Osaka, and from this manifest, could direct the workers as to where the stones had to be taken and how it was to be used. Upon completion, Takatora gathered his vassals and together they catalogued all the remaining stones. Of the many hundreds of thousands of stones used at Osaka, only 520 excess rocks were listed, proving that Takatora was not one to waste resources.

Beside Imabari's main *honmaru*, to the north-east, was the *ni-no-maru*, and these two baileys were surrounded by a triple set of moats. Unfortunately, the outer two moats no longer exist, having long since been filled in and paved over. Most castle stone walls would slope down into the waters of the moat itself, but at Imabari, the base of the *ishigaki* was set on a narrow piece of flat land between the moat and the walls. This strip was known as an *inubashiri*, or literally a 'dog run'. Ranging from

3m to 5m, these *inubashiri* were quite wide. There are various reasons for having these *inubashiri* which can also be found at other Takatora-produced castles. One reason is that Imabari Castle, being beside the coast, was built primarily on sand, and to prevent the heavy stone *ishigaki* from settling or falling easily, were set on dry soil. The *inubashiri* acted as a retaining wall of sorts. Another reason is that the *inubashiri* sped up construction of the castle. Because *ishigaki* construction could not begin until the moats had been done, in order to complete both projects as fast as possible, leaving the narrow *inubashiri* space allowed work crews to do both – dig the moats and build the stone walls – simultaneously.

The castle's *san-no-maru* enceinte was designated the living quarters for the castle's higher ranked samurai. To the west of this large and imposing castle was the *joka machi*, the castle town. Takatora decreed that numerous temples were to be built along a stretch of land on the outskirts of the town, the rows of high-walled temples acting as a further protective barricade around the town and its castle.

The square Imabari Castle design would become another signature design feature of Takatora's castles, and the style would later be used at Tamba Sasayama Castle, Tsu Castle in Ise, and Ieyasu's Sumpu amongst many others. As per Todo Takatora's preferences, the *uchibori*, inner moat, is exceptionally wide – amongst the widest at around 80m – and fed by sea water channelled from the ocean, allowing sharks to swim in the moats.[7] The moats were crossed by way of a narrow 70m-long *tsuchibashi* earthen bridge leading to a *masugata* gate system around the main *Kurogane mon*, or literally 'Black Metal Gate', an impressive wooden gate covered in thick protective steel plates, lacquered black to prevent rusting in the salty sea air. Above the gate was a protective gatehouse-styled *yagura* watchtower. Outside of the *Kurogane mon*, beyond the *tsuchibashi*, adding protection to this important gateway, was an *umadashi*.

Umadashi were a most effective style of defensive barrier and compound complex built in front of castle gates as a first line of defence. They were situated outside of the main moats, and like a barbican gate system, they

---

7. Fed directly by the sea, there are often sharks in the moats of Imabari. Also poisonous fugu blowfish, even bream, rays and other fish can often be found in the moats. That being said, admittedly the sharks are not the ravenous man-eating, *Jaws*-like monsters of the deep you are probably imagining, but smaller, less dangerous varieties. But you must agree, it does sound cool having sharks in the moats!

worked like an airlock for a castle, allowing attack parties to sally forth and safely return without letting the enemy in. *Umadashi* varied in size from small earthen walled sections to huge moat-surrounded stone and earth embankments with towers and walls. Most *umadashi* featured a wet or dry moat in front. The largest examples of *umadashi* were at Nagoya, Shinoyama and Hiroshima Castles. Unfortunately, at the end of the Edo period, *umadashi* were among the first castle features destroyed, and so very few remain. Some of the best remaining examples can be found at Takatora's Sasayama Castle (Hyogo Prefecture), Odawara Castle and Suwahara Castle in Shizuoka.

When building the stone walls of Uwajima Castle in 1595, Takatora had used both large and small unprocessed natural stone in a very random pattern, forming walls of *nozura*, un-hewn natural stone, styled in *ranzumi*, randomly laid patterned stonework. The corners of these walls featured stones of various size stacked on a slight angle to form the corners. As has been mentioned, although these early styles of wall construction look rickety, they are in fact very sturdy, and hold up well in earthquakes. Seven years later, in 1602, we find Takatora's *ishigaki* construction methods to have not only advanced, but surpassed those of any other *daimyo*. Here we see the perfection of the cornerstones in a technique known as *sangizumi* 参議済み, where alternate long side-short side cornerstone stacking techniques form a strong corner. Takatora had rectangular blocks of stone cut, at a ratio of one length wide, two lengths long, and would build his walls in this manner.

Imabari Castle's five-storey keep was not only the main focal point of the impressive castle, but one of Takatora's greatest innovations. Samurai castle keeps are classified as *borogata* or *sotogata*, and are defined by their shape and construction techniques. Imabari was the first to feature an ingenious *sotogata*-styled *tenshu*. Until now, the various *tenshu* keeps were built in what is called the *borogata* style. Basically, *borogata* keeps are built along the lines of a single or two-storey temple-like base structure with *irimoya zukuri* or gable and hip-styled roofing, with a single or twin-storey watchtower added to the top. The advantages of a *borogata*-type *tenshu* was that a tower keep could be constructed even if the lay of the land required the keep's base to be of an uneven shape, such as trapezoid, pentagonal or even, in the case of Oda Nobunaga's towering Azuchi Castle keep, an uneven octagon. This was beneficial during the civil war period, as vital time was not spent on evening-up the base, and a strong keep could be erected relatively quickly.

Sotogata, literally 'layer tower' type keeps, resembled a modern-day wedding cake, being basically square shaped and built in tiers, each ascending level smaller than the supporting floor below, and separated by roofing. The third shogun, Tokugawa Iemitsu, would also plan on using a similar design for his version of Edo Castle's keep. Because the *sotogata* was a simple design, it was cheaper and faster to build, and very strong defensively. With *borogata* keeps, a single main carpenter lead his team in step-by-step construction, which could be a time-consuming practice. When building *sotogata* keeps, one would know in advance the shape, the size and therefore how much timber was required. A number of different carpenters could fabricate separate floors simultaneously, and later put them all together at once, greatly speeding up the construction process.

Imabari's keep is recorded as having the first floor measuring 9 *ken*,[8] 4 *shaku* or around 17.57m square, relatively narrow for a keep. The second floor was 8.5 *ken*, or 15.45m², the third floor at 6 *ken* measured 10.91m², the fourth floor was 4 *ken*, equalling 7.27m², and the top floor was 3 *ken*, or 5.45m². The keep had 765 joists supporting the floorboards. Imabari's keep had a steel-plated front entrance and featured twenty-four standard-sized *sama* gunports and a much larger upper gunport to accommodate a cannon. The fifty-four windows around the keep's walls were of the *tsuki-age* type, being opened from the bottom with a hinge along the top edge. The roofing was of layered wooden shingles, held in place with bamboo nails. Apparently Takatora referred to this keep structure not as a *tenshu* like other castle lords but as a *to-date*, a 'standing tower'.

This original Takatora design although in various sizes would be used time and again in many early-modern period castles to follow. Of note was that this keep was possibly built not on a raised stone base like most castle donjons, but directly upon flat foundation stones laid out on the *honmaru* ground. No sign of a stone base ever having been used at Imabari has been found, however. Mie University Professor Fujita Tatsuo in his book *Edo Jidai no Sekkeisha* (2006) notes that just as Takatora dismantled the keep to take with him, it is possible that he also took the stone base

---

8. A *ken* is a traditional Japanese unit of length still used in architectural designs. A single *ken* is now standardised as being 1.82m in length, and used as the guide to explain the above-listed sizes

with him too. The records of the *Kouzan Kojitsu Roku* make mention of Takatora later donating the keep to Kameyama Castle, and along with a detailed list of all the parts included, was the addition of '100 large stones, 11 corner stones', and '80 *tsubo* of *kuri ishi*'. A *tsubo* is approximately 3.3m², so around 264m² of *kuri ishi*, literally 'chestnut stones', the small, roundish stones 3 to 5cm in diameter and used to fill between the larger outer wall stones and the inner earth, was included.

The bulk of the construction and defensive work on Imabari was completed by 1604 and Takatora himself relocated here from Uwajima in 1608 when the elegant *honmaru goten* was finally completed. He would not enjoy the fruits of his labour long, as later that same year he was to be transferred to Tsu in Ise Province, and so his adopted son, Takayoshi, took over command of Imabari. Interestingly, while most *tozama daimyo* were being sent further away from Edo, Takatora was slowly being brought closer.

Haishi Castle had been constructed around 3km away from Imabari. Kato Yoshiaki's younger brother Tadaaki was the castellan of Haishi, and it is speculated that it was erected to keep an eye on Takatora, suggesting that Kato Yoshiaki may have been wary or even fearful of him due to their falling-out stemming back to their days in Korea. Tensions rose between the Todo and Kato clans in the late summer of 1604 when Takatora and Yoshiaki were absent from their estates, and their clansmen Todo Takayoshi and Kato Tadaaki almost came to blows on the domain borders. Both backed down before serious trouble commenced, but this incident shows the degree of ongoing animosity between the Todo and Kato clans.

When ordered to transfer from Imabari, Takatora had the innovative keep dismantled and planned on rebuilding it at his new fief in Iga Ueno. However, as explained, Takatora was later to be involved in the construction of Tamba Kameyama Castle and, wanting to complete that project as quickly as possible, he donated the tower to its master, Ogasawara Hideaki. The keep parts were then transported to the Tamba Kameyama Castle construction site in 1610 where it was re-assembled. This was also the first time a *sotogata tenshu* had ever been relocated. Old Meiji-period glass plate photographs dated 1872 of Tamba Kameyama showing Takatora's original *tenshu* before its destruction in 1877 still survive.

In 1635, Takatora's eldest adopted son Todo Takayoshi was reassigned and in his place, the *Bakufu* made Matsudaira Sadafusa Lord of Imabari. The Matsudaira would continue to rule Imabari until the Meiji Restoration.

Takayoshi was sent to Nabari (Mie Prefecture), and in decommissioning the small castle there, constructed a *jinya*, a fortified mansion, from which to administer the area. The impressive Todo clan villa remains there to this day.

Edo Castle

While he was engaged with development of Imabari, Tokugawa Ieyasu requested Todo Takatora undertake the enlargement of the Shogunate's headquarters, Edo Castle, in particular the *ni-no-maru*, *san-no-maru*, *higashi-no-maru* and *nishi-no-maru* compounds, in 1603. Takatora at first declined, saying to Ieyasu that such important work should only be undertaken by a higher-ranked vassal, or at least a *fudai daimyo*, someone who had served the Tokugawa clan longer, rather than a *tozama daimyo* such as himself. It is recorded in the surviving *Koshitsu Nenpu Ryaku* that Ieyasu is said to have replied, 'Your designs and skills are most excellent, I encourage you to try your best.' Takatora then refused to eat or sleep until the designs were completed and presented to Ieyasu, who was most pleased with his efforts. Once the plans had been accepted by Ieyasu, construction commenced almost immediately.

Since Ieyasu ordered the construction of Zeze Castle in 1601, that castle and subsequent castle construction used the *tenka bushin* system. Not only did this system work in Ieyasu's favour, but by employing Todo Takatora to oversee the design and construction ensured that Ieyasu's castles were among the finest ever built. These castles were a symbol of Tokugawa authority and would ensure the dynasty could control the nation strongly and effectively through force if need be.

Kuroda Nagamasa's castle-building skills were also recognised, and so the Kuroda clan, also classified as *tozama daimyo*, were also regularly called upon to assist. The role of *ishigaki bushin* (commissioner for stone wall construction) was entailed to Takatora, Yamauchi Katsutoyo and to Kinoshita Nobutoshi. The *soto-guruwa*, outer baileys, and *ishigaki* stone walls were also entrusted to Kato Kiyomasa, Hosokawa Tadaoki, Maeda

Toshitsune, Ikeda Terumasa, Fukushima Masanori, Asano Yoshinaga, Kato Yoshiaki, Ikoma Kazumasa, Horio Yoshiharu and others as superintendents.

Ieyasu had witnessed first-hand how the first man to attempt to unify the nation, Oda Nobunaga, was cut down early with no contingency plans to continue the family line. He watched as the Oda lands and power were usurped by the cunning and shrewd Hideyoshi. He then watched a similar situation unfold with the second unifier, Hideyoshi, dying and leaving a five-year-old son as his heir and little more than a council of five antagonistic elders to rule in his stead. Ieyasu was not going to let the Tokugawa clan suffer such a fate.

Not long after being made Shogun, Ieyasu established the *Go-sanke*, the Three Noble Houses. By forming the *Go-sanke*, effectively three branches of the Tokugawa clan headed by three of his many sons, and having one based in Mito, another far south in Kii at Wakayama and the financially and politically strongest of the three, the Owari branch, centrally located in Nagoya, the Tokugawa clan would remain stable. Should the main Edo clan for any reason, be it attack, earthquake, fire or through natural death, become extinct, a direct descendant of Ieyasu could be selected from the three branches to serve as Shogun and continue the Tokugawa family line. Now he needed a system by which he could maintain a firm grip on the security of his land.

The Systems Engineer

In the Sengoku period, the *daimyo* fought great battles amongst one another to take and defend their lands. Under the authority of the Toyotomi administration, land ownership was well understood, but still an unclearly defined concept. Rather than clearly-delineated territories, the domains of the *daimyo* were loosely based on periodic land surveys and projected agricultural yields. This Toyotomi-style feudal system remained basically in place after the Battle of Sekigahara, but with the commencement of the Edo *Bakufu* under the Tokugawa, major political reform was called for.

After the Tokugawa victory at the Battle of Sekigahara, the approximately 300 various-sized domains became the de facto estates of the *daimyo*, ruled by them as governors, at the pleasure of the Shogun. While some of the *shinpan* (*daimyo* of Tokugawa or Matsudaira blood) and *fudai daimyo* clans managed to hold and govern their domains throughout the Edo period, many other *daimyo*, particularly the *tozama*, were transferred at irregular intervals for a variety of reasons, including reward, punishment, or to simply keep them on their toes.

When the Tokugawa came to power, there were no set rules on how to create or operate these domains. That system is believed to have been organised by Takatora on behalf of Ieyasu. Indeed, the only person with sufficient political and managerial acumen to be able to formulate such a system within Ieyasu's circle of advisors and be influential enough to have other *daimyo* follow suit was Todo Takatora. Once established, his fine administrative skills were regularly called upon and he would serve as an advisor to many other *daimyo* eager to succeed in their new roles in the hopes of not just pleasing their Tokugawa masters, but for self-preservation. Likewise, a system to ensure the *daimyo* remained loyal to the Tokugawa and to prevent uprisings or wars was required.

Todo Takatora was in Edo in 1604 when he proposed a plan to Ieyasu that, once eventually adopted, would come to define the Edo period and samurai society under the Tokugawa. The plan involved every *daimyo* in the realm being required to build and maintain a residence in the Shogun's capital. Ostensibly, this was a show of compliance. The proposal was supported by the 'One-Eyed Dragon of the North', the *daimyo* Date Masamune. Takatora set an example of what was to follow by bringing his wife and concubine to Edo and having them reside in his mansion there permanently. His own younger brother, Todo Masataka, had earlier been sent to live in Edo as a show of subservience, by which Ieyasu was most pleased. Asano Nagamasa soon followed suit, bringing his wife and their children. Four years later, Takatora suggested that not only the wives and children of the *daimyo* should reside in Edo, but the sons of the chief retainers of all domains should do also. The Tokugawa readily accepted his advice, and again, Edo's population swelled.

This led to the *Sankin Kotai* policy being adopted, a system originally initiated by Toyotomi Hideyoshi during the Sengoku period and perfected by the Tokugawa Shogunate during the relative peace of the Edo period. *Sankin Kotai* required the *daimyo*, or nobility, to spend alternate years between their home domains and residences in Edo. In principal, the practice was to provide military services to the Shogun. A set number of the *daimyo*'s samurai would accompany him to Edo, and while stationed there would perform castle and civic policing and guard duties, administrative and other services for the Shogun. *Sankin Kotai* service was made compulsory for *tozama daimyo* in 1635, and for *fudai daimyo* from 1642.

In reality, Takatora's strategy had been to create a nationwide security system to maintain peace. It was a way to impoverish the *daimyo*, making them spend twice as much to maintain two households, as their wives and heirs were to remain in Edo as representatives (read, 'hostages') and the added expense of the *daimyo gyoretsu*, the lavish processions in and out of the city, would also prohibit them from being able to afford weapons, armour, extra samurai and from staging an insurrection.

The size of retinue in these parades were decided by the Tokugawa government. *Daimyo* of 100,000 *koku* value would have to furnish at least 250 men, including 10 mounted samurai, 80 *ashigaru* and another 150 assorted personnel. As the processions were a status symbol, extra staff would be included (the *daimyo* of Kaga, valued at 1,000,000 *koku*, once had some 4,000 people in his procession!) and an appropriate amount of splendour was expected, with the required amount of samurai guards, administrative staff, servants, porters and horses all dressed in the finest attire. All had to be fed and lodged during the procession, thus creating a further financial burden on the *daimyo*. It has been estimated that as much as 25 per cent of a *daimyo*'s annual net revenues was allocated to the *Sankin Kotai* system including maintaining the Edo mansions as well as funding the processions.

Takatora's suggested plan had other beneficial implications. During these processions, the *daimyo* would use one of the many highways, the *kaido*, with the five main routes being those of the Tokaido, Nakasendo, Koshu-kaido, Oshu-Kaido and the Nikko-Kaido. Another twenty-five minor routes were also used. Along each of the highways were designated stops, post towns, featuring special inns reserved for the *daimyo* and nobility called *Honjin* and *Waki-honjin*, while *Hatago* were officially sanctioned lodging establishments for everyone else. The processions encouraged cultural and economic growth along the highways, which in turn improved road maintenance and was beneficial to local industry, and they aided and enhanced communications across the country. The *Sankin Kotai* system was also imitated by the *daimyo* within their own domains, ensuring peace through the subservience of their retainers.

The *Sankin Kotai* can be seen as another reason for Takatora's reputation having been sullied by some of the other *daimyo* – it was his suggested plan for peace that caused them all personal, financial and logistical hardship. This system remained in place until it was practically abolished in 1862 near the end of the Edo period, when the Tokugawa Shogunate was in danger of collapse. Within six months, the population of Edo had halved as the *daimyo*, their families and their retinues returned to their provinces. In 1868, the 15th Tokugawa Shogun resigned his position, ending 260 years of Tokugawa rule and the nation abandoned feudalism as it entered the Meiji period. Through the *Sankin Kotai* system, peace and Tokugawa supremacy had been maintained.

To further enforce the peace and maintain authority, the Tokugawa Shogunate had created the *Buke Shohatto*, or Laws for Military Houses, a series of decrees and codes of conduct issued in 1615 and continually updated by the Tokugawa Shogunate for the *daimyo* and the samurai caste. These were first issued in August 1615, and read aloud to a gathering of *daimyo* by Tokugawa Ieyasu at Fushimi Castle. Created to protect the peace forged by the Tokugawa, to maintain their control and to limit the powers of the *daimyo*, these rules were conceived, compiled and written by Ieyasu's political advisor, the priest and scholar Ishin Suden, with suggestions from Todo Takatora and other trusted advisors.

Decree of 1615
1. All samurai are to devote themselves to archery, swordsmanship, horsemanship, literature, and pursuits appropriate to the warrior.
2. Entertainments and such expenses are not to exceed limitations.
3. Domains shall not harbour fugitives nor outlaws.
4. Agitators and cut-throats are to be expelled from service and from the domains.
5. *Daimyo* must not engage socially with people from other domains.
6. All castle repairs must be reported to the Shogunate. Structural innovations and extensions are banned.
7. Coalitions involving scheming or conspiracy in neighbouring domains, the increasing of defences, fortifications or forces must be reported to the Shogunate immediately.

8. Privately arranged marriages among *daimyo* and other persons of importance are prohibited.
9. All *daimyo* are to present themselves in Edo regularly to provide services to the Shogunate.
10. Formal attire regulations are to be observed.
11. Only persons of rank and standing may use palanquins.
12. Samurai are to practice frugality.
13. The *daimyo* are responsible for appointing men of ability to serve as officials and administrators.

These rules were reissued in 1629, and again in 1635, by the third Shogun Iemitsu, with the implementation of additional laws, including;

1. All roads, bridges, boats and docks are to be maintained to facilitate rapid communications.
2. Non-Shogunate checkpoint barriers and tolls, and the cancellation of current ferry services are forbidden.
3. Construction of ships able to transport over 500 *koku* is prohibited.
4. Shinto shrine and Buddhist temple lands may not be confiscated.
5. Christianity is strictly forbidden.

These decrees were again reissued upon the succession of each Shogun, with minor amendments.

The Sanmon Gate

Among the many influential personages in Tokugawa Ieyasu's inner circle was a Rinzai sect Buddhist priest by the name of Ishin Suden (1569–1633). He was the second son of Isshiki Hidekatsu, a close retainer of the Shogun Ashikaga Yoshiteru, and as a relative of Todo Takatora's wife, he was therefore on very good terms with Takatora. Like Takatora he too closely served Ieyasu, Hidetada and Iemitsu as a political advisor and chancellor. Suden was sent to Kyoto's Nanzen-ji, an ancient temple that had been destroyed by fire in the Onin Wars of 1467–77, but never completely rebuilt. In 1605, aged just 36, Ishin Suden took over the temple, and in commemoration, Todo Takatora rebuilt and donated the magnificent and still extant Sanmon Gate. Most temples have a large and impressive outer gate, and this particular one is Kyoto's largest. Hidden away inside the second floor is a wooden statue of Takatora beside that of Ieyasu, along with the funerary tablets of seventy-one of his men killed in action at the Siege of Osaka.

Of interest, the often-staged and very popular Kabuki play, *Sanmon Gosan no Kiri* includes a much loved scene in which the bandit and ninja Ishikawa Goemon is sitting on the balcony of this great Sanmon Gate, enjoying the view. The flamboyant thief is seen smoking an oversized pipe, and claims; 'They say the spring view from up here is worth a thousand gold pieces, but a thousand is too little, yes, too little. My own eyes rate it worth at least ten thousand!' The play remains popular despite the fact that Ishikawa Goemon was executed at the temple on the orders of Toyotomi Hideyoshi in 1594, nine years before Ishin Suden took over the temple and long before Takatora commenced reconstruction of the extant Sanmon Gate.

Sumpu Castle

In April 1605, Ieyasu relinquished his position as Shogun and his son, Hidetada, was sworn in as his successor, allowing Ieyasu to retire to Sumpu Castle. Reconstruction of Sumpu began in 1607. Ieyasu had asked Takatora to assist with its new layout and features, but Takatora was occupied with work on Edo Castle, and therefore was unable to offer little more than advice on the layout of Sumpu. This was done via messenger. The early mornings and days were spent overseeing work on Edo Castle, and the evenings on the design of Sumpu. The castle's *honmaru* appears typical of Takarora's work, with its square-shaped layout, *so-tamon yagura* around the edges and reinforced with *masugata* gate systems. The bulk of the fortress was built based on Takatora's designs and set rules for castle construction, although he had suggested wide moats around the castle Ieyasu had decided on narrower ones.

Upon completion of Sumpu, Ieyasu suggested his giant of a friend relocate to the area in order to be nearer to him, and to encourage the move, provided Takatora with a large tract of land immediately in front of Sumpu Castle's *otemon* gates. This was a great honour indeed, a sign of total trust on Ieyasu's behalf. In April 1609, Takatora began construction a large *yashiki* residence on the land and according to contemporary diaries Ieyasu and Takatora enjoyed each other's company in their later years watching Noh plays and taking tea together.

The exceptionally large living quarters contained an entertainment area complete with a Noh stage. Four months later on 16 September, the villa was completed, and Takatora welcomed a very important guest when Shogun Hidetada came to Sumpu to pay his respects to his father and to inspect Takatora's new estate. About the same time, Ieyasu asked Takatora to oversee the final stages of Sasayama Castle, which took him back to Sasayama and also to Tamba Kameyama, where Takatora also took control of redesigning the *nawabari* ground plans and the rebuilding of the *ishigaki* stone walls.

The Diaries

Although the contents of the diaries may seem of little significance at times, they are listed here in chronological order, along with episodes in Takatora's life to better explain his importance to the Tokugawa clan and their government.

The diaries mention that on 26 September 1608 Shogun Hidetada visited Sumpu and came to Takatora's house.

One day, not long after Hidetada had become Shogun, he asked Takatora advice about the key to governing the country. Takatora replied as follows:

> In order to rule the nation, it is essential to know people. Each person has his or her own strengths and weaknesses. If a person is appointed to a position well suited to his strengths, he will devote all of his time and strength to that position. If you already have such a person in place, then don't ever doubt them or their appointment. If there is any sign of doubt from the upper echelons, the lower ranks will also begin doubt those above them, and if the upper and lower levels doubt each other, people's minds will be divided. If doubts arise in the morning, slander will be introduced in the evening. If groups of people then gather to advise the Shogun, no matter how wise the lord, he will be confused. Disturbances across the nation have been caused by slanderers in all ages, so please be very careful about this.

On 30 April 1609, Takatora met with Ieyasu at Sumpu for official talks, but the diaries fail to say what these involved. Takatora met with the Shogun Hidetada at Edo Castle in May 1609, then on 18 June, Hidetada was a guest at Takatora's Edo *yashiki*, where they enjoyed Noh together. At the end of the month, as the cherry blossom bloomed across the land, Ieyasu again called on Takatora to visit him at Sumpu Castle. Takatora obliged, and it was there that Ieyasu requested that Takatora take control of the construction of Sasayama Castle.

By the 3rd day of the 10th lunar month (29 October 1609), records show that Takatora was back at Sumpu Castle and while visiting Ieyasu partook in a tea ceremony with tea master Oda Yuraku, younger brother of the first unifier of Japan, Oda Nobunaga. Tea was served by Ieyasu himself. It is most possible that talk at the time turned to the works being undertaken at Tamba Kameyama Castle, and of the events that had unfolded there. It may be remembered that Kameyama was the castle from which Yuraku's brother Nobunaga's lead retainer Akechi Mitsuhide had departed from prior to the attack on the Honno-ji temple in 1582.

The following year, in around February 1610, Takatora again met with Ieyasu and the Shogun Hidetada at Sumpu Castle. Six months later, Takatora again went to Sumpu Castle to meet with Ieyasu and Hidetada and reported to them on the situation with Kameyama Castle.

Reports dated July 1611 show that Takatora was invited to Fushimi Castle where he met with Ieyasu to plan a party to be held in honour of Toyotomi Hideyori. Two months later, on 11 September 1611, Tokugawa Yoshinao, Ieyasu's 9th son and master of the recently completed Nagoya Castle, came to Sumpu and visited Takatora in his *yashiki* in front of the gates of Sumpu, where, despite a 45-year age difference, they enjoyed a meal and watched *sarugaku* together.

Takatora was a very good host, often entertaining guests with performances of *sarugaku*, a comedic form of the more austere performing art of Noh. During such times his sense of humour would shine forth as he enjoyed a laugh and showed an open, friendly side. Ieyasu would be the next guest at Takatora's home on the 27th day of the 9th lunar month (1 November). They would be joined by Yoshinao and twelve others, including Ieyasu's 12th son Tokugawa Yorinobu, Honda Masazumi, Ando Naotsugu, Naruse Masanari, Nagai Naokatsu, Matsudaira Masatsuna, Mizuno Shigenaka, Nishio Tadanaka, Takekoshi Masaharu, Akimoto

Yasutomo and Itakura Shigemasa. They were entertained by the noted Noh performer Konbaru Dayu. Ieyasu stayed until evening, when he returned to his quarters within Sumpu Castle. Takatora visited Ieyasu the following day to thank him for coming.

At New Years 1612, Takatora went to Edo and paid his respects to the Shogun, Hidetada, and reported on the situation in Kyushu. On the 28th day of the 3rd lunar month (28 April), Shogun Hidetada and his younger brothers Yoshinao and Yorinobu visited Takatora in his *yashiki* in Sumpu, where they enjoyed a *sarugaku* performance together.

Ieyasu again served tea to Takatora on the 18th day of the 7th lunar month, or 14 August by the modern calendar, at Ieyasu's residence in Sumpu Castle. Ten days later on the 28th day (24 August) Ieyasu went to Takatora's home where they enjoyed watching a *sarugaku* recital.

Diary notes from 1612 also show Takatora met with Ikeda Terumasa, Tokugawa Ieyasu's son-in-law and master of Himeji Castle in the Sukiya *yashiki* at Sumpu. Terumasa was nicknamed the 'Shogun of the West' as he earned around one million *koku* and wielded considerable power in the Kansai and western Japan region. Both Todo Takatora and Ikeda Terumasa were considered the foremost experts in the creation of high drystone walling, and no doubt their common interest in castle construction gave them something to talk about. Ikeda Terumasa and Takatora would soon have more to talk about, however.

Negotiator

Takatora was known to have been a fair and forthright man, and while details are scarce, at one stage he became involved in a long-running land dispute between the powerful lord of Himeji Castle, Ikeda Terumasa, and the ancient Rokuo-in Temple of Kyoto that began in 1609. The feud simmered before bubbling over in 1611. The diplomat priest Ishin Suden and the Tokugawa-appointed Chief Magistrate of Kyoto Itakura Katsushige jointly intervened in an effort to reconcile the two parties but to no avail. When the problem escalated and threatened to become a major issue, Takatora was called in. His keen sense of justice and negotiating skills brought about a compromise and the problem was solved with Lord Terumasa maintaining his honour and the Rokuo-in's elderly head priest's entering retirement. That two of the Tokugawa's top advisors and negotiators failed to resolve the problem, yet Takatora was able to arbitrate shows the level of his negotiating abilities.

At the request of the Shogun, Hidetada, in the late summer of 1612, Takatora commenced work on the stone base of Edo Castle's keep, known as a *tenshu dai* and also on the *ishigaki* walls of the *ni-no-maru* enceinte. The light-coloured stones for the keep base were specially mined from the Izu Peninsula.

Shogun Tokugawa Hidetada again visited Takatora's *yashiki* at Sumpu in early January 1613, where he was treated to a fine performance of *sarugaku*. On 15 February 1613, Ieyasu invited Takatora to Sumpu Castle for secret talks.

On the 5th day of the 3rd lunar month, 24 April 1613, diaries show Takatora invited the priests of the Tendau-shu sect of Buddhism to his home, where he treated them to a performance of *sarugaku*.

The Okubo Incident

The *Bakufu* would again call on Takatora in July 1613 to oversee investigations into the sensitive Okubo Incident. Okubo Nagayasu (1545–13 June 1613) was originally in the service of Takeda Shingen of Kai, and then his son, Katsuyori, leaving the Takeda after the disastrous Battle of Nagashino in 1575, and not long after relocated to Mikawa Province. With the collapse of the Takeda clan, the Tokugawa gained parts of Kai province as a spoil of war, and knowing the man's administrative skills, put the former Takeda samurai to work reorganising the province. He did a most impressive job. Nagayasu built levees along major rivers within the former Takeda lands, he developed new farming land and improved the yields from the old Takeda gold mines all within a few years under the Tokugawa. Nagayasu proved himself most capable, an excellent bureaucrat, and through his work became a close and trusted vassal of Ieyasu.

After the 1590 Siege of Odawara, Ieyasu accepted Edo and the Kanto region as his domain. Nagayasu created a Kanto area land registry which became an asset when Ieyasu later distributed the territory to his vassals. Impressed by his accounting skills, Ieyasu appointed financial control of the 2.5 million *koku* of the Kanto region, and another one million *koku* under the direct control of Ieyasu, to the trusted Okubo. He was also made one of the four magistrates of Edo, and later deputy magistrate of other regions too. Okubo Nagayasu developed the Kanto region's transportation networks and the construction of *ichirizuka*, milestone marker mounds, along the major routes.

For his excellent services, Ieyasu awarded Nagayasu with Hachioji domain, Musashi Province (now Hachioji City, Tokyo) with 8,000 *koku*, where he proceeded with the construction of the post station town, and built the Iwami bank to prevent the Asa River from flooding.

At the time of Sekigahara in 1600, Okubo Nagayasu served as a commander in Tokugawa Hidetada's army. Following the battle, Nagayasu was placed in charge of the former Toyotomi gold mines on Sado Island and the Ikuno silver mines. Other appointments followed, further increasing Nagayasu's power, influence and personal connections with various *daimyo*. However, in his later years, he lost favour with Ieyasu due to a decline in output from the gold and silver mines, and his failure in various positions.

Okubo Nagayasu died aged 69 on 13 June 1613 and his body was hurriedly prepared for burial, but Ieyasu called a halt to the proceedings when it was discovered that Nagayasu had misappropriated a substantial amount of money. This was a more than a financial blow, it was a stain on the reputation of the Tokugawa, and a personal slap in the face for Ieyasu. Ieyasu was naturally furious at this, and ordered an inquiry into Nagayasu's affairs. Okubo's sons and heirs refuted all knowledge of the discrepancies and shied away from investigating, claiming lack of skill and immaturity as an excuse. As such, the man Ieyasu truly trusted, Todo Takatora, was summoned to Edo and asked to examine the Okubo ledgers and review the situation. In his usual methodical way Takatora undertook a thorough examination of the incident and made a full and detailed report to his master. The result was Nagayasu's guilt was proved, his properties were seized, and some 5,000 items, including many gold and silver tea utensils, were confiscated. The Okubo clan were dismissed. Five of Nagayasu's sons, two other men associated with the incident and, the following year, another commissioner involved in the dealings, eight people in all, were ordered to commit *seppuku*. Takatora was able to complete the inquiry quickly and conscientiously, maintaining secrecy so as not to cause any further embarrassment to the Shogunate. This again shows Takatora's dedication to the serving of the Tokugawa.

Records show Takatora was at a *sarugaku* performance in Sumpu Castle on August 23. Takatora is also listed as being among the guests at the Tokugawa clan *uta-kai*, a poem writing-party staged on 10 February (second day of the first lunar month) 1614.

Another page of surving notes shows that Todo Takatora met with Tokugawa Ieyasu on the 5th day of the 11th lunar month at Sumpu to talk strategy, tactics, formations and military action prior to the first attack on the remaining Toyotomi clan, for the Winter Siege of Osaka.

Todo Takatora had been involved in the reconstruction efforts of various baileys within Edo Castle, and his excellent designs for the strengthening and improvement of these were highly appreciated. As a reward, 20,000 *koku* was added to his income, bringing his value to 223,000 *koku*. With this came an opportunity to change his title from Sado no Kami to Izumi no Kami. The Izumi area of Tokyo's Kanda district is so named because Takatora had a villa there, and his new title was adopted as the area name. In the meantime, Takatora was also writing exhaustive directions to his staff in Imabari working on his castle there. Much of his time was spent on the road travelling between his domain in Shikoku, Edo at the service of the Shogun, and Sumpu, assisting Ieyasu.

Imabari Castle was completed in March 1608. That year saw many *daimyo* relieved of their fiefs or transferred to other domains. This was particularly so in the lands around the Osaka region, the areas west of Nagoya, and along the vitally important Tokaido, Yamato Kaido, Sanyo-do and San'in highways, and around the Seto Naikai Inland Sea routes. New castles continued to be established, and older castles were improved and brought up to battle status. The new *daimyo* of these areas were all close Tokugawa allies. The changes were a sign from the Shogunate, a message to Toyotomi Hideyori that the Tokugawa were watching.

Among the changes were Todo Takatora's transfer to what is now Mie prefecture and the lands of Iga and Tsu. Iga Ueno Castle came with 150,540 *koku*. The order to transfer was received on 25 August, and Takatora entered Iga on 28 September, an exceptionally fast changeover. Less than two weeks later, on 8 October Takatora entered Tsu Castle with 200,000 *koku* making for a total income of 243,000 *koku*.

Tsu Castle

Tsu was originally a lively port town, but a severe earthquake in August 1498 destroyed the harbour, and the area never fully recovered its position as a major trading centre. In 1568, Oda Nobunaga attempted to annex the Ise region, now Mie Prefecture, by force, and attacked the ruling Nagano clan's retainer Hosono Fujimitsu who had built a castle known as Ano Castle. Hosono was ensconced within Ano when Nobunaga's forces attacked, but were unable to bring the castle down. Later, peace between the clans was achieved, and Nobunaga's younger brother Nobukane was adopted by the Nagano clan. It was Nobukane who first constructed Ueno Castle around 1570, but soon realised it was too small, and so in 1571, work commenced on the larger Tsu Castle. During construction, the Nagashima Ikko Ikki, a series of uprisings involving the militant monks of the Ishiyama Hongan-ji Temple's associated Gansho-ji monastery of Nagashima, broke out. That prolonged war and Nobunaga's attack on Echizen in which Nobukane took part in, meant the castle wasn't completed until around 1580, when the five-storey keep – influenced by his brother's Azuchi Castle – was finally built.

When Nobunaga was killed in the Honno-ji Incident of 1582, Nobukane's forces came under the control of Toyotomi Hideyoshi, who had basically usurped his former master Nobunaga's power and lands. Nobukane and Hideyoshi later had a falling-out over the planned invasion of Korea, and so in 1594 Nobukane was demoted from 150,000 *koku*, down to 3,600 *koku*, and transferred from Tsu to Tamba.

In his place, Hideyoshi installed Tomita Nobuhiro[9] in Tsu Castle with 60,000 *koku*. Nobuhiro retired in 1599, and his son Nobutaka[10] became lord of Tsu. The following year, in the build-up to the decisive Battle of Sekigahara, Nobutaka would choose to support the Tokugawa clan, taking part in the attack on the Uesugi before returning to Tsu, and coming under attack himself from a large contingent of 30,000 under the Western-allied Mori Hidemoto, Kikkawa Hiroie, Ankokuji Ekei,

---

9. Tomita Nobuhiro (?–15 December 1599) was also known as Tomita Kazunobu, Tomonobu, Nagaie and even Ippaku.
10. Tomita Nobutaka (?–7 April 1633) was also known as Tomokatsu, Tomoharu and Nobuyuki.

Chosokabe Morichika and Natsuka Masaie. Tsu Castle was defended by just 1,700 samurai. So fierce was the fighting that even Lord Nobutaka's wife donned light armour and took up arms, using a spear to fend off attackers. The attacking Western forces, concerned at the loss of life and excessive damage to the castle, offered terms of surrender.

A priest from holy Mount Koya was called in to act as an adjudicator and ordered the battle to end. Nobutaka would temporarily retire to Mount Koya, shave his head and enter the priesthood, before being offered an extra 20,000 *koku* from Ieyasu for his services at Sekigahara, bringing the Tomita back into service with 70,000 *koku*. In 1608, he would be offered Uwajima Castle and relocated there.

When Todo Takatora was awarded Tsu Castle in Ise, he immediately commenced improvements, and set about reconstructing the castle and its layout. At the time, he was engaged with assisting Ieyasu at Sumpu, and so just as he had done when working tirelessly on Edo Castle while assisting with Sumpu's redevelopment, every evening he would write detailed instructions and send them to his vassals in Tsu, explaining how and why to build the castle and what improvements had to be made to the surrounding area in order to not only protect the castle, but to be of benefit to the townsfolk. This included the relocation and improvement of roads.

He ordered that the Isebetsu Kaido, a roughly 90km-long roadway between Tsu and the Tokaido linking Kyoto, be improved, making it Kyoto's link to the Pacific Ocean. At the time of Tsu Castle undergoing reconstruction, the busy Ise Kaido route ran along the sea front. Takatora ordered the course of this important pilgrimage route to be altered and brought inland so the many travellers to the Great Ise Shrine would go through the town centre, enlivening the town, and the increased traffic benefited the townsfolk economically.

Two smaller castles within the Tsu area, Kouzubeta and Mineji, both believed to have been constructed by the Nagano clan, original founders of Tsu, were reformed and improved. Both castles were basically the same shape and design, although Mineji was slightly larger. Both had a square shaped *honmaru*, with large *horikiri*, deep trenches, behind the *honmaru*, and an *umadashi*-styled *kuruwa* enceinte to the front. Both castles overlooked the Isebetsu Kaido.

Takatora had secured the Iga and the Tsu regions by reducing the number of smaller castles and fortresses within his domains. Any defensive outpost no longer required, he had demolished. At the same time, any government facilities not up to military standard he had rectified and rebuilt. This reduced the chances of insurrection occurring or of enemy making use of the old military facilities. Takatora was looking to the future.

His attention to detail and his excellent communication with his men were noted by Ieyasu, who, recognising his genius, requested he take charge of work on the new Tamba Sasayama Castle, then on the reformation of Kameyama Castle. Having overseen the design and construction of those two strongholds, Takatora was finally ready to work on his own Iga Ueno and Tsu Castles.

Orders were finally issued for the reconstruction of Tsu Castle in the spring of 1611. For this reconstruction, Todo Takatora once again returned to his tried and tested designs. First, he changed the direction of the castle, from opening towards Ise Bay to a north-facing entrance and shored up the castle walls. The current Tsu City courthouse is believed to have been built on the site of the main Otemon gate. The long earthen bridge leading to the Otemon gates was constructed with two cranks along its length, preventing any attacking enemy from having a direct approach, and the corners allowing the defenders a better chance at shooting at them. With the threat of Osaka looming, Takatora changed the main entrances to the east and west positions, and built three-storey *yagura* on the north-eastern and north-western corners. There were a total of eleven *yagura* and *tamon* surrounding Tsu Castle. On the south-western corner and along the central western side, he constructed two-storey *yagura*. There was a *tenshu dai*, but he was yet to build a *tenshu*. The original five-storey keep had been destroyed in the fighting at the time of the Battle of Sekigahara and was not rebuilt, although in the 10th lunar month of 1662, a great fire broke out, destroying over 700 homes in the town. Records tell how at the time of the fire, the winds were extremely strong, and the flames had spread to a *yagura* and mentions a 'three-storey *tenshu*', suggesting a small keep had been rebuilt.

Typical of Takatora's designs, Tsu Castle's *uchibori* inner moat was 80m wide at its narrowest point, and between the moat along the base of the *nishi-no-maru* stone walls and other sections were the *inubashiri* walkways in common with Takatora's Imabari and Sasayama Castles. These stone walls were straight and high as per Takatora's artistry. The *honmaru* was surrounded by *tamon yagura*, with Higashi and Nishi Kuromon, east and west *masugata* gates leading to the *Nishi-no-maru* and the *Higashi-no-maru*. As mentioned, although the stone foundations for the keep were constructed, a tower keep never graced Takatora's Tsu. Interestingly, despite being made in the relative peacetime of the early Edo period, the stone base of Tsu Castle's main keep was constructed in the older *ranzumi* style, in which large stones are roughly laid in a random pattern, but without *sangizumi*, the alternate interlocking of long stone blocks firming up the corners. This suggests that Takatora was in a hurry to complete the castle in time for it to be in commission by the time Ieyasu was ready to attack Osaka.

Extending Tsu Castle's *honmaru* precinct by 25m to the east and to the north made it even wider than that of Imabari, and while Imabari was surrounded mostly by *tamon yagura*, some parts were the thick, wattle-and-daub walls known as *dobei*, whereas Tsu's *honmaru* was completely surrounded by strong *tamon yagura*. The castle's stone walls below these were also very well constructed. Takatora himself lived in the *honmaru*'s fine *goten* palace, complete with a Noh stage, and a small annex taken from Fushimi Castle, now preserved in Tsu City's Senju-ji Temple where it is used as a tea ceremony room.

Both the Ushitora *Yagura* and the Inui *Yagura* were the same size, each watchtower's first floor measured 5 x 5 *ken* (9.1m x 9.1m), the second floor 4 x 4 *ken* (7.28m) and the uppermost floor 3 x 3 *ken* (5.46m). The *tamon yagura* connecting both the Ushitora and Inui *Yagura* was 3 *ken* (5.46m) wide, and 48 *ken* (87.36m) long. The Iga *Yagura*, Taiko *Yagura* and the Tsukimi *Yagura* were the same size, with the first floor being 4 x 4 *ken*, and the second floor 3 x 3 *ken*.

A new *honmaru* was constructed with new *ishigaki* stone walling built along the northern and eastern sides. On the north-eastern and north-western corners, large three-storey *yagura* watchtowers were built, with *tamon yagura* running along the tops of the walls between the two towers.

Edo Castle and the Tokugawa's Osaka Castle had moats 50m wide, while Tsu Castle's northern inner moat was a most impressive 80m across. The southern moat is believed to have been around 100m wide, but as archeological excavations have not been carried out, this remains to be proven. Even then, the northern moat puts Tsu Castle in a position of being on par with Imabari as having the widest moats of all castles. The wide moats and its southern access to the sea via the outer moat also place it in the category of being a rare example of a *mizujiro*, a water castle. This would all suggest that Takatora's Tsu was an even more formidable and stronger castle than his previous masterpiece, Imabari.

It was still a time of uncertainty, but Takatora realised that the age of war was almost at an end. He rebuilt not just the castle, but the surrounding towns too, widening the streets and improving the roads for trade and commerce to flourish. Takatora recognised that the future held peace, and peace was good for prosperity. To encourage that potential prosperity, town planning went ahead with a peaceful, prosperous future in mind. To ensure that his plans went well, Takatora called upon the merchants and talked with them about ways to improve business and conditions within the town. At the same time, he worked to help and protect the farming communities, sending his men with earth-working skills to commence public works projects.

Such projects as riverbank levee construction, bridge building, developing farmland through land reclamation works etc, had all been undertaken by other warlords during the troubled Sengoku period, but the outbreak of war had seen such works neglected as men rushed off to battle, or the works had been damaged by the fighting. For a *daimyo* of those times, Takatora was among the very, very few who actually talked with the people of his domains to learn about their hardships and their needs, and then addressed them. For the people to be happy, the government had to be effective. Takatora's thinking was that the castle was no longer simply a military installation: its new future role was that of an administrative centre, a fortified town hall at the centre of the domain. Takatora's desire for peace was some time off, but his strategy for the future was already in play.

The castle town of Tsu was also reconfigured, with the townsfolk's housing positioned to the north, east and south of the castle. The samurai residential areas were also in the north and south, but mostly to the western side of Tsu. Around both residential areas was a moat. On the opposite side of the moat was the Teramachi, the temple town, where numerous temples were lined up to form a protective barrier to guard the castle town. The outer moat to the south of Tsu Castle was deep and wide, and the extensive embankments and waterworks connected directly to the sea, allowing for ships to enter and berth. This area became the base of the Todo's naval forces. Although they were operational, these waterworks were not completed during Takatora nor his son Takatsugu's lives.

Another fine example of Takatora's forward thinking can be found in a comparison of castle towns and their contemporary redevelopments. Takatora and his close friend Gamo Ujisato (1556–17 March 1595) were both the same age, born in the same year, and both from Omi Province. Both men had had similar lifetime experiences, facing hardships and death countless times in a number of violent battles. Both were *daimyo* of a similar ranking. Their ties were made even stronger when Gamo Ujisato's grandson and Takatora's adopted daughter married. (Takatora was shocked when his friend Ujisato died of an illness aged just 39 in the Gamo villa at Fushimi Castle.)

Both men had castles in the Ise area. Gamo Ujisato was master of Matsusaka Castle, a large, impressive and strongly fortified castle. When re-organising the town around the castle, Gamo thought about defence. The streets were narrow to prevent large bodies of troops moving through them, and featured numerous junctions, turns and *kagi no te*, cranks, in which to lay ambushes and interrupt the flow of attackers. Not only was the castle town complicated for attackers, but for traders and shoppers too. For that reason, the Edo period township of Matsusaka was not a very popular place to live.

In later years, Takatora accepted Ieyasu's offer to reside in Sumpu in order to be closer to his friend, as well as be closer to Edo so as to be of support to the Shogun. He left command of the Tsu area to his son. Takatora's descendants ruled competently the area from Tsu Castle for 263 years until the end of the Edo period, when Japan abandoned its feudal society, and the castle, except for its stone walls and innermost moats, was demolished in 1871.

Tsu Castle's ruins are now a city park. The tall *ishigaki* stone walls of the *honmaru* and *nishi-no-maru* remain in well preserved condition, as do parts of the water-filled moats to the north and west. A reconstructed three-storey Ushitora *Yagura* guards the entrance to the park. When it was reconstructed in 1958, certain features of the turret, such as extra roof gables, were added to make it more visually appealing. Meiji period photographs taken before the castle's destruction show the original turrets to be of a simpler design. A fine statue of a mounted Takatora can be found in the *honmaru*. Tsu City's town hall stands on the *ni-no-maru* enclosure and a communications company building now fills the Yuzoukan area where the clan's samurai school once stood. At the time of writing, Tsu City is considering plans to have parts of Tsu Castle, including various *yagura* and gates, authentically reconstructed in the traditional manner.

Less than six months after commencing the renovation of Tsu Castle, Takatora was able to report by letter to Ieyasu that the major changes were complete, and Tsu was back in active status. Although Takatora was the master of Iga Ueno and Tsu Castles, he would receive countless orders daily from Ieyasu and the Shogun, and his work for Ieyasu and the Shogunate meant that he was rarely at either castle.

As previously mentioned, with the coming of spring 1609, Takatora had also commenced the building of a large *yashiki* residence in front of Sumpu Castle's grand Otemon main gates on the land provided by Ieyasu so as to have Takatora close at hand. The stately home was to be more than a residence and office, it would serve as a place to entertain many VIP guests, and so it was not only gracious, but well-fortified for safety too. The residence's large front gate, being in front of Ieyasu's castle gates, was most elegant, lacquered and covered in parts with gold leaf in keeping with the decorum of Sumpu Castle. The *nagaya*, literally 'long gate' fronting the property and reminiscent of a *tamon yagura*, was two storeys high, unusual in that a two-storey building was permitted so close to Sumpu's main gates as used by Ieyasu, the Shogun and visiting dignitaries. It was usually deemed unacceptable to have a structure that allowed one to be able to look down upon the elite. The *nagaya* also featured tatami mat flooring on both levels. This too was a consideration for war, as warriors could be billeted here in times of attack. The project was an important one for Takatora – it *had* to be perfect. The *Nagai Bunsho*, a diary collated by one of Takatora's vassals, records Takatora as getting frustrated by the builders' simplest of mistakes, scolding them openly, telling them to 'Stop being foolish, think about the design, image and the usage of space!'

Takatora's allotment was not just in the prime location in front of the castle, but it was the largest of Ieyasu's immediate vassals. His neighbours included the commissioners Honda Masazumi, Naruse Masashige and Ando Naotsugu, Ieyasu's finance minister, Matsudaira Masatsuna, and the governors Ina Tadatsugu, Okubo Nagayasu and Hikosaka Motomasa. The Buddhist monks and advisors Suden and Tenkai, and the revered scholar Hayashi Razan also had homes in the vicinity as did Ieyasu's foreign advisors, the English samurai William Adams and the Dutchman Jan Joosten. Basically, the area was home to the Tokugawa's political think tank, and Takatora's private quarters would regularly become a place for the elite to gather and communicate. The luxurious house covered over 50m by 30m and was made with quality, fragrant hinoki cypress and cryptomeria wood. A Noh stage was built in the sprawling gardens, along with a well-designed tea house, and both facilities were often used to entertain the many regular guests. The site of the stately home is now the Shizuoka Police Headquarters complex.

As with many of the *daimyo*, particularly those of Takatora's standing, Takatora had other residences around the country. He had four in Edo, homes in Kyoto, Fushimi, and even Osaka besides those located in his castles. Todo Takatora's Tatsunokuchi Yashiki residence in Edo, closest to the Shogun's castle, became the hostage house. Todo Takatora had sent his wife and son to live in this mansion in 1605, and in 1611 had the sons of his vassals come to live there too. Included among the roster were Todo Takatsugu, also Todo Takayoshi's son, Nagahiro, Todo Takahiro's son Naohiro, Todo Takanori's son Takatsune, and Todo Motonori's son, Motozumi. Ostensibly, this was done as a show of solidarity with the Shogunate, proof that Takatora, despite being a *tozama daimyo*, could be trusted. When Takatora had sent his younger brother Masataka to Edo in 1595, Ieyasu had been most pleased, and in turn, had provided Masataka with a 3,000-*koku* stipend and Shimosa Domain in modern-day Chiba Prefecture.

Takatora's Kyoto mansion was south of Nijo Castle. This property he would give to his daughter and son-in-law, Kobori Enshu. His next-door neighbour there was the warrior, potter, artist and tea master Furuta Oribe, who was later to be accused of communicating with the enemy during the Siege of Osaka and was ordered to commit *seppuku*. Takatora would receive his late friend's old house right beside that of his daughter. The Furuta mansion was architecturally superb, a two-storey villa with elegant gardens surrounding it and a fine tearoom attached. Furuta Oribe had chosen the area because of the quality spring water, ideal for the tea ceremony. Takatora would later purchase other properties adjoining this one to create a peaceful and private sanctuary. The area's Todo Inari Shrine, established by Takatora, still survives.

Takatora's Fushimi residence, located in an area known as Rokujizo, and his Osaka home were both very large and beautiful properties. The Osaka house at Nakanoshima was accessible by boat along a canal. After Fushimi Castle was destroyed, Takatora would dismantle his residence there and use the timbers to create a new villa, the Tenma Yashiki, in Osaka. He purchased one of Oda Yuraku's tea houses in the area and had it relocated to his Tenma property.

As previously mentioned, the mansion at Sumpu became a place to entertain. Official diary entries for that period show that on the 26th day of the 3rd month, Takatora formally met with Ieyasu at Sumpu. Interestingly, these diaries only mention official meetings held between these two friends, and it can be speculated that being on such close terms and proximity with Ieyasu having asked his friend to relocate to Sumpu, that they would have met more often privately.

These same diaries mention that on 16 September (18th day of the 8th lunar month) Shogun Hidetada visited Sumpu and spent time at Takatora's house. On the 2nd day of the 10th lunar month, 29 October, Takatora visited Ieyasu, and they both partook in a tea ceremony with Oda Yuraku.

Sumoto Castle

Wakisaka Yasuhiro, one of the lords who had defected during the Battle of Sekigahara, was the original master of Awaji Island off Hyogo Prefecture, and Sumoto Castle, a *hirayamajiro* with a large keep and *honmaru* built atop a small mountain, with the official and residential quarters established on the flat ground below it. In September 1609, Wakisaka was reassigned to Ozu in Iyo Province. His replacement, Matsudaira Tadakatsu, had died young and without an heir, ending his clan line. In his place, the *Bakufu* offered Sumoto Castle to the Todo clan. Takatora accepted and sent one of his vassals as a temporary caretaker. Later, Ikeda Terumasa's third son Tadakatsu became the master of Sumoto Castle in 1609.

Early in the cold February of 1610, Takatora is recorded as having had an official meeting with both Ieyasu and Shogun Hidetada at Sumpu where he explained how the first ever *sotogata tenshu* keep, originally developed for Imabari Castle, was to be re-erected at Kameyama Castle. A few months later, in August, Takatora would return reporting directly to both Lord Ieyasu in Sumpu and then the Shogun Hidetada in Edo on the situation at Kameyama. Both were pleased with the progress. The diaries note that on the 27th day of the 9th lunar month, or 12 November, 1610. Tokugawa Ieyasu, his son Yoshinao and twelve other guests were entertained at Takatora's Sumpu *yashiki*.

Oka Castle

Shortly after completing the magnificent *tenshudai* stone base for the keep of Ieyasu's Nagoya Castle, Kato Kiyomasa passed away in 1611 while his son Tadahiro was quite young, and so Takatora became both a minder and advisor to the youth. For that reason, Takatora travelled to Kumamoto Castle. At the time, Nakagawa Hidenari was master of Oka Castle in Taketa, Oita, and asked Takatora to advise him on ways of strengthening the castle. His advice was to change the easterly-facing Otemon main gates to the opposite side of the castle, making the gates westerly facing. His advice was gratefully accepted, but unfortunately the reason for Takatora suggesting this change remains unknown.

Sasayama Castle

Sasayama Castle was built for war! Constructed on a site near the former Yagami Castle, whose master, Maeda Gen'i's son Maeda Shigekatsu, had suffered from mental problems and having killed a samurai in his employ, one Oike Kiyozaemon,[11] was therefore dismissed from his position and imprisoned. In his place, Ieyasu's son Matsudaira Yasushige was given control of Yagami. Upon Ieyasu's orders, a new castle was to be constructed, and Yasushige chose the current site, within an easy-to-defend basin. It was an ideal position. Like Yagami, Sasayama Castle watched over the main route to Kyoto, and so it was a strategically important castle. Construction of Sasayama utilised the *tenka bushin* system to ensure quick turnaround. Naturally, the *nawabari* was drawn up by Todo Takatora, with a *tenshu* planned for the south-eastern corner. The castle's main central baileys featured three *masugata* gates.

---

11. Oike Kiyozaemon was known to Ieyasu, and may have been a spy for the Tokugawa. Maeda Shigekatsu was an underground Christian, and it is possible that Oike had discovered his secret, hence being executed.

The overall design was a square shape, and although there was a *tenshudai*, stone keep base, there was no *tenshu*. Instead, there were two three-storey *yagura* towers, and thirteen two-storey watchtowers protecting it. The wide *ni-no-maru* bailey was surrounded by huge *dorui* earthen walls, and a staggered *byobu-ori* or folding screen wall. The wall featured small right-angled bends at various positions along the wall, giving it the appearance of a folding screen, hence the name. These angled sections were flank defence ports, allowing for the firing along the longer segments of wall. It also had three large *umadashi* protecting the Otemon main gates, the eastern and the southern gates.

Sasayama was surrounded by wide moats, and at the base of its high stone walls – the highest being 18m below the tower keep's base – were narrow spaces about 7m to 10m wide from the base of the angled stone walls to the edge of the moats. These *inubashiri* were similar in design to those of Takatora's Imabari Castle, serving as retaining supports for the high stone walls, and for work crews complete the castle in as little time as possible, allowing both moats be dug and stone walls built at the same time.

The basic outline and design of Sasayama was done by Todo Takatora, while the details were left to his vassal, Watanabe Kambei. Construction was supervised by the *sofu shinbu bugyo*, the superintendent, Ikeda Terumasa, and supported by former Toyotomi clan adherents, Mori Terumoto, Fukushima Masanori, Oda Nobukane, Arima Toyouji, Ikeda Tadatsune, Asano Yukinaga, Yamauchi Yasutoyo, Hachisuka Yoshishige, Kato Yoshiaki, and others totalling twenty *daimyo* in all. Construction of Sasayama was started at the end of May 1609, and completed four months later in September. Matsudaira Yasushige was able to enter and take residence that December.

The castle's wide moats and *ishigaki* stone walls are most impressive, as is the general layout. The three main gates are well positioned, and even now, the remainders of the *umadashi*, special defensive ramparts on the outside of the main gates, can still be seen. As mentioned, the castle has a *tenshudai*, tower keep base, but a keep was never constructed. One of the rumours regarding the lack of a tower keep was because the design of Sasayama was so well made, Ieyasu feared that it could be used against him if ever taken. In truth, plans for the keep were abandoned as Ieyasu was in a rush to commence construction of his next major project, Nagoya

Castle. Takatora's Iga Ueno keep had recently been destroyed during construction by a typhoon, and as Ieyasu was desperate to wipe out the Toyotomi as soon as possible, he cancelled the rebuilding of that keep too. This suggests that the tower keeps were more symbols of authority than necessary military structures, and that a samurai castle could operate just as well without one.

Nagoya?

As soon as Sasayama Castle was completed, Tokugawa Ieyasu ordered the same twenty *daimyo* to commence work on an even bigger, grander castle, that of Nagoya! In using the same *daimyo*, no doubt Ieyasu would have employed his trusted friend, castle design specialist and architect Todo Takatora for this job too. It almost seems implausible that he would not engage the talents of the best and most trusted of castle designers and architects to work on his finest castle to date, second only to Edo Castle. Yet it is interesting to note that while there are reams of meticulously-kept documentation extant, architectural drawings, ground plans, and detailed records of who participated, the numbers of people and materials they supplied, and what parts of Nagoya Castle they worked on, and the fact that Todo Takatora's son-in-law, the equally talented designer Kobori Enshu, was responsible for the design of the magnificent keep, there is no mention of Todo Takatora's name in any of them. Nor are there any suggestions in the detailed Todo clan diaries of Takatora's involvement in Nagoya Castle.

As has been noted, Nagoya's layout is typical of Takatora's work. The baileys have a square-shaped layout. Tamba Kameyama's *san-no-maru* is the identical shape and design of Nagoya Castle's. Nagoya's *honmaru* was completely surrounded by strong *tamon yagura*, with large *sumi yagura* corner watchtowers, and with gates positioned in the same way as other Takatora-designed castles, such as Sumpu. Nagoya Castle's large *umadashi* were of the same design and shape as Imabari, Sumpu and other Takatora castles, and featured the same style of *tamon yagura*-surrounded *masugata* gate system with smaller *korai mon* gates in front.

Entry to Nagoya's keep was via the smaller sub-keep in a design the same as that of Sumpu Castle. These and many more points suggest that although not mentioned in any of the surviving documents regarding the design and construction of Nagoya, Takatora would most probably have had a hand in Nagoya's development.

For many years after the end of the Edo period, because of anti-Tokugawa sentiment, locally-born hero Kato Kiyomasa was suggested and promoted as the architect of Nagoya. In fact, while there are currently no statues of Tokugawa Ieyasu within the city of Nagoya, there are two large statues of Kato Kiyomasa, one just outside the current main gates of Nagoya Castle beside the Noh theatre, and another mounted statue of him on the corner of the *ni-no-maru* and *honmaru* precincts within the grounds of Nagoya Castle. A third statue of Kiyomasa within the city limits can be found at his birthplace in Nakamura Ward. The castle's largest stone, located inside the *honmaru*'s eastern facing *masugata* gate, is also known as 'Kiyomasa's Stone', despite that particular area having been designated for construction by Kuroda Nagamasa and his men.

There are stories and woodblock prints of Kiyomasa standing atop a giant stone, spear and folding fan in hand, dramatically encouraging the hundreds of workers dragging it through the streets of Nagoya to the castle to pull harder. Yet there is no such huge stone as depicted in the many portraits anywhere within the walls of Nagoya Castle. Even now many falsely believe the old stories that Kiyomasa created Nagoya Castle, but what is obvious is that its wide moats, large square-shaped baileys, the extensive use of *tamon yagura* surrounding the *honmaru* and *ni-no-maru*, the use of *masugata* gates and their positioning, the distinct lack of multiple *yagura* turret use – Nagoya had just ten watchtowers – and straight-sided walls are definitely not of Kiyomasa's design. His were much more complex. The simple yet effective elements of Nagoya, shared with castles such as Imabari, Sumpu and Sasayama, are typical of Takatora's designs, leading this author to believe that without doubt, Takatora too had a hand in the development of what is seen as the Warring States' period's ultimate castle.

Kato Kiyomasa was apparently upset that he had not been asked by Ieyasu to design Nagoya.[12] When he saw the plans, Kiyomasa believed the design to be too simple. Fukushima Masanori had complained openly to Kiyomasa that he did not want to participate in the construction of Nagoya, and had done so begrudgingly, straining his relationship with

---

12. According to researcher Togawa Jun in his article (*Rekishijin* No. 77 (May 2017), p. 36).

Ieyasu. For this project, Kiyomasa was responsible for both the main and adjoining sub-keep's *tenshudai*, stone base only. This he completed within three months of commencing, and to keep other *daimyo* from discovering his secrets, did so behind huge cloth screens set up to hide his work.

Nagoya Castle contains quite a few innovations and design elements that further suggest Takatora had a hand in its formation. Such innovations include a device known as an *U-no-kubi*, a Cormorant's Neck. Not far from Nagoya in Inuyama, and particularly in the Gifu area, a form of fishing known as *Ukai* has been practiced for centuries. This involves a handler with as many as ten trained and well cared-for cormorants tethered to long ropes, and with a metal ring around their necks. At night, a bonfire is lit and suspended from the bow of a riverboat to attract *ayu* sweetfish, which are scooped up by the birds. The metal ring prevents the birds from swallowing the bigger fish, which they regurgitate in the boat for collection. Around Nagoya Castle's innermost citadel, the *honmaru*, are five locations known as *U-no-kubi*, where, like with the cormorant, the enemy are sent down narrow paths (necks) between the deep, stone-lined moats, in clear view of the 'metal rings', being the archers and matchlockmen in the *tamon* and *sumi yagura* watchtowers and other defensive facilities. Such a simple, yet highly effective design could only have come from the brilliance of Todo Takatora.

It has been mentioned that Takatora had a number of regularly used rules and devices, including square-shaped ground plans, wide moats, high stone walls, use of *masugata* gate systems and *tamon yagura* running between corner watchtowers etc, and while such devices were regularly incorporated into his castles, Takatora was also a flexible designer, not confined to one particular style. He would consider each and every castle or construction project on an individual basis, and take into account various circumstances, such as its positioning and surroundings, its role, i.e., was it to be a castle for war, in which case it had to be a very strong design, or simply as a symbol of authority, in which a larger keep and fancy watchtowers and gates would show its master's dignity and power. Was it to be a residential and administrative castle or a support facility guarding a particular area? Each and every castle he recognised as unique, and was able to adapt his compositions to suit. It was this wide range of understandings and skill that Ieyasu recognised and took full advantage of. Construction of Nagoya Castle began with the roping off of the grounds in late 1609 at a time when Takatora was busily engaged with numerous castle designs for the Tokugawa. That his name is not recorded alongside that of Nagoya would appear to be one of history's greatest mysteries.

In early February the following year, the Shogun Hidetada once again made the 173km, five-day trip from Edo along the Tokaido to Sumpu, where he exchanged New Year's greetings with his father, Ieyasu, and later entertained both Ieyasu and his special guest, Takatora. The castle architect would not stay long in Sumpu and was soon on his way back to the areas north of Kyoto where work on Kameyama Castle continued.

Tamba Kameyama Castle

Tamba Kameyama Castle had originally been built by Akechi Mitsuhide. During Toyotomi Hideyoshi's time, it was a very important castle, guarding the north-eastern districts of Kyoto under the command of Maeda Gen'i (1539–9 July 1602). In 1609, the Tokugawa clan *fudai daimyo* Okabe Nagamori was made the lord of Tamba Kameyama. To enlarge and strengthen the castle, Todo Takatora was tasked with redesigning the *nawabari* ground plan, and rebuilding parts of the *ishigaki* dry stone walls.

Akechi Mitsuhide had built Kameyama Castle in haste. Being an older style castle, the shapes of the various baileys, positioning of gates, walls and moats conformed to the shape of the mountain, meaning many rounded and strangely shaped baileys were created. One of Takatora's first tasks in reconfiguring Kameyama was to square up much of the ground plan.

Once again, the castle was completed quickly with the forced assistance of Ikeda Nagayoshi, Shimazu Mochihisa, Asano Yukinaga, Mori Tadamasa, Akitsu Tanenaga, Ito Sukenori and others under the *tenka bushin* system. Around twenty-five different types of *kokuin*, identification marks, carved into the rocks to prevent the misappropriation of stones during construction, and to show proof of their work in the way an artist signs his paintings, can be found in the walls of Tamba Kameyama.

While the Akechi had built Kameyama roughly, Takatora was to do a thorough job, redesigning the layout to a *rinkakushiki nawabari*. *Rinkakushiki* layouts position the important main *honmaru* in the centre of the *ni-no-maru*, providing the greatest of protection on all four sides. *Rokabashi*, covered bridges, spanned the considerably widened water-filled moats of Kameyama. Above the moats Takatora built high *ishigaki* stone walls, topped with double-storeyed *tamon yagura*. Two-storey *tamon yagura* are very rare, and the wider moats, high walls and even higher *tamon* meant that infiltration was nigh on impossible. Takatora also had earthen embankments running along both sides of the bridge spanning the moat to the strong *masugata* gate system. This too was a Takatora innovation used only at Imabari, Kameyama and Nagoya Castles. The gates were further protected by large *umadashi*.

Tamba Kameyama's new design was to have elements used in both Sumpu and Nagoya Castles.[13] As mentioned, Tamba Kameyama's is an identical shape and design as Nagoya Castle's, suggesting that although not mentioned on any of the surviving documents regarding the design and construction of Nagoya, Takatora may well have been involved in Nagoya's development. Todo Takatora was also responsible for constructing Tamba Kameyama's keep, a very simple Takatora original *sotogata* design with no decorative *hafu* gables.

It may be remembered, Tamba Kameyama's five-storey keep had originally been constructed by Takatora for his Imabari Castle. It was dismantled initially for use at Iga Ueno, but instead, Takatora had realised the strategic value and importance of Tamba Kameyama, and although a tower keep had neither been planned nor budgeted for, to improve Kameyama's strength and image, he had donated the keep. While the keep had been built without a stone *tenshudai*, raised base, at Imabari, a special high stone keep base was built for Kameyama.

This particular keep was closely surrounded on two sides by corridor-like *tamon yagura*. There were no *ishigaki* at Kameyama in Akechi Mitsuhide's day, nor were the surrounding moats very wide. The wide moats and high *ishigaki* walls were added at this stage using the *tenka bushin* system. In particular, *daimyo* considered 'dangerous' were called in to work on the project. The only two working on the project not deemed a concern to the Tokugawa were Todo Takatora and Ikeda Terumasa. Takatora because of his close relationship to Ieyasu and many years of service to the Tokugawa, Ikeda Terumasa because he was the son-in-law of Ieyasu.

---

13. Incidentally, in the very late Edo period just before the arrival of America's Commodore Perry and his Black Ships in 1853, plans were afoot to redevelop Tamba Kameyama Castle. Three plans dating from the 1840s survive.

Once again, all the hallmarks of Todo Takatora's successful designs were most evident. The general straight lines of the various baileys, the *honmaru* location being in the safest central area, the large *tenshu* being surrounded by *tamon yagura* featuring plentiful *teppozama* gunports along the walls. The *ni-no-maru* bailey being surrounded by *dobei*, large thick clay walls with rows of gunports and arrow slits along its length. The castle was very much a typical Takatora school castle. Simple in design, easy to defend but most effective against attack.

The only elements at this castle not attributed to Takatora were, the *niju masugata*, twin story death-box, and the large *umadashi* barbican located outside of the main Ote and Karamete Mon gates. The *umadashi* idea is believed to have been suggested by Tokugawa Ieyasu, who had noted their effectiveness and often adopted the features employed by the once-feared Takeda clan in their castles. Imabari Castle, Sumpu Castle, Sasayama Castle and Nagoya Castle – built in this order – also had the same style of large square-shaped *umadashi*. By August 1610, Takatora was able to report directly to Ieyasu and the Shogun Hidetada that most of the construction work on the strategically important Tamba Kameyama had been completed.

Four photographs of Tamba Kameyama Castle are known to exist from just before it was demolished in 1874. Much of the outer stone walling was pulled down and used at the Higashi-Hongan-ji Temple in Kyoto, even more was removed for use along the early Meiji period railway lines being built across the country. The ruins of Tamba Kameyama were purchased in 1919 by a religious organisation that rebuilt many of the *honmaru*'s walls, meaning that little of the original stonework by Takatora remains. The site of the *tenshu* keep is now a shrine dedicated to the sect founder and is off-limits to non-members, but visitors are allowed to wander the well-maintained grounds.

With work on Tamba Kameyama completed, reconstruction of the equally important Iga Ueno Castle then began in earnest from New Year 1611.

Iga Ueno Castle

Todo Takatora had been sent by Tokugawa Ieyasu to Iga Ueno in Ise (modern-day Mie Prefecture) in 1608, with orders to improve the castle against possible attacks from Osaka, and to prepare for the planned siege of Osaka. During his initial work on Iga Ueno, Takatora was then sent to work on Sasayama Castle in 1609, and then possibly Nagoya in 1610, and was then involved in Tamba Kameyama's rebuild including the construction of the keep.

On arriving at Iga, Takatora first repaired and rebuilt the Kimon Gates of the Iga Ichinomiya Aekuni Shrine, then the main prayer hall and Kanetsuki-do Hall at his own expense, but for the benefit of the townsfolk. In 1612, he would donate some 1,074 *koku* to the shrine for upkeep and to ease the burden on the people of the area.

Iga Ueno Castle was built on a steep hill between three rivers, and had been controlled by the Tsutsui clan for over 20 years. Hideyoshi himself had made Tsutsui Sadatsugu master of Iga in 1584. The Tsutsui castle had a large three-storey keep at the low mountain's highest point, but it was destroyed by a typhoon well before Takatora received the castle. When Todo Takatora took over control of Iga Ueno Castle from the Tsutsui, he had to quickly and effectively completely redesign the entire layout of the castle. One of the major reasons for the redesign being that initially Iga Ueno was a Toyotomi-allied castle, designed to face and to repel the Eastern armies of the Tokugawa. Now it was a Tokugawa fortress with the enemy expected from the opposite side, and so everything had to be reconfigured to face west towards the Toyotomi. For starters, Takatora called for a large-scale redevelopment of the entire grounds. The area directly south of the hill, around 100m and 300m wide running east-west, was also fortified. This area, the Maru-no-uchi precinct, now the site of Ueno High School, the Ueno Nishi Elementary School and the former Iga Ueno City Council Offices, had two south-facing *masugata* gate systems near either end and watchtower turrets along its length. Old maps of Iga Ueno show the area once had a street named the 'Daimyo Koji'. The Todo clan and their elite vassals lived along this street. To the west of the *honmaru*, across the wide moats in what is now the school's sports ground, was the *O-yashiki*, a palatial living quarters for the Todo family, accessed via the Nishi Otemon, western *masugata* gates.

A large trench was dug across the *honmaru* and a north-south running *yaguradai* base for a *tamon yagura* was constructed. A new *honmaru* was also developed, the *tenshu* keep was demolished and a new base was constructed on the opposite side of the complex. Takatora made the moats along the western face wider and deeper and the walls much higher. Having conceived the idea of building stone walls twice the height of the record Toyotomi Osaka Castle, and receiving approval from the Shogun, Hidetada, the stonemasons of Anoshu were called in to work on the walls which rose directly from the waters of the moat. At around 27m high, plus another 5m below the moat's waterline, they became the tallest in Japan at the time, and remained so until Osaka Castle came under Tokugawa control and was re-constructed under the control of Toda Takatora in the 1620s. The high *ishigaki* were harder to attack and impossible to scale, and the height too gave the defenders an advantage. Takatora had begun constructing high stone walls while working on Uwajima Castle, particularly around the Tomei-maru compound. No other *daimyo* would surpass Takatora's skill in achieving such high and sturdy walls. The elegantly curved walls of Kato Kiyomasa's Kumamoto Castle only averaged 10m in height.

The corners of a castle's bailey can be compromised where 45-degree blind spots prevent the defenders from being able to fire upon an attacking enemy and provide the enemy with a narrow window of cover. Long sections of wall needed a central or multiple staggered ports for security. To protect the corners and improve defensive capabilities along the walls, protruding *desumi* or depressed *irisumi* sections of *ishigaki* or *dorui* walling is configured into the design. *Desumi* in particular must be properly fortified and ideally require a defensive *yagura* be built in order to be fully effective. Known collectively as *yokoya*, literally 'Side Arrows', these defensive flank ports are considered difficult to properly construct, particularly at the corners. Takatora's vassal Todo Ukyo, who had developed skills in forming *desumi*, and Watanabe Kanbei, who was equally skilled at creating *irisumi*, were called in to oversee work on the walls.

In four locations along the stone walls of Iga Ueno are stones with numbers carved into them at various levels. This was done to maintain the straight edges preferred by Takatora, and to determine the wall's height. Overlooking the important Iga Kaido route, these high stone walls hurriedly built along the western edges used a mixture of *nozura zumi* techniques featuring natural unprocessed stone and *uchikomi-hagi* techniques in which the stone is roughly cut and fitted in place.

The all-important corners employed well-developed *sangizumi* techniques, where well-stacked long, squarish stones lying at an angle facing inwards, formed straight, sharp corners, laid with an overlap of long or short length stones to make a zipper-like effect while eliminating consecutive vertical joints. Takatora used the longest corner stones of all *daimyo*. The average corner stone block was one width (averaging a metre) and twice as long, whereas Takatora opted for one width, 2.5 to three times as long. This meant very large stones had to be sourced, but it also meant a very firm corner could be constructed. According to Japan's premier castle specialist, Professor Miura Masayuki, Takatora was not only the most skilled at *sangizumi* corner construction, but he perfected it at Iga Ueno Castle.

At the time of Iga Ueno's reconfiguration and reconstruction, *borogata*-type keeps were still the norm. Todo Takatora was responsible for the innovation that led to *sotogata* keeps being constructed. *Sotogata*-type keeps were cheaper, easier and faster to build. Iga Ueno's keep was basic, like that of Tamba Kameyama, consisting of five floors also bereft of the *hafu*, triangular roofing features that lend grace to the castles of the samurai.

Takatora often used recycled timbers and stone in his castle construction to reduce costs and construction time. Newly-cut wood required time to dry and so old timbers were considered handy. Takatora would often direct his carpenters to build his keeps and other structures by completing the frame first, then quickly fitting the roofing and tiles, followed by the wattle-and-daub walls to prevent the internal timbers from getting wet. Once the lattice and mud walls were complete, they would be encased in white *shikkui* lime plaster, or protective *itabari* lacquered wooden panels. Once the exteriors were complete, work on the internal flooring, stairs, windows and gunports would commence. The final stages saw internal walls, ceilings, skirting boards and finally tatami mats fitted. Iga Ueno's keep was around 34m high. He wanted a large keep as a show of strength, and so that should the Toyotomi ever try to attack, they would be able to see the castle from a distance.

Tragedy struck on 7 October 1611, when Iga Ueno's near-completed keep collapsed in the violent storm-force winds and the lashing rains of a great typhoon. The *kawara* roof tiles had been set in place, and the walls had dried, such was its state of near completion. When the keep fell, Hiramatsu Kizo, the *sakuji bugyo*, and a team of carpenters were killed while still working on the interior. Hiramatsu's funeral was held at the

Jokyo-ji Temple, the Todo clan family temple, where his name is recorded and remembered. The funerals of the carpenters killed in the collapse were held in Iga Ueno's Sairen-ji Temple with Takatora covering the expenses for all of them.

Takatora had reported the incident to Ieyasu immediately and promised to rebuild the fallen *tenshu* as quickly as possible. Ieyasu considered Takatora's promise, but impatient to complete other castles quickly and to make a final assault on Osaka, decided that Iga Ueno could do without a keep for now. The castle would be bereft of a keep until 324 years later when a local businessman had the current wooden keep constructed in 1935 as a local museum and tourist attraction. Incidentally, James Bond author Ian Fleming had Iga Ueno Castle in mind when he penned *You Only Live Twice*. Unfortunately, in the 1967 movie starring Sean Connery, instead of Takatora's Iga Ueno Castle, we see Himeji Castle being used as the site of the secret ninja training grounds.

Iga Ueno Castle's palace, the *goten*, was positioned in the western section of the *honmaru*. An old photograph of the palace remains. Takatora was well known for his love of the performing art of Noh and the comedic form of *Sarugaki*, and this grand *Oyashiki* residence and government offices featured a Noh stage built to the east of the main living quarters. Among the many structures within the *honmaru* was a smaller *yashiki*, brought from Kyoto and reconstructed in the castle grounds. This particular home had once belonged to the warrior and tea master Furuta Oribe. The south-western corner of Iga Ueno Castle's central *honmaru* compound had a special storeroom for the keeping of weapons in it.

Many years after Takatora's death, in June 1662, a great earthquake struck the Iga Ueno region. Much of the castle's walls and features remaining from the Tsutsui period collapsed, but those parts designed and constructed by Todo Takatora remained standing. Iga Ueno was to suffer further quakes in 1707, and again in 1854 when the *Shoin*, a section of the palace consisting of the highly decorative formal reception rooms including the lord's audience chambers and waiting rooms, was badly damaged.

Iga Ueno Castle's Higashi Otemon and Nishi Otemon gates were large-scale *uchi-masugata* gates surrounded by *tamon yagura*. Interestingly, the Higashi Otemon's *masugata* gate was configured with a right turn to the second gate, which is the norm in most Japanese castles. The Nishi

Otemon, however, had a left-hand turn. In the Meiji Period, the Higashi Otemon became the site of the Mie Prefectural Offices, and the Nishi Otemon was used as a storage facility, but was later demolished in 1907.

Iga Ueno Castle's Maru-no-uchi bailey had an outer earthen wall, a *dorui*, topped with ten *yagura* watchtowers. Each of these *yagura* were named after personnel from within the Todo camp. The first was known as the Todo Shoden no Yagura, later renamed the *ni-no-maru* Yagura. Second was the Nozaki Genzaemon Mae no Yagura, later to become the Higashi Dote Kita Yagura. Third was the Kuwana Yajibei Ushiro no Yagura, subsequently called the Higashi Dote Minami Yagura. Next was the Nozaki Shinpei Mae no Yagura, becoming the Tatsumi Yagura, then the Umehara Gen'emon Mae no Yagura, afterwards called the Higashi Otemon Kiwae Yagura. The seventh one was the Todo Shikibu Sumi Yagura, later known as the Higashi Yagura. The eighth watchtower was the Wakisaka Saburoemon Mae no Yagura, which was also called the Taiko Yagura, or Drum Tower, used for the regular signalling times, shift changes and in times of attack for sending warnings and orders via the huge drum inside.

The ninth *yagura* was the Niju Yagura, which being a two-storey structure later became the Hon-taiko Yagura, or Main Drum Gate. To the west of the castle's rice storehouses was the Kura Seinan Yagura (*kura* being storehouse and *sei-nan* meaning south-west). This and other castle structures along with 2,576 other houses and buildings were damaged in the magnitude 7.25 Iga-Ueno Earthquake in July 1854 that killed 995 people and injured 994. More damage was caused in the Great Tokai Earthquake of 24 December that same year. Six of the *yagura* positioned near the *buke-yashiki* samurai homes, including the Tatsumi and the Higashi Dote Yagura, the Taiko Yagura and Minami Dote Yagura all survived the quakes, and were still standing well into the Meiji period.

The Maru-no-uchi and the Nishi-no-maru areas were part of the *jokamachi*, the castle town. There were eighty-eight samurai homes located within these areas. These samurai were of higher rank, and were expected to protect the castle in times of attack. Lower-ranked samurai not allocated living quarters within the castle grounds built their smaller homes to the south of the castle. Their role too was to protect the town should an enemy approach. There were eight temples within the *jokamachi*. The Kofuku-ji Temple, located in the western corner of the Nishi-no-maru, and the Atogo-sha Shrine to the south of the castle were readied and designated *toride*, forts, in times of attack.

The township itself was designed along a simple checkerboard plan. South of the *Soto-uma-ba* area were the Iga Mono no Yashiki, also known as Shinobi-cho, being the houses of the regions famed ninja corps lay. South of that was Teppo-cho, the area allocated to the matchlock corps. Other *ashigaru* foot soldiers and gunners were housed to the south-east of Shinobi-cho.

Iga Ueno is well known as the birthplace of Japan's most famous wandering poet master, and rumoured ninja, Matsuo Basho (1644–28 November 1694). According to the researcher Onishi Shinsaburo, there is an interesting connection between Takatora and Matsuo Basho. The poet's mother was the daughter of one of Takatora's vassals, and she was born in Uwajima during Takatora's posting there. Matsuo Basho's father is believed to have been a *musokunin*, a class of landowning peasants with certain samurai status privileges, under Tsutsui Sadatsugu, master of Iga Ueno before Takatora was transferred there. When Takatora moved to Iga Ueno, naturally his vassals followed. Basho's mother and father met and married in Iga Ueno, where the poet was born. As a youth, he served as a page to Todo Yoshitada, and shared Yoshitada's love for collaborative *haiku* poetry composition. When Yoshitada (pen name Sengin) died suddenly in 1666 aged 25, Basho abandoned hope of living the life of a samurai, becoming a poet instead. He would travel the nation extensively, returning to Iga Ueno on occasions where he maintained close connections to the Todo clan.

At the time of the first Siege of Osaka, contingency plans had been made that should the Tokugawa fail in their efforts, and the Toyotomi triumph, Shogun Hidetada was to go directly to the Ii clan's Hikone Castle, while Ieyasu would seek refuge with Todo Takatora at Iga Ueno, such was the importance of the Ii and Todo clans, as well as their respective castles.

Takatora was in Edo on New Year's Day 1612, and visited Edo Castle to pay his respects to the Shogun, Hidetada. Once again he was warmly greeted by the Tokugawa. As the winter passed and the world once again started to show some greenery, on 28 April Shogun Hidetada, his younger brothers Yoshinao, lord of Nagoya and Yorinobu, lord of Mito, visited Takatora in his *yashiki* residence in Sumpu.

For even a *hatamoto*, one of the closest vassals of the Tokugawa clan, to be visited in their private home by not only lords of Yoshinao and

Yorinobu's standing, but by the Shogun himself, would have been a very great honour indeed. To have been visited by all three at once, triply so. For a *tozama daimyo*, this was unheard of, and simply reinforces the degree of intimacy between Takatora and the Tokugawa clan.

Another episode that clearly shows the strength and depth of the remarkable relationship between Takatora and Ieyasu took place in his later years. While being towed into port, an incident occurred in which one of Takatora's ships accidentally collided with the ship bearing the flags of Ieyasu's 6th son, Matsudaira Tadateru, damaging the Matsudaira ship's tower.[14] Which of the ships was in the wrong remains unknown, but the captain of Takatora's ship and his men on seeing the Matsudaira/- Tokugawa crest immediately offered their sincerest apologies to Lord Tadateru. Greatly angered by the mishap, Tadateru paid them no attention, ignoring their words of remorse and went straight to his father to make his claim. However, when Ieyasu heard this, he said to his son, 'You know that Takatora's navy are highly trained and achieved many great victories against the Korean blockades during the war in Korea. If the Todo ship's crew apologised, then the shame is on you for not having accepted it as an accident.'

Diary notes show that on the 18th day of the 7th lunar month (14 August) Takatora was again a guest at Ieyasu's private residence, within the confines of Sumpu Castle. Takatora also met with the master of

---

14. Although Matsudaira Tadateru (16 February 1592–24 August 1683) was Ieyasu's 6th son, he was seen as somewhat of an outsider by the Shogunate. Tadateru was ordered to remain in Edo during the Winter Siege of Osaka in 1614. He was, however, permitted to fight in the Summer Siege the following year, but for some reason his brother, Shogun Hidetada, later had him removed from his position of command, and exiled to Ise Province, then Hida Province and later transferred again to Shinano Province. One reason for this treatment was that Tadateru's wife was Iroha-hime, the eldest daughter of Date Masamune, the One-Eyed Dragon of the North. Although the Tokugawa had used the Date clan to keep the Uesugi from attacking Tokugawa interests just prior to the Battle of Sekigahara, the Tokugawa never fully trusted them. Tadateru's marriage was arranged by Ieyasu to form and maintain ties between the once rival clans, but also came to be seen as a growing concern as the father and son-in-law formed close and friendly terms, with both having a keen interest in foreign affairs and technology. There were even rumours that through his wife's influence, Tadateru had accepted the Christian faith. As it was, when Tadateru was stripped of his position in 1616, she divorced him, and returned to her father's estate in Sendai. Incidentally, in 1610, Tadateru was made Lord of Shinano and Echigo Provinces, and Takatora was employed to instruct him in politics and methods of domain administration

Himeji Castle, Ikeda Terumasa, at Sumpu that December, and not long after, Shogun Hidetada again visited Takatora's *yashiki* at Sumpu.

The 26th day of the 12th lunar month (15 February) would have been Tokugawa Ieyasu's birthday. He had been born on the 26th day of the 12th lunar month of the 11th year of Tenbun, or 31 January 1543 by the modern-day calendar. On that particular day Ieyasu had invited Takatora to Sumpu Castle for secret talks. These concerned Ieyasu's plan to finally seize total control of the nation. Ieyasu had been victorious 12 years earlier at Sekigahara. He had been made Shogun and established his Shogunate in Edo, but despite having achieved all this, still the Tokugawa did not have 100 per cent control of the country. Not while the Toyotomi clan remained in Osaka. There were still many warlords, particularly in the western districts, who remained loyal to the Toyotomi, and secretly hostile to the Tokugawa, and as Ieyasu feared his life was coming to an end, he wanted to ensure that not only peace but Tokugawa authority would remain unchallenged. His plan was to eliminate the Toyotomi once and for all. Takatora understood that necessity well.

Takatora was still in Sumpu on the 5th day of the 3rd lunar month (24 April by the Gregorian calendar) when he invited the local priests of the Tendau-shu sect of Buddhism to his home and spent an afternoon entertaining them with performances of Takatora's favourite *Sarugaki*. Diary entries from the 8th day of the 7th lunar month, or 23 August, show Takatora was among those invited to such a performance staged at Sumpu Castle and hosted by Ieyasu.

Another party staged in the Sukiya Yashiki at Sumpu was attended by Takatora and Ikeda Terumasa. Two months later, Shogun Hidetada would again journey to Sumpu and enjoy another *Sarugaki* performance at Takatora's home. The year seems to have been one of relaxation and entertainments, but it appears that there may have been some urgent behind-the-scenes talks going on, as later that year the meetings would begin to take on a darker tone. On the 5th day of the 10th lunar month (16 November) Takatora and Ieyasu are known to have met at Sumpu to talk strategy, tactics, formations and military action prior to the first attack in what would become the Winter Siege of Osaka. During this year, Takatora was able to report that work on his castles at Tsu and Iga Ueno was completed, bringing both castles to peak battle-ready status. Ieyasu was pleased. Both castles were to be vital to the Tokugawa cause.

Takatora was in Edo for New Year 1614, paying his respects to Shogun Hidetada at Edo Castle, and the next day took part in a private traditional poem-writing party held by the family of the Shogun. To have been included in a family event such as this shows the closeness of the Tokugawa clan to Takatora. It also suggests that besides being on familial terms, he was also cultured enough to have written such poems, something a common soldier would naturally have known about, but rarely participated in.

While based in Iga Ueno during 1614, Todo Takatora recognised a need for extra security, and so he granted ten plots of land and dwellings to ten local *shinobi* or ninja, in an area of the *jokamachi*, castle town, that is still known as Ueno Shinobi-cho. The word 'ninja' was rarely used in those days, instead the men specialising in espionage and guerrilla tactics were known as *shinobi*, or *Iga-no-mono*, amongst other names. By 1645, the numbers had swelled to twenty families. The men of these households served as guards around Iga Ueno Castle, and security during the Todo clan's *Sankin Kotai* alternate attendance trips to the Shogun's capital in Edo. Once there their task was to guard the main central palace, and to secure the various gates around the castle grounds.

These warriors had family names, and were permitted to carry *katana* in the manner of the samurai. They were supplied with armour and long battle spears, but unlike samurai, were not paid a stipend from the provincial lord. Instead they were *nomin bushi*, farmer warriors also known as *musoku-nin*, with land allocated for their house and plots to farm. Their produce sustained them and their families, leaving a fair portion that could be sold at markets for cash. Some also engaged in crafts such as umbrella and fan making to help enhance their meagre incomes. Records show that in 1741 there were 1,936 such *musoku-nin* in Iga Ueno, but another record dated 42 years later shows there was a sharp decrease to less than 1,200.

Men required for ninja stealth missions were chosen from their ranks and paid a reward on successful completion of their tasks. During the Siege of Osaka, Takatora had twelve of these men at close hand, and provided them with homes in Iga's Shinobi-cho afterwards as a reward. In order to maintain secrecy, the majority hid in plain sight, serving as members of the matchlock corps. That these men were trusted enough to be allowed to guard not just Iga Ueno Castle but the palace of the

Shogun in Edo speaks volumes. Despite their low status and income, these families were fiercely proud of their roles, and were extremely loyal.

These *musoku-nin* also guarded prisoners too. In 1623, Matsudaira Tadanao, a grandson of Tokugawa Ieyasu, was banished to a small island off Funai Domain in Bungo Province (Oita Prefecture, Kyushu). Tadanao had fought well at Osaka in 1615, but was displeased at his meagre reward, and so in 1621 he claimed to be ill and failed to appear in Edo for the mandatory *Sankin Kotai* service. He was also accused of heading wild groups of rioting samurai through the streets and even through the houses of the townsfolk. The following year he attempted to murder his wife by poison, but one of her maids discovered the plot and took the potion in place of her mistress, saving her life. Shogun Hidetada ordered the banishment and requested Todo Takatora escort Tadanao to his place of exile. Takatora raised a unit of fifty *musoku-nin* warriors of Iga to accompany them. Tadanao remained on the island for three years before being brought to the mainland for closer observation in fear of his attempting to escape. He died aged 56 in 1650.

Imperial Connections

As the Tokugawa clan had revived the once-dormant position of Shogun, and a hereditary system had been organised to maintain the future of the Tokugawa clan by way of the *Go-sanke*, the Three Houses of the Tokugawa (see above), Tokugawa Ieyasu now firmly believed that his family should also have imperial connections, and so in 1614 he began to arrange the marriage between his granddaughter, Shogun Hidetada's 5th daughter Masako, to Emperor Go-Mizunoo.[15] Ieyasu would turn to his trusted Todo Takatora to negotiate the delicate arrangements for this enterprise between the Tokugawa and the Imperial Family. From Ieyasu's choice of negotiators, it is obvious that Takatora possessed the dignity, communications skills and refinement required, while fully

---

15. Emperor Go-Mizunoo (29 June 1596–11 September 1680) was the first Emperor of the Edo period and according to the traditional order of succession, Japan's 108th Emperor, reigning from 1611 until 1629. Tokugawa Masako (23 November 1607–2 August 1678) was a patron of the arts and as Empress supported the restoration and reconstruction of a number of important historical structures in and around Kyoto that had been damaged by wars in the preceding years.

understanding the protocol, etiquette and decorum of the Imperial Court. Takatora had already formed prominent and influential contacts within the Imperial Family. Emperor Go-Mizunoo's younger brother, Prince Konoe Nobuhiro, was a close friend of Lord Hidenaga, and Takatora too had formed a friendship with him through Hidenaga's introduction. The prince was also close friends with the influential priest, Ishin Suden, a relative of Takatora's wife O-Ku, and this also served to tighten the bonds of familiarity. These contacts helped Takatora to achieve an agreement of marriage between the two great houses later that year, but it was still not to be an easy negotiation.

To begin with, the young Emperor Go-Mizunoo resented the idea of marrying the daughter of a samurai, even if it was the daughter of the Shogun. He felt the child – she was only seven at this time – was being forced upon him in an effort to improve the Tokugawa's lineage. Indeed, it is known that Tokugawa Ieyasu had some years earlier had his family tree 'researched', and conveniently 'discovered' a noble Minamoto clan ancestor, enabling him to claim the title of Shogun. Relations between the Shogunate and the Imperial Court had soured over the years. Treating this as he would a military encounter, Takatora found an opening and made his move.

He knew the Emperor was in financial difficulties. The Emperor's annual stipend was only 3,000 *koku*, equal to that of a mid-ranked *hatamoto*, and far less than even the negotiator kneeling before him, Takatora, was receiving. He pointed out that the 10,000-*koku* dowry offer that came with the wedding would bring the Emperor up to the stipend of the lowest-ranked *daimyo*. The political and financial power of the Tokugawa, and the lack of political and financial clout of the Imperial court, was such that Go-Mizunoo had to accept this humiliating matrimonial alliance.

Takatora's success was to his credit, but the wedding was postponed due to the Winter Siege of Osaka later that year, and again because of the final assault on Osaka in 1615. It was further postponed when Ieyasu died in 1616, followed by the death of Emperor Go-Mizuno's father. In the meantime, Emperor Go-Mizunoo had sired heirs with another woman, which greatly angered Shogun Hidetada and his wife. Finally, as per the late Ieyasu's wishes, Masako entered the Imperial household in 1620. The bride was aged 13, the groom then being 24.

Tokugawa Masako arrived at the Imperial Palace on 18 June for her wedding in a gorgeous procession worthy of the Tokugawa and Imperial clans. The procession was about 2km long, starting from the Tokugawa's Kyoto residence, Nijo Castle. Her ox-drawn carriage was guarded closely by Todo Takatora and several hundred samurai. She was followed by thirty-two elite ladies-in-waiting also riding in ox carriages and thirty-six lower-ranked hand-maidens carried in beautifully-decorated enclosed litters. Her vesture, carried by twenty-nine groups of bearers all dressed in matching light blue robes, featured treasures, kimono, furniture and belongings including 260 cedar chests, and 30 sets of folded art screens in boxes. The entire 2km route was securely lined by the major *daimyo* and their warriors. The citizens of Kyoto had built viewing stands and set up mats along the route through the city streets, decorating them with gorgeous curtains and screens. Dressed in their finery, they enjoyed the spectacle which was recorded for posterity on two extant folding screens.

Takatora accompanied her as her escort, staying directly by the side of her enclosed carriage. The story goes that when they arrived at the great gates of the Imperial Palace, a high-ranking lady-in-waiting came forward and demanded rather haughtily to inspect the contents of the palanquin and to observe Masako before they entered. Takatora raised an eyebrow, and refused her, telling the lady that she could not. The woman is said to have countered him coldly asking, 'On whose orders?', to which Takatora answered in a firm voice, 'By order of the shogun, and backed by my sword.' As he said this, his feet slid naturally into a fighting position and his hand moved menacingly towards his sword hilt. The court lady quickly and quietly shrank back and retreated, allowing the procession to resume unhindered.

The Tokugawa *Bakufu* had spent the equivalent of 700,000 *koku* on the wedding and for Masako's new palace built right beside the emperor's own residence. In 1623 a daughter, the first of three children, would be born to Masako and Emperor Go-Mizunoo. That child would become the future Empress Meisho.

Chapter 5

The Sieges of Osaka Castle

lthough Tokugawa Ieyasu had been victorious in the Battle of Sekigahara, had been made Shogun less than two years later, a role he then passed on to his son Hidetada some three years later, and had established his government in Edo, he still did not have complete control over Japan.

Toyotomi Hideyori and his mother, Lady Yodo, remained in Osaka Castle, and there were many *daimyo*, particularly those in western Japan, still sympathetic to the respected Toyotomi clan. Those who had lost at Sekigahara too wanted to see a reversal of fortunes, and so peace remained fragile. Ieyasu was ageing and realised he would not be around forever. He wanted to impose total Tokugawa power over the nation, and so he was looking for a reason, any provocation that could legitimately be used to destroy the Toyotomi once and for all.

Eyebrows were raised when Osaka underwent reconstruction during early 1614, and the castle's leaders actively began recruiting *ronin*, masterless samurai. At the same time Toyotomi Hideyori openly supported the reconstruction of the Hoko-ji Temple in Kyoto. His father, Hideyoshi, had attempted to build a Great Buddha there from around 1588, about the time he commenced his famed 'sword hunt' using the melted-down weapons to form nails and clamps for the huge wooden structure and for the great statue of the Buddha. This was all destroyed by a massive earthquake in 1596, and work to rebuild began but was halted with the death of Hideyoshi in 1598. Twelve years later, Hideyori decided to complete his father's plans with the intention of recreating the Great Buddha and temple structures, and as part of the rebuilding, had a huge bell cast.

The bell featured an inscription praying for peace and prosperity throughout the nation, but it was two particular passages that Tokugawa Ieyasu took great offence at. Part of the inscription read '*Kokka anko*' (家安康), or literally 'The country and house, peace and tranquility'. The character 安, in this case referring to peace, was positioned in between the characters 家 and 康, which together read 家康 – Ieyasu's personal name! Feigning great offence, Ieyasu accused Osaka of suggesting that that peace could only be forged through Ieyasu's dismemberment. Another passage carried the inscription '*kunshin horaku*' (君臣豊楽), literally 'Masters and servants, abundant pleasures' but if read backwards 'the pleasures of the Toyotomi lords', which could be interpreted as meaning the Toyotomi (豊臣) would rise again, i.e. against the Shogunate.[1] Naturally it was taken as a pretext for war, and despite repeated attempts by Hideyori and his envoys, Ieyasu's wrath, real or imagined, could not be placated. The die was cast, along with the bell.

In October 1614, Tokugawa Ieyasu and his army of 164,000 men departed from Sumpu Castle and travelled the Tokaido route first to his 9th son Yoshinao's Nagoya Castle, where the traditional *shutsujin-shiki* pre-war ceremony was staged. Heavy rain on the day of this important bond-forming ceremony meant that it was held indoors, within the confines of the sprawling *ni-no-maru goten* palace. From Nagoya the great army continued on to Nijo Castle in Kyoto. At Nijo, he was joined by Todo Takatora and – most surprisingly – Toyotomi Hideyori's former right-hand man, Katagiri Katsumoto. Hideyoshi's mistress, the shrew-like Lady Yodo, had been angered by Katagiri's inability to control the situation regarding the accusations over the bell incident and on the eve of war had coldly dismissed him from service. Now suddenly masterless, the resentful Katagiri had then approached the Tokugawa and offered his services. Together, Ieyasu and Takatora, with intelligence supplied by Katagiri, devised tactics by which to launch an attack on Osaka Castle and bring down the rival Toyotomi clan.

Following the Battle of Sekigahara, Takatora had played a major political role in controlling the other *tozama daimyo*, particularly those who still had pro-Toyotomi leanings. His work as a mediator had meant a smoother transition into the position of power for the Tokugawa, but it was understood that while the Toyotomi clan remained in existence

---

1. It was the Rinzai sect Buddhist monk Bunei Seikan (1568–16 May 1621), the Head Priest of Kyoto's Tokufu-ji Temple and later of the Nanzen-ji Temple, who had been commissioned by Osaka's Katagiri Katsumoto in April 1614 to write the bell's poem-like inscription, while the casting craftsmen of the Tsuji family were contracted to cast the giant bell. Knowing that both men and their families were in danger for their part in the fall of Osaka, Todo Takatora contacted them and offered them asylum in his domains.

in Osaka and while there were still many loyal to them, war was a real possibility.

Ieyasu had met regularly with Takatora, and the two had mulled over various contingency plans. Ieyasu then announced to his general staff that he was appointing Todo Takatora and Ii Naotaka as head of a battle-planning committee. To many, this was a surprise. This teaming of Takatora and Naotaka, a *tozama daimyo* sharing equal status with a *fudai daimyo* in such an important role was, until then, unheard of.

Being awarded the vanguard position in battle was a great honour for any samurai and his men. It meant that one was more than well trusted by the liege lord. In the case of the Winter and Summer Sieges of Osaka, Todo Takatora was placed in the van by Ieyasu, a role he shared with the equally trusted Ii Naotaka.

The Winter Siege of Osaka, 1614

The Tokugawa forces commenced their attack on Osaka on 8 November 1614, lasting until 22 January 1615, during which time all armies under Tokugawa command made a full-scale assault on the castle. Todo Takatora had been made commander of the leading Kii, Mino, Owari and Mikawa Tokugawa forces.

A month after hostilities commenced, Takatora's men alerted him to some suspicious activity. Fukushima Nagakado, son of Fukushima Masanori's retainer Fukushima Tamba, and a unit of samurai were caught making a beach landing at Sumiyoshi and attempting to join the Toyotomi defenders in Osaka. Takatora quickly led his men against this detachment, and they were soon defeated in a minor gun battle and bloody close-quarters skirmish.

Not long after, in late December a shocking incident took place, when an intercepted letter from within Osaka Castle was brought to Ieyasu's immediate attention. It was addressed to Todo Takatora. It read;

> Lord Takatora, thank you for arranging to have the father and son, Ieyasu and Hidetada brought to Osaka. As per our mutual desire, we can now destroy the Tokugawa together. As I promised you when we last spoke, once we have become victorious, you shall be granted any lands you wish. I will give you anything you desire. Please accept this letter as proof of our pact.

It was signed and stamped with the official black seal of Toyotomi Hideyori.

A scowl crossed Ieyasu's face, and he called for Takatora to present himself immediately. When the giant of a man came before Ieyasu he bowed low. Ieyasu maintained eye contact with Takatora. Holding up the letter, he simply asked 'How low,...How low can they stoop?' Showing a surprised Takatora the letter the great lord laughed. Ieyasu didn't believe the letter for a minute and recognised it for what it was; a poor attempt by the Toyotomi to cause dissent and mistrust amongst the Eastern forces in the hopes it would deprive Ieyasu of a friend and advisor, and the Tokugawa army of one of their finest warriors.

Already, other letters had been conveniently intercepted, suggesting that Todo Takatora and Asano Nagaakira[2] had been in direct communication with the enemy, meeting in their curtained war camps. When various Tokugawa allies came across these notes, most took them straight to Takatora, none of them believing for a moment that a man of Takatora's character could ever betray the Tokugawa. That Takatora was the target of such slander shows just how important to Ieyasu and the Tokugawa forces he really was, and how the Toyotomi obviously feared his influence.

The story goes that early in the campaign at Osaka, Ieyasu would turn to bribery first, contacting Sanada (Yukimura) Nobushige, who openly exposed the offer made through the contact to embarrass Ieyasu. Next on the list was Nanjo Tadashige, whom Ieyasu offered considerable riches in turn for opening the gates to the Tokugawa forces. Nanjo's dealings were discovered, and he was executed for his treachery. Ieyasu then turned to diplomacy to hasten the end of the siege. On 20 December 1614, a letter was sent to Ono Harunaga and Oda Yuraku, suggesting they encourage Toyotomi Hideyori to come to an arrangement. As no reply was forthcoming, further letters were sent over the following few days, until finally on 7 January 1615, Ieyasu received replies from Ono and Oda enquiring about the terms being offered. In his reply to them, Ieyasu offered a pardon to all troops within Osaka and offered Hideyori

---

2. Asano Nagaakira (18 March 1586–16 October 1632) was the *daimyo* of Wakayama Domain, and later Hiroshima Domain. He was the son of Toyotomi Hideyoshi's retainer Asano Nagamasa of Omi. Nagaakira had also served Hideyoshi, but allied with Tokugawa Ieyasu just before the Battle of Sekigahara. Nagaakira distinguished himself in the Winter and Summer Sieges of Osaka.

the adjoining provinces of Kazusa and Awa in modern-day Chiba, close to Ieyasu's Edo.

Hideyori instead demanded two provinces in Shikoku, far from Edo, which angered Ieyasu, and so on January 15 he had his best gunners fire what is believed to be one of four English-forged culverin ship's cannons at the inner residences of Osaka Castle in a show of strength. The 83mm diameter, 13lb (6kg) shot made a direct hit on the castle's apartments, killing two of Lady Yodo's ladies-in-waiting. The shock had her imploring Ono and Oda to assist Hideyori in making immediate peace with the invading Tokugawa.

In the lead-up to this peace being brokered, the Todo troops had seen frantic action in attacking the castle. Takatora had brought sappers, professional gold miners from Sado Island, to Osaka Castle, and had them dig under one of its vital corner *yagura* watchtowers in the hopes of bringing it down. All the while his gunners used the large-bore *ozutsu* matchlocks and standard guns to maintain a barrage of fire on the *yagura*.

Watanabe Kanbei, the samurai general Takatora had secured for a controversial 20,000 *koku*, was in the van of the Todo force on a freezing cold 4 January 1615, when Takatora led an attack on the Tanimachiguchi gates along the outer south-western wall of Osaka Castle. These gates were defended by troops under the command of Oda Nagayori, a grandson of the great Oda Nobunaga. Prior to the skirmish, Watanabe had clashed in heated discussions with his master Takatora over tactics, souring the once strong relationship between them. Exactly what the differences were have been lost to history, but the troops defending Osaka managed to keep up continual gunfire and hails of arrows, preventing the Todo units from advancing any further than the edge of the moat. While Takatora's men returned fire, it had little effect as the men of Osaka were well protected by the high, thick walls and turrets of the castle. Takatora's men, on the other hand, being in the open, suffered heavy casualties. It was discord amongst the defenders that eventually allowed Takatora and his men to breach these outer gates, and having partially entered the castle grounds, faced a fierce counter-attack by Chosokabe Morichika's men. In the fierce attack on these gates, Watanabe Kanbei was hit by matchlock fire and fell wounded, being dragged back to safety. With Watanabe down, and the Chosokabe matchlockmen and archers making a desperate bid to prevent the Eastern troops' entry, the Todo forces were driven out of the castle, and into a short retreat. However, Takatora's *hata bugyo*, a bannerman named Kuki Shirobei, played a major role in rallying the Todo troops.

According to records in the *Shahon Heiyo Roku*, as the vanguard of the Todo army were facing rout, Kuki Shirobei took three of the large battle flags he was entrusted with and ran back towards the enemy and kneeling at their base, set the flags in a position not far from where the Todo troops had just been turned back. The retreating men saw this and, greatly encouraged, quickly reformed their ranks and returned to fight the enemy from where the banners fluttered

For this battle, Todo Takatora once again used his dark blue-based *shiro-mochi sashimono* battle flags featuring three large white circles on a blue background. His main *O-uma jirushi*, or great battle standard, was a large white flag with a red circle in it, rather like the national flag of modern-day Japan.

Various skirmishes had occurred around Osaka Castle over the previous weeks, and the defenders of Osaka were beginning to tire. It was four days after Takatora's men had smashed their way into the Tanimachiguchi gates that Ieyasu had used artillery taken from foreign ships and made a direct hit on Lady Yodo's quarters. This incident, and the stress of having been completely surrounded and suffering the continual racket of matchlocks and cannon fire, gradually wore down the Toyotomi forces inside Osaka, and so on the 18th day, the Toyotomi signed the terms of surrender.

The terms with which peace were settled included Ieyasu promising that the *ronin* of Osaka not be punished, that Hideyori be allowed to maintain Osaka with all current revenues, Lady Yodo was not expected to be sent to Edo as a hostage, and that if he should wish to vacate Osaka, Hideyori could choose any domain as a fief. Hideyori also promised not to entertain ambitious ideas against the Tokugawa, and that Ieyasu be consulted above other council in all matters. The solemn vows were signed with blood from the tips of one another's fingers.

Part of the peace terms demanded the castle's outer moat, and the moats around the *ni-no-maru* and *san-no-maru* precincts were to be filled in – 'After all, if peace was to be concluded,' suggested Ieyasu, 'there would be no need for such defences.' Also, to maintain the peace, the Toyotomi warriors Ono Harunaga and Oda Yuraku were to supply hostages. For agreeing to these demands, Tokugawa Ieyasu promised to protect Toyotomi Hideyori, his lands and property.

A few days later, Takatora and his men began the work of filling in the moats. The ever-loyal Honda Tadamasa and Honda Masayuri were left in charge of supervising the demolition of certain walls and the filling in of moats. Other parts of the outer moat and those surrounding the *ni-no-maru* were filled in by Takatora and his troops within days and the work was completed by mid-January.

Takatora was renowned for taking great care of his vassals, and there is only a single incident recorded where he physically punished one. That was Kan Hiraemon Michinaga. Kan had long been a comrade in arms and had fought alongside Takatora in the Korean expedition, but he had left his post and sided with the Western Army at the Battle of Sekigahara. For this, he was neither executed, nor made to commit *seppuku* as he would have been under any other warlord, but simply cast out and exiled. Later Takatora had taken pity on him, and not only offered him his position back, but promoted him too. Kan Hiraemon Michinaga quickly accepted the generous offer and returned to the Todo clan roster of samurai. As part of the Osaka Winter Campaign ceasefire, Kan was assigned to supervise the filling-in of sections of the moat as a condition for peace. However, Takatora noticed that his work was lagging far behind that of the other teams. Expressing his disapproval of Kan's work, Takatora asked him to explain himself. Kan claimed they had already gone beyond filling in the required moats and went as far as accusing Takatora of being a sycophant, a flunky to the likes of Ieyasu. Shocked and angered by the remarks, Takatora made a hasty judgment, and ordered Kan to cut himself open on the spot. The site of Kan's *seppuku* is believed to be in front of the Oteguchi Gates of the castle's *ni-no-maru*, where the Osaka Police Headquarters building now stands. Prior to the building's construction in 2002, an archeological excavation was conducted in which a wooden memorial tablet inscribed with Kan's name was discovered in the remains of the old moat.

By 24 January, Ieyasu had left Osaka for Kyoto where he met with the Emperor on the 28th. Takatora and his men also returned home to Tsu Castle. Although the Tokugawa claimed victory, it was still not the result Ieyasu had wanted. However, it would not be long before the troops were recalled. Another opportunity to destroy the Toyotomi had presented itself.

The Summer Siege of Osaka

By 13 March 1615, the Toyotomi clan were once again gearing up for battle. More *ronin* were being hired, and the moats filled in by the Tokugawa allies were being re-dug. Todo Takatora had only returned to his domains in Tsu less than two months earlier, and yet he ordered provisions be prepared, weapons readied and, leading his men, again departed for Osaka where he hurriedly set up a command post at Yodo, south of Kyoto. Once again, Ieyasu had nominated Takatora as the vanguard of the Tokugawa forces, a great honour indeed, particularly for a *tozama daimyo*.

At the time of the Osaka summer campaign, Takatora's younger brother Takakiyo was left in charge of Nabari. Masataka, his other younger brother, was ordered to stay at Iga-Ueno Castle, and another samurai named Chou Renbo, Todo Takatsugu's tutor, was ordered to remain in control of Tsu Castle. All three then appealed against Takatora's decision and begged to be allowed to join his forces and fight at Osaka. Takatora again ordered them to remain at their posts in their respective castles. Chagrined at not being given permission, the three men surreptitiously made their own way to Osaka, where they joined the fighting on the front lines. The battle went in their favour, and all three performed exceptionally well. Despite their having distinguished themselves in action, when Takatora learned of their transgression, he refused to acknowledge them as they had disobeyed him. Because of their violation of orders and the abandoning of their posts, Takatora ordered each of the three men be placed under house arrest for five years. Even though they were close relatives, they were treated like any other vassal. Takatora treated all equally and fairly.

Ieyasu had left his castle in Shizuoka on 3 May, stopping in Nagoya for the wedding of his son Yoshinao on the 11th, and the following day met there with another traitor to Osaka, Oda Yuraku. Yuraku would spend only a short while in secret talks with Ieyasu at Nagoya before rushing back to Osaka. Ieyasu again held a *shutsujin-shiki* pre-war ceremony at Nagoya Castle, moving on some days later, arriving in Kyoto on the 17th, when he held a council of war, with Takatora by his side and his most senior generals all in attendance. Shogun Hidetada had left Edo on the 10th and arrived at Fushimi, south of Kyoto, 11 days later, having sent a letter to Takatora, asking him to inform his father, Ieyasu, that he had arrived. On receiving the letter and informing Ieyasu of the news, Takatora and a select unit of guards immediately rode out to Fushimi to greet the Shogun and escort him safely into Kyoto. Hidetada and Takatora arrived in Kyoto on the 22nd, where the Shogun, his father and Takatora held a meeting to discuss the second attack on Osaka. By this stage, the Toyotomi were well aware of the Eastern forces' actions and of the impending attack, and so they had stepped up their preparations for the upcoming siege.

Osaka was indeed well prepared for this next onslaught. Over 200,000 *koku* of rice, just a fraction of what was already in the castle's warehouses, had been brought into the castle prior to the attack. Over 90,000 battle-hardened samurai and *ronin* – only too happy for an opportunity to fight – manned the castle walls. Osaka was among the strongest of castles in Japan at the time. As Takatora had rightly pointed out in his meetings with Ieyasu and Hidetada, there was very little chance of taking such a castle by assault. Ieyasu too eventually gave strict orders that any reckless attacks would be met with severe punishment.

One of the major concerns at this time was that if the garrison within Osaka could hold out long enough, it was possible that the resistance would encourage former Toyotomi loyalists in the Tokugawa ranks to again defect. The Tokugawa possibly faced greater jeopardy now than they had while being surrounded at Sekigahara almost a decade and a half before. At the *shutsujin-shiki* pre-war ceremony, and subsequent councils of war prior to this Summer Siege of Osaka, Ieyasu had clearly expressed his will that engagements with the enemy were to be kept to a minimum. The reason for this was that the Toyotomi-held Osaka area had just 650,000 *koku*, so this was to be a battle with very little financial gain. It was merely a battle to eliminate the Toyotomi, and cement Tokugawa control over the nation. There would be very little direct profit from this engagement, and the potential for loss was great. Takatora obeyed that command as he would any made by Ieyasu. Except when he noted certain troop movements.

Takatora set up camp at the Joko-ji Temple while other Todo clan commanders had made base at the Kyuho-ji at Chizuka Mura, a small village in Yao, about 10km south-east of Osaka. Here, Takatora's men would be faced with a contingent of samurai from the Chosokabe clan. Takatora was now 59 years old, and had had experience fighting against the Chosokabe during the conquest of Shikoku 30 years earlier. At that time, three years after the death of Oda Nobunaga in the Honno-ji

Incident, Toyotomi Hideyoshi had complete control of the former Oda lands and forces. Shikoku, then under the control of the Chosokabe clan, lay within his grasp. Fighting under Hidenaga's banners, Todo Takatora, it may be remembered, was one of the 100,000 warriors sent by Hideyoshi to conquer Shikoku. Despite the Chosokabe army's valiant efforts, they succumbed to the might of the overwhelming Toyotomi forces. Chosokabe Motochika's lands were reduced to Tosa Province and his third son, Chosokabe Chikatada, was sent to Osaka as a hostage of the Toyotomi, being left to the care of Todo Takatora. Because of this a bond of friendship had been formed between Takatora and the Chosokabe clan. Indeed, after the Battle of Sekigahara, Todo Takatora and his vassal Kuwana Kazutaka had absorbed many of the abandoned Chosokabe troops into their own forces. For Takatora, this was now a cause for concern: this was going to be a particularly difficult fight, as many former Chosokabe troops now serving Takatora were facing their old comrades in battle.

The Battle of Yao and Wakae

The Battle of Yao and Wakae was to be one of the bloodiest engagements of the Osaka campaign. The Tokugawa forces had already filled in the outer moats of Osaka Castle after the previous siege, greatly reducing its military capabilities. The Toyotomi loyalists were now forced to sally forth and fight in the fields around the castle to defend it. Tokugawa Ieyasu saw this as an advantage, as his forte lay in field battles, not in sieges, and so he gained confidence knowing that the enemy would be forced to come to him.

The Tokugawa forces approached Osaka Castle from three directions, Kawachi in the north-east, Yamato directly east, and Kii, from the south. The Kawachi-based Tokugawa samurai, a total of 55,000 men in all, were spearheaded by Todo Takatora and Ii Naotaka, and followed by Honda Tadacho, Maeda Toshitsune and Matsudaira Tadanao. Behind them came Tokugawa Ieyasu and the Shogun, Hidetada. The Eastern forces had entered the area via the Tateishi-kaido route bound for the Buddhist Shingon sect's Domyo-ji Temple, where it was planned they would set up an encampment.

On 2 May, the Toyotomi forces planned to ambush the Shogunate troops around Kawachi-guchi, a low-lying wetland area east of Osaka

Castle considered unsuitable for the manoeuvring of large forces. Some 6,000 samurai under Kimura Shigenari had left Osaka Castle, with another 5,300 under Chosokabe Morichika and Mashita Moritsugu setting out shortly afterwards. Three days later, on 5 May, Osaka-allied commander Kimura Shigenari made an inspection of the area around Imafuku Village along the north-eastern approach to Osaka and considered it unlikely that the Shogunate forces would pass through this area. Instead, in an effort to attack the Eastern forces' flank and possibly take the heads of Ieyasu and Hidetada, he chose to move his men to the Wakae area and wait. To remain unseen, Kimura had planned to depart at around midnight on 6 May, but due to delays in assembling his troops, he finally left at around 2 a.m. The march did not proceed smoothly as Kimura's men got lost in the dark and found themselves stuck in a swamp.

Meanwhile, the Eastern troops were also on the move. At 1 a.m., Ii Naotaka, realising it was going to be a long night, ordered his troops to rest, eat and wait for further orders to march. Around 4 a.m., just as the sky was beginning to brighten in the east, the Todo army's right flank, led by Todo Yoshikatsu, spotted the Toyotomi-allied Chosokabe army heading towards Wakae. The Shogunate forces had been ordered by Tokugawa Ieyasu himself to refrain from entering combat when possible, but on hearing the report the concerned Takatora decided to attack, explaining to Yoshikatsu that 'Considering the direction they're heading, the Chosokabe army would most probably be plotting an attack on the main camp, putting Lords Ieyasu and Hidetada in grave danger, and so it is necessary for us to take action immediately', and so ordered each corps to advance.

The Chosokabe forces' front-line leader, Yoshida Shigechika, had advanced as far as the village of Kayafuri-mura when the early morning silence was shattered by the sudden report of many tens of matchlocks. Yoshida's units had been fired upon by Todo Takeyoshi's gunners. Thrown into action, Yoshida quickly despatched messengers back to his main force alerting them of the attack, prompting Chosokabe Morichika and his men to take up a strategic position along the Nagase River in which to intercept the Todo units. Meanwhile the thunderous peal of gunfire had been replaced with the roar of men's voices as the Todo and Chosokabe forces then ran screaming at each other through the clouds of white smoke and engaged in fierce hand-to-hand combat, during which Yoshida Shigechika was killed.

Hearing the gunfire and hellish cacophony from a distance, the Todo forces' left-flank vanguard under the command of Todo Takanori and Kuwana Yoshinari, who were heading for Domyo-ji Temple, quickly turned around and crossed the Tamakushi River to confront Chososokabe Morichika's main force at the Nagase River to the west of Yao Village. Takatora's *hatamoto* bannerman Todo Ujikatsu's units followed in support.

Upon receiving reports from his scouts, Chosokabe instructed his cavalry to dismount, and spears in hand, lie down behind the river embankment and wait. As the Todo forces searching for them unwittingly came alongside them, the Chosokabe samurai suddenly rose and with a bloodcurdling war-cry fell upon the Todo. The three Todo units were thrown into confusion by the Chosokabe's successful ambush. Matchlocks roared at near point-blank range in the savage combat. Swords, spears and glaive-like *naginata* polearms clashed as armoured men crashed into one another, grappling like steel-encased judo practitioners spilling one another to the dirt before spilling their blood with a quick slash of a blade across the throat, then removing their heads. The Todo were routed. Todo Takanori and Kuwana Yoshinari were killed, while Todo Ujikatsu, also known as 'Devil Kageyu' for his ferocious fighting skills, had been badly wounded and would soon succumb to his injuries during the retreat. Todo Takayoshi had rushed his troops to the rescue, but he and his men were soon overwhelmed in the attack and they too were defeated. The Todo clan's long-serving retainer Nagauchi Genbei was also cut down and killed during this skirmish.

Todo Takanori was 39 years old. He had begun life as Suzuki Jinemon in 1577. His biological father was the warrior Suzuki Yaemon and his mother was Takatora's elder sister. He had commenced his career as a 15-year-old serving in his uncle Takatora's units, and first saw action against the Korean navy in 1592. Takanori distinguished himself in Korea, capturing a number of enemy ships, for which he was given the honour of receiving the Todo surname, thus nephew Suzuki Takanori had become Todo Takanori. His wife was the biological daughter of Oda Nobukiyo, and an adopted daughter of Todo Takatora. Takanori was around 24 at the time of Sekigahara when he took the head of General Otani Yoshitsugu's lieutenant, Yuasa Gosuke. Later, when this battle against the Chosokabe had ended, Takanori's headless body was claimed and prepared for burial. It was discovered that there were over thirty-six fresh cuts and wounds on his body from this particularly violent fight alone! Not long after, a single Chosokabe samurai by the name of Nakauchi Yogozaemon, a known brave and skilled fighter, approached the Todo camp and requested an audience with Takatora. Permitted into the presence of Takatora, and kneeling before him, Yogozaemon presented him with the *horo*, the large balloon-like cloth carried by Takanori on the back of his armour in battle. The *horo* had been taken as a trophy along with Takanori's head. Grateful for the return of the keepsake, the ever-generous Takatora gave the man 150 *koku*, and knowing the man to now be masterless, offered him a position in the Todo army. Todo Takanori's grave is located at the Joko-ji Temple in Honmachi, Yao City, Osaka Prefecture. Generations of Takanori's descendants later served as the Jodai priests for the Todo clan of the Ise Tsu domain.

By around 5 a.m., Kimura Shigenari's forces had extricated themselves from the swamp and had arrived at Wakae, where he ordered his force be divided into three groups and prepare to engage the enemy. Kimura Shigenari was only 21 at the time of his first battle, being the previous year's Winter Siege of Osaka. His father had served the Toyotomi, and his mother had been a wet nurse to Toyotomi Hideyori, hence his rapid rise in the Toyotomi forces. He had distinguished himself in this first battle and was later awarded a certificate from Hideyori proclaiming him a 'Peerless hero of the nation' along with a short sword forged by the master swordsmith Masamune. However, because of his loyalty and absolute trust in the Toyotomi, Kimura humbly returned these rewards immediately. During this Summer Siege of Osaka Kimura Shigenari wore an old-styled suit of armour made of gold and silver-covered *kozane* scales, laced together in colourful silk braiding. He rode a fine black horse and carried a 5.5.m-long spear.

The right-hand vanguard of the Todo forces, Todo Yoshikatsu and Todo Yoshishige's companies, attacked the Osaka allies, and an exceptionally fierce encounter commenced. The action was so close and so violent that the Todo forces lost half of their men, including Yoshikatsu and Yoshishige who were killed in the onslaught. The remaining Todo forces retreated, allowing the much-emboldened Kimura Shigenari to reposition his guns on the west bank of the Tamakushi River where he planned to trap and destroy the Eastern armies by luring them onto the narrow earthen causeways between the rice fields.

At approximately 7 a.m., aware of the situation with the Todo divisions, Ii Naotaka decided to challenge the Kimura units in Wakae and moved his front-line troops west. Heading the Ii forces was Ihara Tomomasa to the right and Kawate Yoshitsune on the left. Advancing to an area close to the Kimura positions, Kawate Yoshitsune's *teppo tai* marksmen fired several rounds from the east bank of the Tamakushi River and then fell upon the enemy.

The Kimura matchlock corps returned fire, and the two armies then clashed in close combat during the reloading. So violent was the fighting that the Kimura troops on the bank were soon put to flight, heading off in a westerly direction, and in their place the Ii occupied the bank. Kawate Yoshitsune and his men pursued the retreating Kimura samurai, but he was soon killed in battle. Ihara Tomomasa took his place at the front, and the fight continued. The retreating Kimura Shigenari then stopped to face his pursuers, and armed with his spear, led a charge directly at them, expecting death or glory. He was quickly engaged, felled and beheaded. His noted warriors Yamaguchi Hirosada and Naito Nagaaki were also killed and so Kimura's main unit was destroyed. The entire engagement had lasted several hours, during which some 600 Osaka troops were killed. In their retreat, they lost almost another 300 including their leader, Kimura. When Kimura's head was later taken to Tokugawa Ieyasu for inspection, it was noted that his forehead had been neatly shaved and the hair properly trimmed and perfumed with incense in the traditional manner. Everything indicated that he had gone into the battle well prepared to die.

Meanwhile, the Tokugawa-allied Sakakibara Yasukatsu, Niwa Nagashige and others had been watching the battle from the sidelines. Seeing an opportunity, they entered the fray and attacked the company supporting Kimura Shigenari's left, the fighting men of Kimura Muneaki. Soon the smell of spent black powder and blood permeated the air between them. Despite putting up a good fight, Kimura Muneaki's troops began to buckle under the relentless waves of matchlock fire, arrows and armed combatants. Muneaki was forced to order his samurai to retreat to the safety of Osaka Castle.

Todo Takatora's general Watanabe Kanbei, who had been badly wounded during the Winter Siege of Osaka in the attack on the Tanimachiguchi Gates, had recovered enough to participate in this second siege of Osaka too. In the heat of the moment during the Battle of Yao, he suddenly led his units forward and ignoring direct orders from Takatora, took off to attack a nearby detachment of more than 300 troops under Chosokabe Morichika and Masuda Moriji. Seeing his general advance on the enemy despite orders to the contrary, Takatora sent a messenger forward demanding Watanabe withdraw. The order was ignored, and yet another messenger risked his life with orders for Watanabe to return. Seven times the order to stand down was rejected, and although his brave actions helped win the overall battle, the rift caused between Watanabe, his master Takatora and the other senior vassals was irreparable. Watanabe had seen the smaller contingent as an opportunity to gain glory for himself, knowing the 300 Chosokabe and Masuda troops to be an easy kill. Takatora too had realised this but had wanted to allow the Tokugawa troops to take the honour, rather than have his men overshadow those of his master. It was not just the rejection of orders, but the righteousness of the situation that appears to have annoyed Takatora the most. As a result, after Osaka, Watanabe Kanbei was dismissed from service and became a *ronin* again. When he left, Watanabe is said to have walked out of Iga Ueno Castle proudly dressed in his armour, his bow was strung and he wore arrows slung across his back in a quiver. His matchlock he carried loaded, primed and with a smouldering match in the serpentine, boldly telling anyone willing to listen that he was ever ready to take on the enemy at a moment's notice. He expected to be offered a new position quickly, but died in 1640 in Kyoto, still a *ronin*.

The intense fighting continued all morning until about noon. During a lull in the action, the Chosokabe forces regrouped and set up a command post encampment on the high ground atop the embankment along the Nagase River and rested. It was then the news of Kimura Shigenari's defeat at Wakae was received. Fearing being trapped and isolated amongst his enemy's forces, Chosokabe Morichika, quickly reconsidered his position and hurriedly withdrew his troops back into the safety of Osaka Castle.

The Todo and the bright red-armoured Ii from Hikone suffered heavy casualties in this battle and although they been awarded the honour of leading the Battle of Tenno-ji and Okayama planned for the following day, Takatora explained to Ieyasu that the deaths and injuries from the battle had weakened their forces, and Ieyasu agreed to their taking a lesser role. It was not just the Todo and Ii who had suffered. Chosokabe

Morichika also failed to appear on the battlefield the following day, preferring to recuperate in Osaka Castle. Of the 5,000 troops stationed at Yao when the surprise attack took place, over 300 or some 6 per cent of Takatora's own men were killed in action. Of the 5,300 Toyotomi-allied attackers, Mashita Moritsugu and Yoshida Shigechika were among the 530 Chosokabe troops killed in action that day. Ieyasu's grandson, the problematical Matsudaira Tadanao, was later reprimanded by Ieyasu for having simply stood by and watched the battle unfold before him. Tadanao objected to the rebuke claiming he was obeying Ieyasu's orders to refrain from fighting without permission. The following day, 3 June, saw the final push against the Toyotomi.

The Battle of Osaka Tenno-ji

On 3 June, the great Battle of Osaka Tenno-ji commenced around noon on the wide open areas south of Osaka Castle between the Hirano River to the east, and the waters of Osaka Bay to the west. The Tokugawa forces made their advance from the south. On the right were the 15,000 Maeda troops, supported by the Katagiri clan and Honda Yasunori. In the centre positions of the Tokugawa, the Akita, Asano Nagashige, Honda Tadatomo and interestingly, Sanada Nobuyuki, brother of the leading Osakan commander, Sanada 'Yukimura' Nobushige, waited. Directly behind them were another 15,000 Echizen samurai under the command of Ieyasu's grandson Matsudaira Tadanao, supported by around 7,000 troops under various lesser *daimyo*. On the far left, beside the bay area, were the troops of Date Masamune, backed up by Ieyasu's 6th son, Matsudaira Tadateru. Behind him stood the samurai of the Mizuno and Murakami. Behind the Mizuno and almost on the beaches were the 5,000 samurai of the Asano clan of Wakayama.

Tokugawa Ieyasu moved into a central position behind the Akita, Asano, Honda and Sanada divisions, positioning his own men as a reserve, while Shogun Hidetada's own army, now being led by Todo Takatora and supported by the Hosokawa and Ii troops, advanced to a position supporting the Maeda front right.

In opposition, looking south, with their backs to the Toyotomi's great castle, the Osaka forces had shrunk to around 54,000 samurai. The bulk of the Toyotomi troops had now advanced to just beyond the Tenno-ji area, with the armies of Sanada Nobushige and Mori Katsunaga threatening the Tokugawa central divisions, supported by various smaller warlords' units. They were ordered to remain stationary for the time being.

Ono Harunaga led his men out of Osaka Castle and positioned his battalion to the far east. The Toyotomi plan was to prevent the main Tokugawa forces from advancing too far, while Akashi was to lead his troops from Semba and work their way around to the rear of the Tokugawa allies for a sneak attack. The Chosokabe were to watch this situation and assail the enemy flanks when the opportunity arose. Once this had been achieved and the Tokugawa forces thrown into panic and confusion, Hideyori would emerge from Osaka Castle with his own troops and join the all-out destruction of the invading Tokugawa.

Things did not go to plan, however. The Akashi troops were discovered, their ambush forestalled and they were cut down. The *ronin* among the Mori troops in the centre then ignored orders to hold steady and attacked the Eastern enemy. These overeager *ronin* were looking to make a name for themselves in the hopes of gaining a permanent position once again. When ordered to cease fighting, they simply redoubled their efforts. Unable to stop them, Mori then thought it best to take advantage of their momentum and push ahead, and so ordered his troops fully into battle. Forming two divisions, Mori's men surged forward into the Tokugawa centre, breaking the Akita, Asano, Honda and Tokugawa-allied Sanada ranks and forcing them and their supporters back.

Concerned that the Mori's advance would ruin the carefully-laid plans, Sanada (Yukimura) Nobushige sent word to Hideyori to start his advance and encourage the troops to fight harder. The Echizen forces under the Matsudaira banners then faced an onslaught from the Osaka Sanada troops based south of the castle. The discharge from the Sanadas' gunners tore into the front lines of the 15,000 Matsudaira troops, who could barely hold them off. Seeing this, Ieyasu ordered his own guard unit to take position behind the men of Echizen to hold the lines steady. Their arrival bolstered the Matsudaira before a serious panic ensued.

Cries of treachery then up went in the Tokugawa ranks as Lord Asano of Wakayama suddenly moved forward and crashed into the left rear flank of the Matsudaira. Asano had once served the Toyotomi, and there had been rumours circulating that Asano had held secret communications with the enemy. Confusion reigned as it appeared the Asano had turned.

The Sanada cavalry ahead of them was now making short work of the Matsudaira, but the Matsudaira were giving back as much as they were taking. The Matsudaira samurai were distracted, those in the front watched the Sanada, while those to the rear were about-facing, and weapons were quickly redirected towards the Asano. Through the entire Sengoku period, one could never fully trust the man next to you. Friends, neighbours, even family could turn at any moment and with no warning. The situation was becoming critical for the Tokugawa allies, then, just as hard and fast as they had hit, the Sanada samurai suddenly began their retreat. The Asano incident now appears to have been nothing more than a simple problem of commanders failing to control their hot-headed samurai eager for a fight.

The Osaka-allied Sanada troops continued to back off. Their lord, Sanada Yukimura Nobushige, mastermind of the Osaka battle plan, horribly injured and brought to the point of sheer exhaustion after nearly three days of continual fighting, had stopped in the grounds of the Yasui Shinto Shrine, and sitting below an old pine tree, waited. When the Tokugawa troops approached, he announced his name, and in saying that he was too tired to continue fighting, asked them to give him a few moments during which he removed his armour and cut himself open, allowing a Tokugawa samurai by the name of Nishio Nizaemon to take his head. A statue of the war-weary warrior now sits below the second-generation pine tree in the shrine grounds.

This respite allowed the Matsudaira and Ieyasu's guard units to concentrate their efforts on the Mori and their *ronin* forces. Takatora's troops and the red-armoured men of the Ii clan pushed across the field from Hidetada's van to reinforce the Tokugawa's central force, and in turn protect Ieyasu himself, all the while mounting an attack on the Mori's left flank. Despite the hardships and losses suffered the previous day, around 2 p.m., the troops under Ii Naotaka and Todo Takatora fought so hard and so well that the Mori were forced back towards Osaka Castle.

Seeing the strong Todo and Ii units taking the central positions encouraged the Osakan samurai of Ono Harunaga, Ono Doken and Naito Tadaoki to make an attempt on the Tokugawas' right flank in the hopes of claiming the ultimate prize, the head of Shogun Tokugawa Hidetada himself. The offense was so savage and so close, Hidetada's life was in peril, and Kuroda Nagamasa and Kato Yoshiaki had to physically prevent

the brave Hidetada from entering the fight himself, until the Todo and Ii
had repelled the enemy troops sufficiently enough to allow Ii Naotaka's
samurai to disengage and assist the Shogun, while Todo Takatora's men
kept the opposing Mori at bay.

The Tokugawa allies fought long and hard. The Osaka forces were
desperate. Gunsmoke filled the air, the clash of steel on steel and the roar
of voices could be heard as the armies battled. An hour later, around 3
p.m., war drum and conch shell signals sounded off across the plains, and
the *ronin* units soon turned and ran back into the safety of Osaka Castle.

Toyotomi Hideyori, prevented by his captains, had failed to make an
appearance on the field, and this can be seen as one of the reasons for the
collapse of the Osaka forces so soon. Had Hideyori appeared before his
troops, they would probably have fought harder and longer. Indeed, his
earlier failure to appear at Sekigahara is seen as another reason for the
Tokugawa being able to claim victory. One of Hideyori's cooks, in disgust
and despair, is then said to have set fire to the kitchens. The strong winds
of the day soon fanned the fire into a conflagration and Osaka Castle was
soon ablaze. The fear and confusion within Osaka simply encouraged the
attackers to increase their efforts, and within two hours Tokugawa forces
had entered and captured the huge *ni-no-maru*.

Hideyori, his wife and his mother, Lady Yodo, sought refuge in a fireproof
storeroom. Ono Harunaga organised the dispatch of Hideyori's wife to
her father Hidetada and her grandfather Ieyasu, in the hopes of asking for
mercy and sparing the lives of Hideyori and Lady Yodo. There was to be
no mercy from either. One story tells that having been safely delivered to
her father's war camp, Hidetada had told his own daughter quite bluntly
that she should return to the castle and die with her husband! The very
next morning, 4 June, Toyotomi Hideyori and his mother, Hideyoshi's
precious Chacha, Lady Yodo, fearing defeat and humiliation at the hands
of the Tokugawa, committed *seppuku* in a small storeroom just behind the
main keep as it continued to burn. Osaka had fallen, the Toyotomi clan
were no more. The Tokugawa were now the undisputed masters of Japan.

The fighting had been particularly violent, and seventy-one of
Takatora's samurai, his top men, including cousins and relatives such
as Todo Takanori, Todo Ujikatsu, Yoshikatsu and Yoshishige, Kuwana
Yajibei and more had been killed in action. Takatora was so shocked by
the losses, it is said that he was unable to eat for days afterwards. Because

of the great numbers of his men that had been killed, Takatora staged a mass funeral at the Joko-ji Temple in Yao. Meanwhile, a *kubi-jiken*, head-viewing ceremony, was held with over 870 heads placed on display, after which the planks on which the heads were arrayed were given to the temple. The bloodied unwashed wooden planks were stored, dried, and later used in the main hall's new ceiling, bloodstains and all. The bloodstained ceiling can be seen to this day. Of those 870 heads, 851 had been taken by the Todo troops. Watanabe Kanbei and his men had taken 63 heads, but because of his argument with Takatora, Watanabe had taken back his unit's 63 heads, and thrown them away in anger, and so only 788 heads went on the official records. Even then, Todo Takatora's men had taken the record number of heads at Osaka, and they had also suffered the greatest losses of any army in the Tokugawa forces during the Siege of Osaka. Following the action at Osaka, Takatora is said to have entered the Nanzen-ji, a Buddhist temple in the Higashiyama foothills of Kyoto, and spent six long days deep in prayer for the souls of his slain men.

One of the reasons the Todo troops were so strong in battle was because of their leader, Takatora. Not only did he ensure they were well armed and properly trained – in fact, the Todo clan's command post design, troop manoeuvres and formations used at Osaka were considered so effective, that they were adhered to and learned by the Todo troops throughout the Edo period – but he showed genuine care and concern for his men. When men fell in battle or during service, he would mourn them afterwards, sparing no expense in ensuring that proper Buddhist funeral rites were offered to the deceased and their families, and that memorial rites were regularly performed. Records show that in 1714, the Todo clan and their men held special services at the Joko-ji Temple to pray for the souls of the men who paid the ultimate sacrifice for the clan 100 years before in the Battle of Yao, and that memorial rites were staged every 50 years after that. Takatora was quick to generously reward his men too, and never forgot a debt of gratitude. The story of the former samurai who ran a *mochi* rice cake shop, and the hiring of former comrades on his rise in stipend and his paying for the erection of a gravestone for the enemy Otani Yoshitsugu, are all indicative of Takatora's fine character, and why his brave samurai admired and respected him, and were willing to give their lives for this man.

The battle had been a close struggle for Takatora, but success here, the losses incurred by the Toyotomi forces, and Takatora's decision to fight to protect the lives of Tokugawa Ieyasu and the Shogun Hidetada served to heighten his already fine reputation. Ieyasu was most pleased with his close friend's actions. Following the battle, it was reported that the prisoners taken had made mention that 'What we feared most was the sight of the Golden Cow's Tongue standard of the Todo units!' Indeed, Takatora's *umajirushi* battle standard had been a large gold-leaf covered, elongated gourd-shaped device. He had also used a red cloth hoop with red tasselled streamers, resembling a modern-day windsock as well as his famed *shiro-mochi* battle flags.

It has been said that during the whole of the Osaka campaign, the Todo forces suffered the greatest number of casualties among the Tokugawa forces. After the battle, while at Edo Castle, many *daimyo*, including those who had not been able to take part in the Osaka campaign, asked Ii Naotaka about his experiences alongside Takatora, and he appeared more than happy to entertain them, regaling them with talk about his adventures and exploits. Later when Takatora appeared at Edo Castle, he too was soon surrounded by many *daimyo* wishing to hear more war stories. To those enquiring, Takatora was quoted as simply saying 'ただ己の職責を、どうにか果たせただけでござる,' – 'I did what I had to do to fulfil my duties'.

Takatora had seen death and destruction time and again throughout his life. He had been in countless battles and situations where his own life had been in danger, yet the violence of the Osaka campaigns seems to have weighed heavily on him. Takatora appears to have been haunted by dreams of those vassals and relatives killed in the battle for nights afterwards. He could only take solace in the knowledge that he had fought hard on the front lines, and his sacrifices had helped to achieve peace throughout the land.

Thanks largely to the efforts of the Todo clan, and the equally fine fighting skills of the Ii, the Tokugawa were victorious, and now held complete authority over the nation. For Takatora's successes in the Summer Siege of Osaka, Ieyasu added 50,000 *koku* and the four counties of Suzuka, Age, Mie, and Isshi of Ise, bringing his stipend up to a total of 270,950 *koku*.

The Death of Ieyasu

Osaka had been conquered. The Tokugawa were without rivals. But on the first day of the 4th lunar month of 1616, Tokugawa Ieyasu fell ill. He had been falconing near Tanaka Castle in Shizuoka and had felt unwell after enjoying a dinner of *tempura*, fried battered fish.[3] Ieyasu soon called in Takatora and Honda Masazumi, instructing them to have adequate forces prepared in order to strike at any rebellion that might break out on his death. The military commander who had long assisted Ieyasu at Sumpu, Hori Naoyori (1577–29 July 1639), was then called to his side, and given the instructions that if anything untoward, such as an insurrection, were to happen upon news of his demise, Todo Takatora was to lead any army against whatever enemy came forth. Takatora was to be supported by Ii Naotaka, with Hori himself to be situated in the middle. While other long-term and loyal retainers were given orders regarding his funeral and burial, it was Todo Takatora in whom Ieyasu put the most trust, and who was left in charge of the important military affairs.

Ieyasu died around noon on the 17th day of the 4th month – 1 June 1616 by the modern calendar – aged 75. Takatora was at his side. In fact it had been Takatora who was most in attendance during Ieyasu's final days. Ten days before passing away, Ieyasu on his deathbed had called for Takatora, and in thanking him for his services, had cried, saying he would miss him in the afterlife. Takatora calmed his friend, promising to serve him in the afterlife.

'But I am of the Jodo (Nichiren) sect, and you are of the Tendai Sect,' Ieyasu reminded him. 'We will be in different heavens.'

Later that day, Takatora sought out the monk Tenkai, who also served Ieyasu closely, and asked that he be made a disciple of the great monk, and be admitted into the Tendai sect. Tenkai agreed, and confirmed him there and then, giving him the sect name of Kanshoin. Takatora was then able to return to the dying Ieyasu's side and told him that he was now of the same sect, and therefore able to continue to serve Ieyasu after death. Both are said to have shed tears. A greatly pleased Ieyasu then decreed that Takatora and Tenkai were to stand on his right and left as tutelary

---

3. Despite theories that he had been poisoned, it is commonly believed that Ieyasu was most probably suffering from stomach cancer and the oily food had simply hastened a further upset of his stomach.

deities of the Tokugawa clan. It was to be one of the last orders given by Tokugawa Ieyasu.

As per his will, Ieyasu's body was carried to his grave atop Mount Kunou, but Takatora was not listed among those escorting his body up the steep slopes. Ieyasu's body was laid to rest in the Kunouzan Shrine overlooking what is today Shizuoka City, and a small shrine was to be erected at Nikko as per his wishes. His grandson, the third Shogun Iemitsu, was a great admirer of his grandfather, and decided that a small shrine was out of the question. For a man of his grandfather's stature, a man who was now a god, only the grandest, most gorgeous of shrines would do. The only man Iemitsu could trust to design and lead construction of such a shrine, was the man trusted by his grandfather, also his father, and now a faithful advisor to himself, Todo Takatora.

Takatora did indeed work hard on the initial design of the Nikko Toshogu, and employed the master carpenters of his home village of Koura, the Koura family, to act as the head carpenters. The first of the Koura carpenters, Koura Mitsuhiro, had been employed by Oda Nobunaga to work on Azuchi Castle alongside Owari-based carpenters, the Okabe family. Mitsuhiro had also built a *yashiki* villa for Ieyasu at Fushimi Castle, and had long assisted Todo Takatora on a number of projects. The Nikko Toshogu took a year and a half to complete, employing 4,540,000 labourers, carpenters and artisans and the timber from 147,600 trees at a modern-day cost estimated to be 58.6 billion yen, the equivalent of around $US542,838,873.20 or 450,884,280.60 Euros (May 2021 estimates).

Almost a year after the death of Ieyasu, on 16 April 1617, Shogun Hidetada and Takatora were scheduled to travel together and pay their respects at the Nikko Toshogu, but Takatora was forced to cancel on account of poor health. For Takatora this would have been almost inexcusable. He had never missed memorial services for Hidenaga, nor his men killed in action, not even the lowly carpenters killed when a typhoon destroyed the almost completed keep of Iga Ueno, and yet his own health prevented him from attending to his master and friend's services.

Chapter 6

The Later Years

Strict Disciplinarian, Man of Principle

One of Takatora's precepts was; 人を斬るばかりが武士ではない。人を生かすのも武士だ。 'It is not for a samurai to take lives. It is for a samurai to save lives'. According to Takatora, a true samurai did not simply cut a person down, but found a way to make the best use of that person.

During a particular battle Takatora had managed to take a high-ranked warrior's head as a trophy, and as the battle continued to rage, instead of temporarily retiring from the battlefield to register it, or have one of his men depart from the battlefield to clean and prepare it for the later head-viewing ceremony, he asked one of his rearguard *ashigaru* to keep the head for him while Takatora returned to the fighting. The *ashigaru* accepted this task, and Takatora left the head with him.

Exhausted from marching and fighting, the weary *ashigaru* soon dozed off while he rested and waited, and in the meantime the valuable head he was safeguarding for Takatora was stolen from him. Later Takatora approached the man and asked for the head back. The nervous *ashigaru* fell to his hands and knees before Takatora, and bowing profusely explained that the head had been stolen from him after he had fallen asleep. As an apology, the *ashigaru* then offered his own head in exchange for the one Takatora had entrusted to him. Taking pity on the low-ranking warrior, Takatora told him 'Your head is no substitute for the enemy! I can take another enemy head, but once you lose your life, it cannot be returned. Your life is more valuable than that of an enemy head.' The *ashigaru* was deeply moved when he heard that and thankful for having been spared, waited only long enough to be dismissed by Takatora before rushing off into the thick of the fighting in an effort to redeem himself. The *ashigaru* boldly took on a samurai well above his own rank, and in killing him took his head while still housed in its helmet. Such trophies, known as *kubi-*

kabuto, were considered an auspicious catch. Having taken the head, the *ashigaru* sought out Takatora before presenting it to him. Again, bowing low to the ground before the giant warrior, the *ashigaru* addressed him; 'Lord Takatora, please accept this *kubi-kabuto* I took in battle in place of the one I carelessly lost. Because you spared my life, I was able to take that of an enemy.' Takatora was very pleased by the man's attitude and bravery.

The Noh Actor

Todo Takatora was a patron of the arts and particularly fond of the performing arts of Noh and *Sarugaki*. His homes often had Noh stages built in the grounds, and he would invite friends and colleagues to enjoy performances as a show of hospitality. Kita Shichidayu (1586–1653) was a descendant of one of the four leading Noh theatre troupes of the Muromachi period. Shichidayu was not just a master of Noh, but a master of the spear, serving Hideyoshi as a samurai. Even after Hideyoshi's death, he remained loyal to the Toyotomi family and had survived both the Winter and Summer Sieges of Osaka. However, when Osaka Castle finally fell, fearing for his life, the actor-warrior sought out Takatora, and begged his acquaintance for assistance. Takatora was concerned that his old friend's actions would cost him his head, and so, suggesting he retire from the life of a warrior, sent him to Kyushu. When Ieyasu later enquired about Shichidayu's whereabouts, Takatora told him what had happened, and suggested that Ieyasu agree to forgive Shichidayu if Takatora would employ him only as a Noh actor. Ieyasu did so. Takatora lived by his own words, 'It is not for a samurai to take lives. It is for a samurai to save lives.' Takatora saved the man's life and protected him as a Noh actor, the life to which he was best suited. Shichidayu would form the Kita Ryu of Noh, now recognised as one of the five main schools of Noh. Instead of taking the man's life, Takatora allowed him to live and use that life to enhance the culture of Japan.

Takatora was an extraordinary man for the times. Among his many traits, his kindness and generosity towards his men were renowned. He told them, 'If you ever wish to leave my employ and join another clan, I will fully understand. Just remember, if you do leave, you are welcome to return if things don't go well.'

There were very few who ever did decide to leave to test the offer, but those that did, he personally invited to a tea ceremony, during which he would present them with a farewell gift of a *tachi* battle sword, and reminded them that 'If it doesn't work out, you will be welcome to return to my service.' He meant it.

Those that did return were usually given more than their old positions and old stipends – they were often given a higher rank and a raise! In the case of one vassal, Okamoto Yaichiemon, after he had resigned from the Todo's employ, he returned meekly only to be offered a 200-*koku* raise, bringing him up to 500 *koku*, and made the *ashigaru taishi*, captain of the *ashigaru* corps. However, some time later, he approached Takatora and told him he was leaving again. Again Takatora thanked him for his service, and on parting told Okamoto that if this new master was not to his liking, he could always return. Not long after, Okamoto returned again with his tail between his legs. This time too Takatora welcomed him home, returning him to his former position as *ashigaru taishi*, but this time with a 1,000 *koku* stipend. Takatora believed in people. He would take care of his men and would forgive those he believed had skills or value.

Bankrupt

Another story that also shows Takatora's wisdom and character tells of how five of his vassals once went bankrupt. Two of the five had frequented the red light district far too often, and falling into debt, were forced to sell their household items. The other three were over-fond of gambling and like their roving counterparts were forced to sell everything to cover their losses and went bankrupt. The two men who had taken to carousing with women were cast out. The gamblers, on the other hand, had their stipends reduced by a third, and were ordered to change their gambling habits.

When asked by an aide about the reason for this differing treatment, Takatora answered: 'A man who loses his home and belongings by falling for the touch of a woman has no merits, no wisdom and no courage. However, gambling is different. It is not desirable, but certainly shows spirit and a vigorous desire to win. That sort of man still has use.'

The Hairdresser

One day, when Takatora was at his residence in Kyoto, he came across a skilled *tokoya*, a traditional hairdresser, and offered to hire him for 13 *koku* and three assistants' allowances, but the hairdresser said, 'Since I support a mother and wife, I would like 15 *koku* and five assistants' allowance'. Takatora refused, saying, 'Fifteen *koku* is the stipend I pay for my infantry. It would be an insult to my warriors to offer that much for such a lowly skill.' This episode shows how much Takatora cared for his retainers.

Samurai Death and *Junshi*

Four months after the passing of his dear friend and master, Ieyasu, Takatora's wife O-Ku passed away on 30 September 1616. She was buried at the historical Shitenno-ji Temple in Tsu where her grave stands to this day. The Shitenno-ji's grounds also contain the grave of Tsuchida Gozen, the mother of Oda Nobunaga.

Death had surrounded Takatora, as it had all who lived and fought in the violence of sixteenth and early seventeenth-century Japan. Indeed, death was a way of life for the samurai. In the Sengoku and early Edo period, when one's lord died, many of his closest vassals would commit *junshi*, an act of self-immolation in order to follow one's master in death. It was a practice known to have existed as early as the seventh century. When Ieyasu's fourth son, Matsudaira Tadayoshi, died in April 1607, seven of his closest vassals followed him in death. Two months later, Ieyasu's second-born son, Yuki Hideyasu, also died and seven retainers followed suit.

Takatora realised that the majority of those that followed this practice were important figures in the clans, usually councillors, elders and others of foremost importance. He had noted that the deaths of these talented people often caused a power vacuum or a shift in the political balance, leading to a weakening of the clan. With this in mind, Takatora had a special box placed in the main audience chamber of his primary residence and instructed his staff that any one of his retainers or servants considering committing *junshi* upon his death were to leave their full names in the box. Over forty names were dropped in the wooden container. When the same command was given at his elegant mansion in Sumpu, over thirty names were left.

Deeply touched by the dedication of his followers, Takatora took the list of seventy-three names to Ieyasu in Sumpu and showed him, telling Ieyasu, 'There are so many willing to die when I die. These people are loyal servants to my family, highly experienced in matters of war, peace and administration, and as such are an asset to the Tokugawa. Please, use your executive powers to ban the practice of *junshi* and end the risk of losing so many important and loyal lives.' Ieyasu quickly grasped the situation and readily agreed, and in accepting the wise Takatora's advice once again issued a decree. This was accepted by many other *daimyo*, but not officially put into effect until the fourth Shogun, Ietsuna, made it so. Even then, in the years following there were known cases of it being violated.

With Ieyasu's consent, Takatora strictly prohibited the act of martyrdom within the Todo clan, believing it to be a waste of loyal human life. He gathered together those who had offered to follow him in death, and in thanking them for their devotion, explained his reasons and then forbid any of them to commit *junshi*, and encouraged them instead to be of even greater service to the Todo and the Tokugawa clans should he, Takatora, die. Of those seventy-three, only one man refused to obey the order. He had lost his right arm in battle, and even though he survived, considered himself useless and a burden on Takatora, and so he prayed that he be allowed to martyr himself to at least be able serve Takatora properly in the afterlife. Takatora had expected such a reaction, and so he showed them a proclamation written by Ieyasu.

The loyal Todo clan is the Advance Guard of the Tokugawa. If anyone refuses to obey Lord Takatora's orders and commits *junshi* on his death, I will be forced to rescind the Todo clan's position. I command you to live!

On seeing this, the man agreed, promising not to compromise the Todo clan's standing.

Of the many famous maxims attributed to the samurai, one of the best known is; 'Live each day as though it were to be your last'. That particular saying has been attributed to Todo Takatora, and it can be seen engraved in stone at Tsu Castle. In Todo Takatora's last will and testament, it is written; 'If you spend every day from the moment you wake up in the morning thinking that today is the day you die, you will never be lost, confused or misled.'This is also the motto of the Todo clan. ·

In the Warring States period, when lives were constantly in the balance, hesitation and indecision were the worst of enemies. An ambiguous attitude, a delay in response or action could lead to one being suspected of treason. Todo Takatora changed his lord seven times in his life, but in each case he served his lord without hesitation, trusting his own judgment. Todo Takatora was also faithful to his vassals once they defected because he judged that they had made the right choice.

Tamaru Castle

Takatora was yet again to be recognised for his efforts and fine service to the Shogunate. In 1617 Takatora received Tamaru Castle, in Tamaki, Mie Prefecture, from Tokugawa Hidetada and an extra 50,000 *koku*, bringing him to 323,000 *koku* in total.

Tamaru Castle was founded in 1336 by Kitabatake Chikafusa during the violent Nanboku-cho civil war (1336–92), a result of the Imperial court being split into two factions. The noble Kitabatake were stalwarts of the Southern Court and built Tamaru as a defence against the supporters of the Northern Court. This *hirayama* castle saw action several times during those turbulent years, and was later to become one of the Kitabatake clan's main castles. It was such a well-built and magnificent castle, it became known as the Tamaru Gosho, or the Tamaru Imperial Palace.

Tamaru and the Kitabatake clan were attacked by Oda Nobunaga's forces in 1569 when attempting to annex Ise, an attack they faced bravely. Nobunaga's second son Nobukatsu was later adopted into the Kitabatake clan as part of the peace process and to strengthen ties between the two clans. Nobukatsu was based in Tamaru Castle, and was responsible for having constructed the stone walls and a small three-storey tower keep in 1575, just before completion of his father's masterpiece castle at Azuchi. As such, Tamaru is believed to have been among the earliest castles to have sported a *tenshu*, tower keep. This was badly damaged in a fire that broke out in the main bailey around 1580 and due to the damage Nobukatsu moved his headquarters to the nearby coastal Matsugashima Castle. Tamaru was soon repaired, and changed ownership a number of times. In 1600, *daimyo* Inaba Michito'o was master of Tamaru. Although Takatora was awarded the domain, and with it both Tamaki and Tamaru Castles, he never up took residence in either of them, instead his representative Kanou Touzaimon took the role of resident castellan of Tamaru. Except for a single remaining gate, Tamaru Castle was mostly demolished in the Meiji period, although the castle's impressive stone walls, baileys and parts of the moats still remain in very good condition. Tamaru is also listed as one of the Extended Top 100 Castles of Japan.

In 1619 Fukushima Masanori was dismissed from his fief at Hiroshima on the grounds of his having repaired a section of wall at Hiroshima Castle that had been damaged by flooding in a typhoon. At the time, there was a strict law against any castle repairs or construction without the explicit permission of the *Bakufu*. Masanori had requested permission on numerous occasions, but a reply had yet to come from Edo. Annoyed at the ongoing delays, he went ahead and had the walls repaired. For this he was severely reprimanded by the Shogunate, and demoted. He was sent instead to Kawanakajima domain, with a great loss of income.

A certain retainer of Fukushima Masanori named Kurushima Wakasa had been released from service in the restructuring following Masanori's downfall, but was soon offered a stipend of 5,000 *koku* by the Asano clan who had been given Hiroshima in Masanori's place. Takatora was also interested in obtaining Wakasa's services and tried to summon him for double that amount, but the offer was refused. When asked by Takatora the reason why, Wakasa replied, 'My old lord, Masanori, and Lord Takatora did not always get along well. It would not be right for me to accept such a generous offer.' Impressed by the man's integrity Takatora recommended him to Wakayama Castle's Lord Tokugawa Yorinobu of Kishu, who hired him for 10,000 *koku*.

Osaka Castle

The first Osaka Castle was built by Toyotomi Hideyoshi on the ruins of the Higashi Hongan-ji Temple, over which the Jodo Shinshu sect adherents and Oda Nobunaga had waged a ten-plus-year war. Nobunaga attacked and burned it all down in 1580. Having taken over the Oda clan's power, Hideyoshi commenced building Osaka Castle in late 1582, the year of Nobunaga's death, as a symbol of the Toyotomi's newfound authority. As has been explained, that castle was attacked twice by the Tokugawa forces in 1614 and again in 1615 in which it was destroyed. Tokugawa Ieyasu's grandson, Matsudaira Takaaki, was then named master of Osaka, and set about rebuilding the town and castle. He would later relocate to Takatora's former place of residence, Nara's Yamato Koriyama Castle, in 1619 and Osaka would become the property of the Edo *Bakufu*. From November of 1619, Shogun Hidetada requested Todo Takatora take charge of the complete redesign of Osaka Castle.

Takatora took around 90 days to conduct a complete survey of the grounds and decide on the redevelopments to be made. The Edo *Bakufu* wanted no remnants of the Toyotomi to exist and so the entire layout of the castle was to undergo major changes. Takatora's plans called for the moats to be made wider and deeper, the *ishigaki* stone walls to be made higher. Takatora extensively redeveloped the castle's *nawabari* layout, and became the overseer on various dry-stone wall projects. Many of the stones for the work came from the now-abandoned Fushimi Castle but, as the reconstruction of Osaka was such an extensive undertaking, there were not enough to complete the work. Extra stone was sourced from Shodoshima, a large island in the Seto Inland Sea and now part of Kagawa Prefecture, where the rock was cut before being shipped to the construction site. More stone was cut from Mount Ono in what is now Kizugawa City in the Kamo region of Kyoto, and also from Kyoto's mountainous Kasagi region. In 1626, the stonework of Osaka was completed. Remaining documents show that around 520 stones were left unused. The size, numbers and details of these remaining *zannen ishi*, or 'Unfortunate Stones' as they were termed, were recorded, such was Takatora's meticulous nature.

Once again the *tenka bushin* system was enforced, in which various *daimyo* were expected to participate in the construction at their own expense. Todo Takatora would set them sections and tasks which he expected to be carried out to his high standards. In the case of the *daimyo* of the northern Hokuriku districts, and Lord Maeda Toshitsune of Kanazawa in particular, Takatora was appalled at the low level of skill and poor quality of the *ishigaki* stone wall construction, and in complaining that they were hindering rather than helping construction, had the Ano-shu stonemasons take over work on the stone walls allocated to the Maeda clan. According to details in the *Chu-kin Roku* documents, many tens of thousands of workers were employed at Osaka. Construction began in 1620 and continued for eight years.

Nijo Castle

Nijo Castle in Kyoto was originally Ieyasu's residence and a highly visible symbol of his authority in the capital. Last refurbished in 1602, just prior to Ieyasu becoming Shogun, it was supposed to have been given another overhaul in 1619 when Ieyasu's granddaughter was betrothed to Emperor Go-Mizunoo. The Shogun Hidetada had directly asked Takatora to oversee the work, but the reconstruction of Osaka Castle being undertaken at the time was deemed of higher military importance and so Takatora was unable to turn his attentions to Nijo until 1621.

Takatora is then said to have drawn up two layouts for Nijo Castle, and shown them both to his son-in-law, the very talented designer, architect, warrior and tea master Kobori Masakazu, better known as Kobori Enshu,[1] and asked him which one he thought was the better of the two. Enshu looked at them both and with a shocked look on his face answered quickly, 'This first design is, . . . dreadful.' Takatora agreed, saying it was done half-heartedly in an effort to improve the image and standing of the Shogun, while putting himself down. 'To propose only a single plan would put one above his master, removing his decision-making role. By submitting two possibilities, the Shogun will choose the best design, proving that he has the knowledge and understanding, while the remaining poor design infers that my abilities and senses are below that of the Shogun. It makes him look and feel intelligent.' Takatora explained to his son-in-law that 'It is a retainer's job to make his master look good.' During the reconstruction of Osaka, while Takatora worked on the general layout, walls and moats, the talented Kobori Enshu was responsible for the design and building of the *tenshu*, various *yagura*, *tamon yagura* and the luxurious palace.

Takatora was in charge of three major elements; designing the overall reconfiguration of Osaka Castle, done around 1620. The reconstruction work took place between 1623 and 1624, and the completion of the high stone walls ended around 1626. Two of Takatora's men, a skilled archer named Yoshida Motonau and an artillery specialist by the name of Yonemura Kazunaga, suggested the *ishigaki*'s uppermost stones, just below the walls that topped them, have battlement-like holes for the

---

1. Other records hint that it may have been Takatora's retainer Shindo Kyuemon who was shown the designs, rather than Kobori Enshu, although it is highly probable that both men would have been shown the same plans.

firing of guns. Takatora accepted the suggestion and designed it so that the stones were carved in a semiconical shape, allowing for repositioning of the guns, and with a small hole on the outer edge. These were known as *hazama-ishi*. The idea was later used in Edo Castle's Ote-mon and Hirakawa-mon gates, and was also adopted by Ikeda Tadao for the walls around the Tsukimi Yagura at Okayama Castle.

While working on the redevelopment of Osaka, Takatora had been approached by Lord Tokugawa Yorinobu (28 April 1602–19 February 1671). Yorinobu, Ieyasu's 10th son, had first been lord of Mito, then the initial lord of his father's estates at Suruga Province and based in Sumpu from the age of eight before being awarded Wakayama Domain in Kii on 27 August 1619, becoming the founder of the Kii branch of the Tokugawa clan. His wife was the daughter of another famed castle architect, Kato Kiyomasa. Yorinobu contacted Takatora and requested his help in enlarging and strengthening the *minami-no-maru* and *suna-no-maru* of Wakayama Castle. Takatora had worked on Wakayama in his early years when his fifth lord, Hidenaga, had built the initial castle. Since then, many changes had taken place, and Takatora agreed to help, seeming only too happy to be of service and visit Wakayama again.

That same year, Takatora become the de-facto lord of Takamatsu Castle in modern-day Kagawa Prefecture, Shikoku. In 1621 Ikoma Masatoshi, Lord of Takamatsu Castle, died aged 37 from an illness. His son and heir was too young to become *daimyo* of Takamatsu, and the future of the domain became a concern. Ikoma's wife was an adopted daughter of Takatora, and so he stepped in to become the official lord in order to support his daughter and grandson. Because of his duties and heavy workload, Takatora was unable to go to Takamatsu himself, and instead sent his trusted vassal Nishijima Hachibei Yukitomo as his representative.[2] Nishijima oversaw the various political and administrative duties and also undertook vital waterworks projects, all the while reporting regularly and directly to Takatora. Despite their best efforts, the Ikoma clan would face further problems in the future. Almost ten years after Takatora's passing,

---

2. Hamamatsu-born Nishijima Hachibei Yukitomo (1596–19 April 1680), became an apprentice to Todo Takatora from the age of 17 with a stipend of 150 *koku*. Nishijima served Takatora and the Tsu clan well, successfully developing many water-use and irrigation projects that benefited future generations, including the Obada Shinden (present-day Nabari City) and the Undei irrigation canals in the Tsu domain, amongst others.

his grandson would be relieved of his duties in 1640 aged just 19 as he was unable to control the actions of a number of the clan retainers, bringing shame on the domain. A branch of the Matsudaira clan, relatives of the Tokugawa, then received the castle. Along with Takatora's Imabari Castle and Nakatsu Castle of Oita Prefecture, Takamatsu Castle was one of the few having seawater moats.

The Second Yodo Castle

Now aged around 67 and when most would be looking to enjoy retirement, Takatora was kept busy working on various castle projects, including Matsudaira Sadatsune's new Yodo Castle.

Shogun Tokugawa Hidetada had awarded the Yodo area in Fushimi, south of Kyoto, along with 35,000 *koku* to his cousin Matsudaira Sadatsune in 1623, and gave orders that a new castle was to be constructed there to strengthen Kyoto's defences. The site chosen was just south of the original Yodo Castle which, it may be remembered, Takatora had completely redeveloped in 1589 as a safe haven for Lady Chacha (Lady Yodo) and Hideyoshi's first child to be born. That same castle had played a major role in the Battle of Yamazaki in which Takatora had taken part when Hideyoshi's forces sought revenge against Akechi Mitsuhide for having attacked and killed Oda Nobunaga in 1582.

Once again, Takatora's trademark design elements can be seen in this castle too. The baileys were carved from the banks of the Katsura River into squares, with an 80m by 80m *ni-no-maru* bailey connected to the north of the large square *honmaru* of around 85m by 125m forming a basic L shape. This was surrounded by three sets of wide moats, the outermost *sotobori* was 70m wide, the *nakabori* or central moat was 20m across and the innermost *uchibori* moat was 30m. To the north-east, facing the L-shaped indent was the *san-no-maru*. Adjoining that and surrounding the main *honmaru* and *ni-no-maru* precincts was a long thin island-like strip of land. Other islands forming baileys were dotted around the main central precincts.

Recycled stones, timbers and structures taken from Fushimi Castle were also used in the construction. The initial plan was to dismantle the main keep for use at Yodo Castle, but it was later decided that it would be used at Kyoto's Nijo Castle, and Nijo's keep would instead be relocated to

Yodo. As Yodo Castle was expecting to receive Fushimi's large tower keep, a wide stone foundation base had been built to house it. As the smaller Nijo Castle keep required much less space, three smaller two-storey *yagura* watchtowers were constructed atop the remaining corners of the keep foundation, and connected by a *tamon yagura* all around, forming a fortified courtyard design, similar to Himeji Castle's main complex. In fact, building materials and structures from Himeji, Fushimi, Shoru-ji, Nijo and the old Yodo Castles were used here. Yodo was protected by thirty-eight *yagura* and twenty-two gates.

Only parts of the *honmaru* with its high, straight stone walls reaching 16.5m in height from the moat's waterline and 20m-wide moats typical of Takatora's work can still be seen at the ruins of Yodo Castle. A 5m-wide *inubashiri* around the east and southern edges of the *tenshudai* keep base also suggest Takatora's design work. Unfortunately, much of the excellent design of Yodo's outer areas have been lost to modern housing and development. Remaining records show that the Todo clan provided stones for the walls, and amongst the 143 different types of *kokuin*, rock identification carvings, Todo clan ones can be found here, further proof that Takatora did indeed take part in the construction of this castle.

Yodo Castle would be among the last of Takatora's castles to see action. In January 1868, the Shogunate was on the verge of collapse. The Emperor Meiji was ready to take the helm of his country, leading to the last civil war between the forces loyal to the Shogunate and those in support of Imperial restoration. In the Boshin War's Battle of Toba Fushimi, the then master of Yodo Castle, Inaba Masakuni, refused the retreating Shogun Yoshinobu and his troops entry into the castle, shutting the gates in the Shogun's face, and instead, offered his allegiance to the new Imperial Forces.

Incidentally, a remaining *shachihoko*, tiger-fish roof ornament, said to have come from Yodo Castle can be seen in the gardens of the Rinsho-in Temple of the Myoshin-ji Temple complex in Kyoto. Another is on display in the Archeological Museum of Kyoto.

Takatora's Last Master

Tokugawa Hidetada retired as Shogun in the summer of 1623, and passed the position on to his son Iemitsu. As the 19-year-old grandson of Ieyasu became Shogun, he became Todo Takatora's tenth and final master. Although 48 years his senior, Iemitsu, like his father and grandfather, thought highly of Takatora and regularly sought his advice. By now the 67-year-old Takatora was having problems with his eyes. His legs were beginning to become unsteady and his back was weakening. Years of hard fighting and stoic service had almost worn him out. Seeing his elderly friend in this state, Iemitsu then ordered Edo Castle's *honmaru goten* palace be remodelled, removing or altering any split-level sections and stairs, straightening out corners where possible, making it what we in the modern world would recognise as 'barrier free' to better facilitate visits by Todo Takatora. No other vassal would ever be afforded such attention.

In 1625 Takatora had written instructions to his son in his will. 'A *Daimyo*'s job,' he explained in his own hand, 'is to look after the lands within a domain at the pleasure of the shogun. The *daimyo* do not own the land, we are merely caretakers.' His son understood the message well. This way of thinking aligns closely with that of the earlier warlord and first of the National Unifiers, Oda Nobunaga, who was of the opinion that the Emperor owned the land, and the *daimyo* were caretakers. With this in mind he had commenced his ambitious project of unification in an effort to end the Sengoku wartime practice of using force to subjugate or take domains, something that could only be achieved with the nation under a single master.

Takatora's extensive redevelopment and rebuilding of the stone walls surrounding Osaka Castle were finally completed in 1626. Very few structures remain at Osaka Castle, and the current concrete keep rebuilt in 1935 is a very historically inaccurate depiction. It was an attempt to build a replica of Toyotomi Hideyoshi's keep, but on the base stones of the later, larger Tokugawa period keep, resulting in an anathema of a structure. One of the remarkable things about Osaka Castle today is the excellent condition of Takatora's work, the stone walls and moats. The area has suffered very few major earthquakes over the last 400 years, meaning that the mighty stone walls and wide moats remain as they were. This is also testament to the excellent skills of Todo Takatora and his ability to properly lead and instruct other *daimyo* in quality construction methods.

The Kato Yoshiaki Story

On 9 February 1627 the husband of another of Todo Takatora's daughters, the second *daimyo* of the Mutsu Aizu domain, Gamo Fushimi, died of smallpox aged just 26. As the couple had no children, the Gamo clan came to an unfortunate and untimely end. The Shogunate offered Aizu domain first to Takatora, who, although grateful, refused it on account of not wanting the extra responsibility affecting his work for the Shogunate. The retired Shogun Hidetada then asked Takatora who he considered the best person for the position. Takatora is said to have answered 'Kato Yoshiaki'. As has been explained, the two were formerly on good terms, but were known to have argued heatedly over tactics during the ill-fated Korean invasion some 30 years before. From that time on they had become bitter rivals and were yet to reconcile. Surprised, Hidetada asked 'Why Yoshiaki? I thought you two had differences?' Takatora answered 'My private feelings and my professional thoughts I keep separate. Kato Yoshiaki is a fine administrator, and an intelligent man. He is without doubt in my mind the best person for such a position.' The domain and position were indeed offered to a very grateful Kato Yoshiaki.

When Kato Yoshiaki later heard about how such good fortune had come upon him, and what Takatora had said about him, he went directly to the Todo clan villa in Edo and on his hands and knees before his giant of a friend, sincerely apologised to Takatora for any problems in the past. Having formally reconciled, Takatora and Yoshiaki were once again on good terms from that time on.

Ueno Toshogu, Edo

It was Todo Takatora who built the Ueno Toshogu, dedicated to Tokugawa Ieyasu and the Tokugawa clan in what is now Tokyo's Ueno Park in 1627. Being a Toshogu shrine, it is dedicated to the Tokugawa, but alongside Ieyasu, his close friend and confidante, Todo Takatora, was also made a deity and is also enshrined here. The 8th Shogun, Tokugawa Yoshimune, and the 15th and final Shogun, Tokugawa Yoshinobu, too were added as deities upon their deaths in 1751 and 1913 respectively.

Although initially constructed by Todo Takatora, the entire shrine was rebuilt in the complex and gorgeous *gongen zukuri* style of architecture by the third Shogun, Ieyasu's grandson Tokugawa Iemitsu, in 1651. The historical Ueno Toshogu shrine has survived numerous earthquakes, fires, the 1868 Battle of Ueno and even Second World War bombing.

The low-lying Mount Ueno was originally known as Shinobi Oka (literally Stealth, or Ninja Hill) and renamed Ueno after Takatora's fief of Iga Ueno. The hill was the site of Takatora's main villa in Edo. To allow his friend the Tendai sect priest Tenkai to build the Kan'ei-ji Temple, dedicated to the Tokugawa on the actual site of his home, Takatora offered to return his land to the *Bakufu* and relocated his residence to Edo's Yanagihara area in 1625. Takatora suggested fellow *daimyo* Tsugaru Nobuhira, lord of Hirosaki, and Hori Naoyori of Murakami Domain in Niigata who also resided on Mount Ueno to donate their lands too. Tenkai's Kan'ei-ji was a magnificent temple. Prestigious, prosperous and powerful, it consisted of over thirty structures, and contained the graves of six of the fifteen Tokugawa Shoguns. (Another six were buried at the Zojo-ji Temple. Ieyasu was buried at the Kunouzan Toshogu in Shizuoka, while Iemitsu's remains were interred in the Toshogu at Nikko. The last Shogun, Yoshinobu, is buried in the nearby Yanaka Cemetery.)

Takatora had three other such *yashiki* residences in Edo. One was located in Chiyoda-Ku not far from the gates of the mighty Edo Castle. Another was at Kanda Izumi town's Komagome Somei Dori. The extant Izumi area received its name from Takatora's title, *Izumi no Kami*, Lord of Izumi. The third residence was at Ryogoku 1-chome, near the modern-day sumo stadium. Here Takatora had a larger plot of land on which he is believed to have grown rice and vegetables, and set up a market to sell the excess produce. This third residence was built on the site of Kimura Shigenari's Edo villa. Kimura Shigenari, it may be remembered, had led 10,000 troops against the Todo and Ii forces in Siege of Osaka 11 years earlier, inflicting heavy losses on Takatora's men. Kimura and his samurai were routed during the Summer Siege of Osaka a year later in which he lost his head in battle.

Emergency Preparations

One day the Todo clan's Edo *Karo*, House Elder approached Takatora and reported, 'There is not a single bird gun [hunting gun] in our Edo properties. We should get a thousand of them from the country [i.e. Iga and Tsu] to prepare for emergencies.'

Takatora replied, 'If you need any guns, we can just ask the shogunate and borrow some'. The old retainer said, 'That may be possible if you are sending one or two men on an errand, but if there is a disturbance in the Shogunate, we will be in need of guns, and I don't think our clan can procure them.'

'If that were the case, it would be recognised as a rebellion, we can go to Maeda Toshitsune's residence across the street and borrow as many as we can,' Takatora replied laughingly. The old retainer looked concerned, but left the matter there, simply asking Takatora to consider it. However, after Takatora's death, an inventory was made of his household and it was found that he had in stock over 1,300 guns and all requirements including accessories down to the smallest of maintenance tools. Takatora may have spoken lightly of the topic but as a true warrior of the old ways, was more than prepared for any situation.

The Death of Todo Takatora

Todo Takatora's eyesight had begun to fail as he aged, and as a result of this his official decorative personal signature, known as a *kao*, became simpler from late 1591. From as early as 1601 he had begun using an *inkan* stamp instead of signing his messages as his eyes, strained from long hours of working on reams of detailed architectural plans and meticulous notes, had apparently weakened to the point where he was having problems writing. In around 1623, he suffered an eye infection that hastened the failing of his eyesight to the extent that he could barely see by 1630, the year of his death. Remaining records suggest that he had contracted an illness, as he had complained of a sore throat and was suffering diarrhoea at the time of his death. This can also be attributed to the elderly Takatora refusing an umbrella and having stood outdoors in the recent cold rains while directing various construction works. Medical records show his caregivers had brewed *Kikyo-to*, a traditional herbal remedy made from glycyrrhiza root and platycodon root extracts, to remedy his ailments.

Todo Takatora passed away in his Yanagihara residence in Edo on the 5th day of the 10th lunar month, or 9 November 1630, aged 74. The average lifespan for a man in those days was 50 years. Todo Takatora had lived a very long life for a warrior of the violent and turbulent Sengoku period, particularly for a man who had participated in the front line of so many battles. Upon his death, his son Todo Takatsugu was finally officially named as his heir and head of the Todo clan.

His adopted son, Todo Takayoshi, was in Imabari Castle at the time of Takatora's death and hurried to Edo to attend the funeral. He and his small entourage had made it as far as Minakuchi in Omi, not far from his father's birthplace in modern-day Shiga Prefecture, when he received a message believed to have come from his brother, Takatsugu, telling him not to come any further, and to return to Imabari. Takayoshi, it appears, had been careless with domain finances, a problem that had come to the attention of his brother Takatsugu and also to the *Bakufu*, to the extent it had become an embarrassment and a stain on the fine Todo family name. Because of this and subsequently on his brother's orders, Takayoshi never made it to the funeral.

Takayoshi would face further shame as part of his mishandling of administrative affairs. In the summer of 1635 he received a missive from his brother informing him that the Shogunate had advised Takatsugu that Takayoshi was to be ordered to vacate Imabari Castle. In his place, Matsudaira Sadakatsu's fifth son, Matsudaira Sadafusa, a nephew of Tokugawa Ieyasu was to become the Lord of Imabari. Takayoshi was ordered to transfer to Nabari in the south of Ise, where his brother ordered him to repair and reside in the old fortified villa there.[3] Takayoshi took up residence in Nabari as ordered, and as a further punishment, was made to split his land holdings between his three sons, awarding them 5,000 *koku* each. Each of those sons were then made vassals of their uncle, Takatsugu. Takayoshi remained quietly in Nabari where he lived to the ripe old age of 93. Eleven generations of the Nabari Todo clan lived in Nabari from 1636 until the Meiji Restoration of 1868. Many of the Todo clan vassals had followed Takayoshi from Iyo (Ehime) and together with an influx of merchants and craftsmen greatly developed the small town.

Todo Takatora had served the Tokugawa loyally for over 30 years. Following his passing, and in the 22 years between 1632 and 1654, the loyal Todo clan were effectively bankrupted by the demands of the Shogunate. The Shogunate first ordered the Todo clan to rebuild Edo Castle's *ni-no-maru* Bailey in 1632. They were then tasked with the rebuilding of

---

3. Parts of the fortified residence and administrative offices survive today. The previous mansion was rebuilt after a great fire in 1710, and according to old floor plans, was said to have been over 1,083 tatami, or about 1,790m², in size.

Edo Castle's main *honmaru* following a devastating fire in 1639, and then the construction of a mausoleum for the 3rd Shogun, Tokugawa Iemitsu, alongside that of his grandfather at Nikko's magnificent Toshogu Shrine in 1652. Ten years later, in 1662 the Todo clan's castle town of Tsu was destroyed in a great fire. The continuous expenditures, as these works were naturally undertaken at the cost of the *daimyo*, unfortunately caused the clan great financial distress. Various fiscal reform efforts were undertaken, and new rice lands developed to increase income, but the clan's difficult financial situation would remain a problem throughout the rest of its feudal history.

On his deathbed, Takatora was measured, showing a height of 6 *shaku* 2 *sun*, or 190cm. His body was covered in battle scars from Anegawa, the attacks on Tamba and Miki Castle, from the Siege of Tottori, the attack on Kanzan Castle, the battles of Shizugatake and Komaki Nagakute, the Sieges of Kizu and Ichinomiya in the subjugation of Kyushu, in repeated action in Korea, in the decisive Battle of Sekigahara, and in both the Winter and Summer Sieges of Osaka Castle to name but a few. According to the report written by the young samurai attendant who washed and prepared his body on death, 'There were no places on Lord Takatora's body without bullet, blade or spear wounds.' The tips of his ring finger and little finger on his right hand were missing, the middle finger on his left hand and his left thumb were short, having lost their nails. The tip of the big toe on his right foot had also been lost to combat. The young samurai attendant had grown up in the peaceful years of the early Edo period and had never experienced samurai warfare, he had only heard the stories, and was shocked at the battle scars. These wounds were testament to the hard life Takatora lived, and the many battles he participated in, more often than not in the very front lines in the thick of the action.

In death, Takatora was given the *kaimyo*, or Buddhist name, Kanshoin Tono Douken Takayama Gondaisozu. The name Kanshoin 寒松院 is written with the *kanji* for 'cold' and 'pine tree', as the evergreen pine tree maintains a strong, rugged image withstanding the severe cold of winter. Like most samurai of the day, there are multiple graves for Takatora. His actual body was laid to rest by the Shogun Iemitsu and priest Tenkai in a grave in Ueno's Jogyo-ji Temple, a Todo clan family temple. Although the temple no longer stands, his grave site and tombstone remains, surrounded by fourteen similar 2m-high Todo clan stone towers located just behind the Tokyo Ueno Zoo's Elephant Forest. Another similar gravestone stands at the Todo clan's family temple, the Kansho-in, in Tsu City. Relics of the man, his fingernail clippings and locks of hair were placed in special memorial graves located at the Kansho-in Temple in Tokyo's Ueno Park, another is at the Takayama Shrine in Tsu City, Mie Prefecture, and yet another can be found atop holy Mount Koya amongst the great samurai graveyard there.

Legacy

Todo Takatora saw action in some of the most violent, history-changing samurai battles of all time. He left over thirty of the finest castles that he either designed, built, contributed to, or at the very least influenced – more than any other man. Having changed allegiances seven times to serve a total of ten lords, Takatora also holds the record for having served the greatest number of masters, more than any other samurai in history. His tribute to his master and friend, Ieyasu, built at the bequest of his final lord, Ieyasu's grandson Iemitsu, the magnificent Nikko Toshogu Shrine, has evolved into one of the world's most spectacular mausoleums and is part of Nikko's UNESCO World Heritage Site. His innovative designs influenced many other castle architects, and the way that castles were planned and constructed.

He can claim responsibility for having suggested a number of political initiatives, including the *Sankin Kotai* system that was to both ensure and maintain peace through the 260 years of Tokugawa rule through the Edo period. The practice of having the *daimyo* travel to and from their domains and Edo also ensured that Japan's highways were well maintained and that the economic benefits associated with the system were enjoyed by all.

Statues of an armoured, mounted Takatora can be found in his hometown of Koura in Shiga Prefecture, with an identical statue positioned within the stone walls of Tsu Castle in Mie Prefecture. Another statue of Takatora is located in the central *honmaru* precincts of Imabari Castle in Ehime, and while this too depicts a mounted Takatora, this statue shows him without armour.

Takatora's noted modern-day descendants include female speedboat racer Todo Rika (born 1987, Ono City, Fukui Prefecture), popular

Japanese comedian Yutti (born Todo Yuta, 1977) and the architect Todo Takanao (born 1983)

Todo Takatora was an exceptionally brave warrior, a respected leader, a skilled diplomat, a thoughtful politician, a brilliant designer, a clever builder, an innovator, a sincere, austere, generous and kind man. Takatora was a man of sincere modesty and unassuming nature. He achieved what he did not to be revered nor remembered, but to be of service.

There is still so much we can learn about, and from, Todo Takatora. He was a man who made a major impact on the history and culture of Japan. That he is not better remembered, nor celebrated for his efforts is a shame. But then again, that is how the humble Takatora would most probably have wanted it. We may not always see the elephant in the room, but Todo Takatora was indeed a giant among men.

Glossary

A

Anoshu – Master stonemasons of what is now western Shiga Prefecture.

Anotsu – Castle and port in Mie Prefecture, now known as Tsu Castle.

Ashigaru – Low-ranking samurai foot soldiers.

Atsuta – The nations' second most important shrine, located in Nagoya.

Awa – Province, modern-day Chiba Prefecture.

Awabi – Dried shellfish used in samurai ceremonies, particularly in the *Shutsujin-shiki*, pre-battle ceremony.

Azuchi – Site of Nobunaga's most glorious castle near Lake Biwa.

B

Bakufu – Literally, 'tent government', refers to the ruling administration.

Biwa – Lake. Japan's biggest freshwater lake, located in central Shiga Prefecture.

Bizen – Region surrounding Okayama in western Japan.

Borogata Keep – An old architectural style of keep building based on temple construction techniques.

Bugyo – Rank. Commissioner.

Buke Shohatto – A collection of edicts regarding conduct, responsibilities and activities, morality, and honour for the *daimyo* and samurai issued by the Shogunate.

Byobu – Decorative folding screen.

C

Chawan – Tea ceremony cup.

Chikuzen – Province, now Fukuoka Prefecture.

Chugoku – Central western regions of Honshu.

Chusei – Medieval period.

D

Daimyo – Title. Refers to the powerful territorial feudal lords.

Desumi – An external corner where two walls join to form an angle.

Dobei – Wattle-and-daub method walls of clay constructed around castles.

Dorui – An earthen wall or embankment.

E

Echigo – Province, now Niigata Prefecture.

Echizen – Province, now Fukui Prefecture.

Edo – City. Tokugawa Ieyasu's seat of power. Currently known as Tokyo.

Edo Period – 1603–1868, named after Ieyasu's Edo Castle, seat of the Tokugawa *Bakufu*.

F

Fudai daimyo – Daimyo historically and closely associated with the Tokugawa clan.

Fushimi – Castle and town south of Kyoto.

Fushin bugyo – Commissioner, magistrate or official responsible for civil engineering public works, construction projects and castle building.

Fusuma – Sliding door.

G

Gifu – Town and site of a strategically-important castle. Capital of modern-day Gifu Prefecture.

Gosanke – The three branch houses of the Tokugawa clan.

Goten – Castle palace.

Gussoku – A suit of samurai armour.

H

Hafu – Triangular roofing devices on *tenshu* keeps.

Hata – Battle flag.

Hata-bugyo – Commissioner, magistrate or official responsible for battle flag and standard positioning on the battlefield.

Hatamoto – Lit. Bannerman. Closest and most loyal of vassals.

Hazama ishi – Uppermost stone of an *ishigaki* carved to allow matchlocks to be fired from below a *dobei* wall.

Himeji – Castle site and city in Hyogo Prefecture.

Hinawaju – Matchlock gun. Also known as *teppo*.

Hirajiro – Castle category. A castle built on flat land.

Hirayamajiro – Castle category. A castle built on a hill and also using the flat land below it.

Hizen Nagoya – Castle in Karatsu, Saga Prefecture built for Hideyoshi's invasion of Korea.

Horagai – Conch shell horn.

Honmaru – The main central, and most important, of castle baileys and walls.

Honno-ji – Temple in Kyoto where Oda Nobunaga was killed.

Hori/bori – Water-filled or dry moat.

Horikiri – Defensive trench cut along mountain ridges to prevent enemy advances.

Horo – Large cloth balloon-like devices carried on the backs of certain mounted samurai.

I

Ichikoku Ichijou Rei – One Castle per Province decree.

Ichirizuka – Milestone marker mounds along *kaido* highways.

Iga Ueno – Castle and city in Mie Prefecture.

Imabari – Takatora's excellent castle in Shikoku.

Inubashiri – Literally 'dog's run', a narrow space around baileys.

Irisumi – An internal corner where two walls join to form an angle.

Ise – Region in modern-day Mie Prefecture.

Ishigaki – Piled drystone castle walls.

Ishiotoshi – Protruding sections of a *yagura* or *tenshu* mistakenly believed to have been for the dropping of stones onto an attacking enemy.

Itabari – wooden panelling protecting the wattle-and-daub walls of castle structures.

Iyo – Province in Shikoku. Modern-day Ehime Prefecture.

Izu – Province. Modern-day Shizuoka Prefecture.

J

Jin – Samurai battlefield war camp, consisting of rudimentary furnishings, and surrounded by *jinmaku* curtains.

Jinbaori – Sleeveless samurai war coat, worn over the armour.

Jingasa – A type of helmet, usually conical, usually worn by *ashigaru*.

Jinmaku – The cotton hemp curtain decorated with crests set up around a battlefield war camp.

Jinya – Fortified command post held by *daimyo* ranked too low to hold a castle, or by *hatamoto*.

Jizamurai – Samurai lords of smaller rural domains or land-holding warriors.

Jokamachi – Castle town surrounding or part of the castle complex.

Jurakutei – Toyotomi Hideyoshi's sumptuous palace complex built in Kyoto.

K

Kabuto – A samurai helmet.

Kachodoki – War cry performed in unison prior to battle.

Kagi no Te – A crank in a roadway to hinder the progress of attackers.

Kaido – A highway. There were five major *kaido* crossing Japan.

Kaishakunin – Assistant to one who performs *seppuku*, administering the coup de grace.

Kampaku – An imperial court title, equivalent to Imperial Regent and Counsellor.

Kao – Official decorative personal signatures.

Karo – Clan or house elder.

Katana – The samurai sword.

Kawara – Roof tiles

Kibatai – Cavalry unit.

Kii – Region and province south of Osaka. Modern-day Wakayama Prefecture

Kinki – Western regions of Japan, around Osaka and Kyoto.

Kinsei – Early Modern period.

Kirigishi – Sides of a mountain or hill cut or carved so as to increase the angle of climb. An artificial cliff.

Kirikomi-hagi – Carefully-carved stone for use in close-fitting *ishigaki* drystone walling.

Kisouma – A type of native short-legged, sturdy horse used by the samurai.

Kiyosu – Town in modern-day Aichi Prefecture and site of a most strategic castle.

Koguchi – A fortified entranceway between baileys, written as 'Tiger's Mouth'.

Koku – A measure of rice, defined as the amount required to feed one person for a year, or about 180 litres. It was by this measure that *daimyos*' wealth (*kokudaka*) was assessed.

Kokuin – (Also *kokumon*) Identification carvings on the stones of castle walls.

Kokumon – see *kokuin*.

Kokushi – Provincial governor.

Komakiyama – Castle built by Oda Nobunaga just north of modern-day Nagoya.

Kombu – Dried seaweed used in soups and in samurai ceremonies.

Korai-mon – A type of simple gate often used ahead of larger main gates in a masugata configuration.

Koshi-guruwa – Lit. 'Waist Bailey'. A narrow strip of flat area around and below baileys, the result of shaving the hillsides to increase the steepness.

Kote – Sleeves on a suit of armour.

Koya San – Mount Koya. A holy mountain, long used as a place of exile for the nobility.

Kozuke – A small steel skewer carried tucked into the sword scabbard.

Kubi Jikken – A post-battle ceremony where the heads of enemy samurai were displayed and inspected.

Kubi-kabuto – An enemy head taken while still encased in its *kabuto*.

Kubizuka – A head burial mound.

Kuruwa – A highly fortified castle bailey, enceinte or precinct, and usually assigned a name or number. An older name for a *maru*.

Kyoto – City. The ancient capital.

M

Masugata – A highly fortified double-gate complex, better remembered as a 'Death Box'.

Maru – Like *kuruwa*, a fortified castle bailey, compound, enceinte or precinct. *Maru* is used as a prefix to a name. For example, *Ni-no-maru*, the Second Bailey, *Nishi-no-maru*, the Western Bailey etc.

Matsugashima – Castle in Mie Prefecture, attacked by Todo Takatora in 1584.

Mizujiro – Castle category. A water castle (see also *Umijiro*).

Mochi – cake made of pounded sticky rice. A favourite food of Todo Takatora.

Mon – A castle gate. *Mon* is used as a suffix, such as *Ote-mon*, Main Gate, *Higashi-mon*, East Gate etc.

Matsuo – Mountain to the south of Sekigahara where Kobayakawa set up camp.

Mikawa – Tokugawa-held domain, now western Aichi Prefecture.

Minami-no-maru – Southern bailey.

Minamoto – Ancient and powerful noble warrior clan of Imperial descent.

Mino – Province. Modern-day Gifu Prefecture.

Momokubari – A small mountain east of Sekigahara where Ieyasu first set up camp.

Muromachi – A period in Japanese history, approximately 1336 to 1573, marked by the governance of the Ashikaga Shogunate, based in the Muromachi district of Kyoto.

Mushatai – Non-mounted samurai.

N

Nabari – City in Mie Prefecture, site of the Todo clan branch domains.

Naginata – A type of glaive-like polearm.

Nagaya – Long gatehouse structure.

Nagakute – City east of Nagoya, site of the Battle of Komaki-Nagakute.

Nagoya – Castle city in central Japan, capital of Aichi Prefecture.

Nakabori – Central moat.

Nakasendo – A strategically important major highway running through the central mountainous regions of Japan between Kyoto and Edo.

Nawabari – Lit. 'rope stretching'; refers to the layout of a castle grounds.

Ninja – See *shinobi*.

Nijo – A castle in central Kyoto.

Ni-no-maru – A castle's second compound or bailey.

Noh – A traditional performing art, often patronised by the samurai class.

Nozurazumi – Form of *ishigaki*, featuring piled unprocessed stone.

O

Obi Kuruwa – Lit. 'Waist Bailey'. A narrow strip of flat area around and below baileys, formed as a result of carving the hillside to increase the angle of the slope.

Ogaki – City and site of a splendid castle in Gifu Prefecture.

Okazaki – Capital of Mikawa Province (Aichi Prefecture), birthplace of Ieyasu and site of his ancestral castle.

Omi – Province, north-east of Kyoto and containing Lake Biwa, currently Shiga Prefecture.

Osaka – City and site of Hideyoshi's most impressive castle.

Otemon – Main gates of a castle.

O-umajirushi – Large battle standard.

Owari – Region now comprising of western Aichi Prefecture.

O-yashiki – Large residence.

Ozu – Castle and city in Ehime Prefecture, Shikoku.

R

Ranzumi – A random stone piling technique used in castle walls.

Rinkakushiki – A basic style of castle layout with the central *honmaru* completely surrounded and protected by other baileys.

Ronin – Lit. 'Wave man'. A masterless samurai.

Ryo – A feudal period gold coin. A pre-Yen unit.

S

Saihai – A short tasselled paper or yak-hair whip used by commanders to direct troops in battle.

Sakamoto Castle – Built by Akechi Mitsuhide on the orders of Oda Nobunaga. It was located on the south western banks of Lake Biwa. The castle was destroyed along with Mitsuhide in 1582.

Sake – A traditional Japanese alcoholic drink made from fermented rice.

Samurai – Lit. 'One Who Serves'. The warrior class of feudal Japan.

Sangizumi – A technique of using a zipper-like arrangement of interlocking horizontally laid corner stones to form strong *ishigaki* corners.

Sankin Kotai – Alternative attendance duties at the Shogun's castle.

Sakuji Bugyo – Commissioner, magistrate or overseer of construction projects.

Sanmon – Lit. 'Great gate'. Usually serving a temple.

San-no-maru – Third compound or bailey within a castle.

Sanuki – Province. Modern day Kagawa Prefecture.

Sarugaki – A traditional comedic performing art.

Sashimono – The battle flag worn on the back of a samurai's armour.

Sasao (Sasaoyama) – Small mountain north-west of the Sekigahara battlefield where Ishida Mitsunari established his headquarters.

Sawayama – Castle, the ruins of which now lie in Hikone City, Shiga Prefecture.

Sekigahara – Major battlefield in Gifu Prefecture, fought in 1600.

Sengoku – Japan's Warring States period, 1467–1615.

Sen no Rikyu – Master of the Tea Ceremony, advisor to Toyotomi Hideyoshi.

seppuku – Polite term for *Hara-kiri*, a form of ritual suicide.

Shachihoko – Decorative tigerfish ornaments found atop castle structures.

Shaku – A measurement of both length and weight. Approx 30cm or 400 grams.

Shikoro – Neck guard below and around the samurai helmet bowl.

Shikkui – White plaster used on castle walls.

Shinobi – Spies, agents and mercenaries. Also known as ninja.

Shinpan – Daimyo related to the Tokugawa clan.

Shizugatake – Mountains in the north of Omi, site of the Battle of Shizugatake

Shogi – A foldable stool used in war camps.

Shogun – Grand General. Hereditary military dictator.

Shoryu-ji – Castle in Nagaokakyo, Kyoto.

Shutsujin-shiki – Samurai pre-battle ceremony.

Sode – Shoulder armour.

Sotobori – A castle's outermost defensive moat.

Sotogata Keep – An architectural style for castle keeps created by Todo Takatora.

Sou Taisho – Title. Commander-in-Chief.

Suigun – Naval forces.

Sumi Yagura – A corner watchtower.

Suna-no-maru – Lit. Sand bailey

Suneate – Armoured shin pads.

T

Tachi – Sword worn with armour, slung with the blade facing downwards.

Taiko – Title awarded to a regent, closely matching that of Shogun. Used by Toyotomi Hideyoshi.

Tairo – Lit. Great Elder. Title. Statesmen and high government official.

Taisho – Commander, general or captain.

Tamon Yagura – A single-storey corridor-like watchtower structure running along the tops of castle walls.

Tanima – Rainwater collection pool within a castle grounds.

Tanto – Daggar under 30cm in length carried by samurai.

Tenka-bushin – System whereby *daimyo* were forced to work on castle construction projects.

Tenshu – The castle's iconic main tower keep or donjon.

Tenshudai – The stone base supporting the *tenshu* tower keep.

Teppo – Japanese matchlock gun. Also called a *hinawaju*.

Teppotai – Samurai matchlock unit.

Teppozama – Port in a wall for firing matchlocks.

Teramachi – Lit. 'Temple town'. Outer sections of a castle town dedicated to temples and forming a protective wall.

Tokaido – The Eastern Sea Route. A strategically important major highway running over 514km between the capital, Kyoto, and Edo.

Tosa – Province in Kyushu.

Tozama Daimyo – *Daimyo* formerly enemies of, or not traditionally associated with, the Tokugawa clan prior to the Battle of Sekigahara.

Tsu – Castle and city in Mie Prefecture.

Tsuchibashi – Earthen bridge spanning moats and *horikiri*.

Tsuke-yagura – An annex adjoining a keep.

U

Uchibori – The innermost moat of a castle, usually around the *honmaru*.

Uchikomi-hagi – A stone wall piling technique using roughly cut and inserted masonry.

Uchi-masugata – A type of walled *masugata* gate system inside the *koguchi* entrance to a defensive installation. The *masugata* has a larger gate in the outer wall, and a second, smaller gate inside at right angles. The *uchi-masugata* is designed to prevent an enemy from breaching a castle directly, and to weaken the attacking force. *Uchi-masugata* are the more common of the two main types of *masugata*, the other being the *soto-masugata*, where the square compound is built outside the larger gate.

Umadashi – Lit. 'horse opening', a fortified barbican-like defence space in front of castle gates for cavalry and infantry to muster and exit.

Umajirushi – Battle standard.

Umijiro – A sea castle.

Utsugatana – A type of common sword, also known as a *katana*, usually worn by samurai with the blade uppermost and carried in the obi belt when not in armour.

Uwajima – Castle and city in Ehime Prefecture, Shikoku.

W

Wajo – Japanese castle built in Korea during Hideyoshi's invasion period.

Wakizashi – A short companion sword to the *tachi* or *katana*.

Washi – Strong traditional Japanese paper.

Y

Yagura – A watchtower.

Yagura mon – A gatehouse.

Yashiki – A single-storey samurai residence.

Yamabushi – Mountain ascetic.

Yamato – Region surrounding Nara.

Yakata – A residence for lords and elite samurai.

Yamajiro – A castle built on a mountain or hill.

Yari – A spear.

Yaribusuma – An effective battle formation consisting of a wall of spearmen.

Yazama – A porthole in a wall, usually an upright rectangle, for the shooting of arrows.

Yodo – Fortress constructed in the south of Kyoto.

Yokoya – Side flank defensive port along a wall.

Yoroi – Suit of armour, also known as *kachu* or *gusoku*.

Z

Zeze – Castle site in Otsu, Shiga Prefecture.

Select Bibliography

Fujita Tatsuo, *Todo Takatora Ron, Shoki Hanseishi no Kenkyu* (2018).

Fujita Tatsuo, *Edo Jidai no Sekkeisha* (Kodansha Gendai, 2006).

Fukui Kenji, *Chikujo no Meishu, Todo Takatora* (Ebisukosyo, 2016).

Gakken History Group Series [Sengoku] Selection – *Gekito Osaka no Jin*.

Glenn, Chris, *The Battle of Sekigahara* (Frontline, 2021).

Hagiwara Sachiko, *Edo Jo no Zenpou* (Sakurasha, 2017).

Iga Cultural Association, *Todo Takatora Ko To Ikun, Ni-hyakka Jo* (Ueno Insatsu Co., 2013).

Ikkojin, December 2013 edition.

香美町の城郭集成 Kami Town Board of Education, Kami Town Historical and Cultural Heritage Revitalization Executive Committee report. March 2015, pp. 72–4 https://www.town.mikata-kami.lg.jp/www/contents/1615449907763/files/kamicyou_jyoukakusyusei.pdf

Kokawa Town, *Kokawa Bunkazai Tsushin*, Vol 24. *Takatora to Kokawa* (1992).

Kokawa Town, *Kokawa Cho-Shi*, Vol. 1 (2003).

Koura Town Board of Education, *Koura no Tamamono*.

Matsumoto Yukio, *Busho ni Manabu Kukyo kara no Dasshutsu* (Sogo Life Publishing, 1992).

Miura Masayuki and Glenn, Chris, *Samurai Castle*, Bilingual Guide (Shogakukan, 2017).

Miura Masayuki – various monthly castle-related lectures attended between 2016 and 2021.

Murdoch, James, *A History of Japan* (Kobe Chronicle Press/Forgotten Books, 1903).

Nakai Hitoshi, Suzuki Masataka and Takeda Kenji, *Tokai no Mei Jo o Aruku* (Yoshikawa, 2020).

NHK - *Eiyu Tachi no Sentaku* 'Todo Takatora' (March 2017 broadcast).

Ota Gyuichi, *The Chronicles of Lord Nobunaga* (Trans. Elisonas and Lamers) (Brill, 2011).

Papinot, E., *Historical and Geographical Dictionary of Japan* (Tuttle, 1992).

Rekishijin, February 2011 edition.

Rekishijin, April 2014 edition.

Rekishijin, May 2017 edition.

Rekishi Kaido, July 2017 edition

Sadler, A.L., *The Maker of Modern Japan, The Life of Shogun Tokugawa Ieyasu* (Tuttle, 1937).

Samson, George, *A History of Japan; 1334-1615* (Stanford University Press, 1961).

Seigle, Cecilia S. Ph.D., 'Some Observations on the Weddings of Tokugawa Shogun's Daughters – Part 1' (2012). Department of East Asian Languages and Civilizations. 7.https://repository.upenn.edu/cgi/viewcontent.cgi?article=1006&context=ealc

Shoku Hoki Kenkyu Kai, *Wajo o Aruku* (Sun Rise, 2014).

Todo Han Itsuka Kai, *Watashi no Todo Takatora Ko* (Tsu City Culture Publishing Association, 2016).

Turnbull, Stephen, *Osaka 1615* (Osprey, 2006).

Ueno City Literature Publishing Association,*Koushitsu Nempu Ryaku* (Todo clan diaries) (Ueno City, 2002).

Ueno City Literature Publishing Association, *Kouzan Kojitsu Roku* (Ueno City, 1998).

Index